STUDIES IN HIGHER EDUCATION

DISSERTATION SERIES

Edited by
PHILIP G. ALTBACH
Monan Professor of Higher Education
Lynch School of Education, Boston College

A ROUTLEDGEFALMER SERIES

OTHER BOOKS IN THIS SERIES:

SAVING FOR COLLEGE AND THE TAX CODE
Andrew Roth

RESOURCE ALLOCATION IN PRIVATE
RESEARCH UNIVERSITIES
Daniel Rodas

I PREFER TO TEACH

An International Comparison of Faculty Preference for Teaching over Research

James JF Forest

ROUTLEDGEFALMER
NEW YORK & LONDON

Published in 2002 by
RoutledgeFalmer
29 West 35th Street
New York, NY 10001

Published in Great Britain by
RoutledgeFalmer
11 New Fetter Lane
London EC4P 4EE

RoutledgeFalmer is an imprint of the Taylor & Francis Group.
Copyright © 2002 by James JF Forest

10 9 8 7 6 5 4 3 2 1

Library of Congress Cataloging-in-Publication Data:

Forest, James J. F.
   I prefer to teach : an international comparison of faculty preference for teaching over research / James J. F. Forest.
     p. cm. — (RoutledgeFalmer studies in higher education ; v. 26)
   Includes bibliographical references (p.) and index.
   ISBN 0-415-93057-X
   1. College teachers—Attitudes—Cross-cultural studies. 2. College teaching—Cross-cultural studies. 3. Education, Higher—Research—Cross-cultural studies.
I. Title. II. Series.

LB1778 .F65 2001
378.1'25—dc21

                                               2001041824

Contents

Acknowledgments

This study was originally undertaken as a doctoral dissertation at Boston College between 1996 and 1998, under the direction of Philip G. Altbach, to whom I am considerably grateful for guiding me through the labyrinth of graduation education and subsequent academic work. Professors Karen Arnold and Ted Youn contributed their expertise in quantitative research to this work as part of my dissertation committee, and I thank them as well. I also wish to send special thanks to the Carnegie Foundation for the Advancement of Teaching for producing the data for this study, and particularly Mary Jean Whitelaw for her assistance with the description of the research design and commentary on the survey data presented in Chapter 3.

Many other colleagues and friends with whom I studied and worked provided a great deal of moral and intellectual support to me during those years, and I sincerely hope they are all aware of my gratitude to them. I have no illusion that my graduate education would not have been such a positive experience without the generous and supportive staff, faculty, and fellow graduate students in the Lynch School of Education at Boston College. An additional debt of gratitude is owed to Judith Gill and the professional staff at the Massachusetts Board of Higher Education, from whom I learned so much. And finally, to all college and university teachers around the world— and particularly those who put a little extra time, heart and soul into their teaching—I offer my deepest respect.

James JF Forest
August, 2000

Preface

University and college teaching, and the assessment and reward of teaching, are among the most important topics in higher education worldwide, and are increasing in importance. This book explores the nature of a professor's fondness for teaching over research, and what impact this preference may have on their perspectives toward other dimensions of academic work and life. While some studies have shed light on this important topic, this is the first to examine how these relationships are shared among faculty internationally. For example, studies of the academic profession have observed how faculty who prefer to teach emphasize their disciplinary affiliations, while those who prefer to engage in research lean more toward their institutional loyalties (cf. Gouldner, 1957; Hughes, 1979). However, where these studies have reflected observations of specific departments or a whole institution, this book offers the first international look at this issue.

The study consists of several analyses of survey data collected from nearly 20,000 professors in 14 countries by the Carnegie Foundation for the Advancement of Teaching. The chapters illustrate associations within the survey data within the context of specific themes, seeking to determine meaningful predictions of teaching preference, as well as the relationship of this preference with how faculty responded to survey items concerning increasingly broader topics—the classroom, the institution, the academic discipline, the academic profession, the role of higher education in society, and the international dimensions of higher education.

This study found that there are significant international similarities in how teaching-oriented faculty responded to the Carnegie survey differently than research-oriented faculty, particularly regarding their views toward the assessment of teaching and toward the international dimensions of higher education. The implications of these findings include the need to improve our training programs for the academic profession in ways that enhance faculty preference for teaching. The findings of this study also demonstrate the need for engaging teaching-oriented faculty in ways that will encourage them to feel more strongly that they are a part of a vibrant international academic profession. Overall, this study is significant in showing that teaching orientation plays an important role in the lives and perspectives of faculty worldwide, and is thus useful for informing our understanding of the choices and decisions faculty make in their daily and professional lives. This understanding can help us develop more useful approaches to the improvement and assessment of teaching at colleges and universities worldwide.

I Prefer to Teach

CHAPTER 1

Introduction

This book is about professors who would rather teach than conduct research, despite the considerable rewards bestowed upon faculty who excel in their research activities. It is based upon the belief that examining members of the academic profession as objects of social science inquiry can lead us to a greater understanding of higher education worldwide. The particular focus of this study concerns whether faculty preference for research or teaching is related to their perspectives toward other dimensions of academic work and life. While several researchers have identified distinct differences between teaching-oriented and research-oriented faculty (cf. Gouldner, 1957; Hughes, 1979), this is the first study to examine these differences on an international level. Using data collected by the Carnegie Foundation's international survey of the academic profession, this study draws on the perspectives of nearly 20,000 faculty from around the world to determine significant trends in survey responses related to faculty preference for teaching or research. Previous studies of the Carnegie data have determined that internationally, teaching-oriented faculty are significantly different from research-oriented faculty in the tasks they perform—faculty who prefer teaching over research teach more than their colleagues, while those who prefer research over teaching engage in more research activities (Altbach & Lewis, 1996; Gottlieb & Keith, 1996). The research questions and analyses described in this study are based on the belief that preference for teaching is an important item to study and can impact the quality of one's teaching. This belief is supported by research which has shown that a faculty member's preferences can often drive their behavior (cf. Clark, 1987; Clark, 1992; Sherman and Blackburn, 1975).

"Because the academic profession is at the heart of the academic enterprise, the views of scholars and scientists must be carefully considered" (Boyer, 1996: xvi). An understanding of factors which influence faculty preferences, particularly their preferences for doing those activities in which they see the most personal reward, can inform new innovations in the assessment of teaching in higher education. Further, as much of today's criticisms toward higher education, and particularly toward faculty, are in reference to questions of teaching effectiveness, it stands to reason that teaching-oriented faculty are an important unit of research. This study adds a new dimension to our understanding of the professoriate by showing that teaching-oriented faculty worldwide are significantly different from their research-oriented colleagues in their views about the assessment of teaching, about the conditions under which they work, about their academic disciplines and the profession, and about the international dimensions of higher education. These findings have implications for our understanding of organizational culture and change within the academic profession, how professors collectively define the work they engage in, and how "excellent" examples of this work are framed. The study also informs institutional administrative policies regarding faculty workload, and contributes to future international and comparative studies of the academic profession. This introductory chapter outlines the primary research questions addressed in the study, followed by brief descriptions of the theoretical framework, the data used for the analysis, and the logic and organization of the chapters.

PRIMARY RESEARCH QUESTIONS

The research questions which frame this analysis are based upon studies of the academic profession described above and in Chapter 2. The areas of analysis chosen for this study are: (1) whether there are meaningful predictors of teaching orientation; (2) whether teaching orientation is significantly related to faculty perspectives toward other dimensions of their work; and (3) whether these predictors and relationships are shared among faculty internationally.

Predictors of Teaching Orientation

The first part of this discussion concerns the question of what the Carnegie data can tell us about who teaching-oriented faculty are. If it can be determined that teaching-oriented faculty are significantly alike cross-nationally, then this would certainly provide a foundation for future research on the academic profession. Thus, the first research question asked in this study is:

> Do teaching-oriented faculty internationally share similar demographic profiles, academic rank, or other background variables that distinguish them from their research-oriented colleagues?

Chapter 4 of this study addresses this research question by looking at whether gender, age, academic rank, working time, professional preparation, or any of several other background data collected by the Carnegie survey has a predictive value for whether respondents indicated an orientation towards teaching or towards research. Multiple regression analyses provide the statistical tool by which it can be determined how much of the variance in response to the "teaching vs. research orientation" question can be accounted for by these variables.

This research question addresses an important dimension of faculty identity. "It is generally accepted that the multiplicity of cultures that shape faculty identities—the culture of the profession, the cultures of the disciplines, the culture of the institution and department, and the cultures of institutional types (Austin, 1990)—make it impossible to conceive of a generalizable faculty essence" (Bensimon, 1996: 38). Nevertheless, it is common to view academics in terms of a generalized class of professionals, and distinctions are often made between those academics who are research scholars and those who have never published anything. The study presented here explores the usefulness of drawing distinctions between teaching-oriented and research-oriented faculty by determining meaningful aspects to the identity of teaching-oriented faculty.

Outcomes of Teaching Orientation

The second part of this discussion concerns the question of whether teaching-oriented faculty were significantly different from their research-oriented colleagues in responding to Carnegie survey questions on a variety of key issues. Here, correlation and crosstab analyses were performed to determine the relationship of teaching orientation with other survey responses. Thus, the second research question asked in this analysis is:

> Do teaching-oriented faculty reflect different views than their research-oriented colleagues toward certain dimensions of academic work?

Chapters 5 through 9 address this question within the context of specific themes, seeking to determine the impact of teaching orientation on how faculty responded to survey items on: (1) teaching and the assessment of teaching; (2) institutional working conditions; (3) life in the academic profession; (4) the role of higher education in society; and (5) the international dimension of higher education. Each chapter thus provides a series of tables and discussion on the strength of correlations found between survey responses within these themes and faculty orientation towards teaching or research.

This research question is based upon a belief that analyses of faculty perceptions of academic work in general, and in particular of faculty characterizations of the teaching-research nexus as complimentary or competitive in nature, have organizational and policy implications for everyday academic life and higher education planning (Gottleib and Keith, 1996). Indeed, while academics are universally engaged in the transmission of knowledge, the way faculty view the kinds of activity in which they are engaged bears particular relevance to our understanding of the academic profession worldwide.

International Dimensions of Teaching Orientation

An international perspective is particularly absent from existing literature on teaching and learning in higher education. This study is thus intended to help fill the void left by the lack of a cross-national or cross-cultural perspective on this important topic. The Carnegie Foundation for the Advancement of Teaching's international study of the academic profession was based on their conviction that in today's interconnected world, an international perspective is essential in understanding how academic life functions and how it might be strengthened both at home and abroad (Boyer, Altbach, & Whitelaw, 1994). The international nature of the Carnegie data is unique—surprisingly little has been done towards providing a cross-cultural perspective on university and college teaching. This study seeks to tap into that uniqueness in a new way, by determining what international trends may exist among faculty whose preferences lie more in teaching than in research. Thus, a third—and central—research question underlies this entire research analysis:

> Are there meaningful international trends in how teaching-oriented faculty responded to the Carnegie survey?

Throughout each chapter of this volume, tables of statistical analysis results provide a representation of a particular trend, related to teaching-oriented faculty, that was found in this study. Where a trend was found to exist in a large proportion of the countries surveyed, that trend was considered significantly international. This study adopts the approach that international similarities among teaching-oriented faculty help to "define priorities that could strengthen the academy worldwide" (Boyer, Altbach & Whitelaw, 1994: 1). Thus, this analysis of the Carnegie data provides a look at faculty that is useful both for current discussions on faculty roles and rewards and for our understanding of the academic profession internationally.

Summary

The primary focus of this discussion revolves around issues of faculty identity and perspectives, which are particularly useful for understanding the intellectual context of faculty work. Each of the research questions outlined above are based on existing research that suggests there are significant differences among faculty related to their orientation towards teaching or research. These research questions provide the framework for developing and testing a set of research hypotheses within the Carnegie survey data.

The purposes of this analysis is to examine the validity of three general research hypotheses (H_1) and their related null hypotheses (H_0):

H_1: Teaching-oriented faculty internationally share similar demographic profiles, academic rank, or other background variables that distinguish them from their research-oriented colleagues.

H_0: There is no difference between teaching-oriented faculty and research-oriented faculty in terms of demographic profiles, academic rank, or other background variables.

H_1: Teaching-oriented faculty reflect different views than their research-oriented colleagues toward: (1) teaching and the assessment of teaching; (2) institutional working conditions; (3) life in the academic profession; (4) the role of higher education in society; and (5) the international dimension of higher education.

H_0: There is no difference between teaching-oriented faculty and research-oriented faculty regarding their views toward these issues of academic work and life.

H_1: There are meaningful international trends in how teaching-oriented faculty differ from research-oriented faculty in responding to the Carnegie survey.

H_0: There are no international trends in how teaching-oriented faculty differ from research-oriented faculty in responding to the Carnegie survey.

Through these research questions and hypotheses, the study helps define teaching orientation as a meaningful way of looking at faculty internationally. Faculty orientation towards teaching is an important item to study, in that it can impact the quality of one's teaching. The implications of this study can inform research on higher education organizations, academic culture, and the assessment and improvement of instruction. Additionally, an understanding of factors which influence faculty preferences, particularly their preferences for doing those activities in which they see the most personal reward, has broad policy implications. It must be remembered here that where teaching orientation plays a significant role in how faculty responded to the Carnegie survey, so must its opposite—orientation towards research. Stronger research orientation is correlated in the opposite manner that stronger teaching orientation is. For example, where teaching-oriented faculty are significantly less likely to indicate that their academic discipline is important to them, the reverse is true for research-oriented faculty. It is envisioned that this study will be particularly useful for informing our understanding of many perspectives shared by academics across cultures and nations.

THEORETICAL FRAMEWORK

In an early study of the academic profession, sociologist Alvin Gouldner (1957) proposed that faculty of major research universities can be categorized as either "cosmopolitans" or "locals"—cosmopolitans are those faculty who identify more strongly with their academic disciplines than their institutions, while locals are faculty whose loyalties are directed more towards their institutions than their disciplines. Gouldner suggested that the further an individual's professional focus moves from research toward teaching, the more that individual is likely to pursue local loyalties and to identify with his or her institution. Other scholars have echoed Gouldner's observations that overall, there is at least some tendency for organizational members who are committed to their profession psychologically to face outwards rather than to stress their local organizational loyalty (Hughes, 1979). However, other studies of the academic profession have suggested that the dichotomy suggested by Gouldner is an oversimplification (cf. Grimes & Berger, 1970; Toomey & Child, 1971), as most all faculty are both researchers and teachers. Certainly, in any particular situation there will also be political and personal factors which will affect the applicability of the cosmopolitan/local construct which Gouldner presents. However, it is clear that every faculty member has some choice over whether they wish to focus the lion's share of their time and energy toward being a teacher or being a researcher, and it is this choice which lies at the heart of this study.

The issue of work preferences is arguably important for the study of any profession. However, empirical data on this topic are scarce, and there is clearly scope for research from differing viewpoints, particularly from an international perspective. A significant aspect of the issue is the perception of the situation held by the participants themselves, the ways in which they construct their own reality (Greenfield, 1975)—for example, whether a faculty member introduces herself as a Biologist or as a professor at Eastern State University. As Tiernery and Bensimon (1996) observed, "the beliefs one holds about the academy inevitably frames how one acts in a postsecondary institution" (p. 5). Indeed, as described later in this book, research on the academic profession has shown that faculty who prefer to teach do in fact teach more than their research-oriented colleagues, and those who prefer to engage in research do more of that than teach.

There are two ideological camps in academe that bear different views toward the relationship between teaching and research in the academic profession. On one hand, there are academics who feel that teaching and research are necessarily complimentary—good teaching informs good research, and vice versa—and, therefore, faculty should be hired and promoted on the basis of excellence in both areas. On the other hand, there are academics who argue that a faculty member's skills, interest, and available time permit excellence in only one arena or the other. Their argument is that, given naturally limited resources, one can excel only in teaching or in research, but not in both. Certainly, they argue, a professor's time is not infinite—more time spent on one activity must certainly leave less time to engage in another.

This decades-old debate between teaching and research has very likely contributed to an informal division among faculty, with some choosing to spend more of their time on teaching, and others choosing to conduct more research. Some faculty love to research, but are told they must also teach. Indeed, regardless of their work preferences or interests, policymakers, legislators, administrators, and the general public all demand that faculty must teach well. Some faculty love to teach, and do it well, but are often rewarded – for example, by salary increases, promotion and tenure – based upon the quality and quantity of their research publications. Gumport (1991) observed that as higher education institutions have increasingly adopted a "research imperative," faculty who are not considered productive researchers are frequently labeled "deadwood." Decisions are made daily at academic institutions which clearly indicate to faculty members what is valued, and what will be rewarded, at that institution. Sabbatical leaves, adjustments in teaching loads, support for attendance at conferences, and grants to support research all give clear indications of institutional priorities.

These dilemmas are not new—the discussion on how a faculty spends their time doing research or teaching has been a part of academe for many decades. Consider the following passage from a 1933 report of the American Association of University Professors' Committee on College and University Teaching:

> When any young teacher, no matter where he [sic] may be located, makes a noteworthy contribution to one of the professional journals, he at once attracts the attention of men in the larger institutions. [Eventually] he gets a call to some better post than the one that he is occupying, whereupon his own college, in order to hold him, counters with an advance in rank or salary. . . [as] good teaching has no such advantages, . . . the young scholars who desire to gain recognition as leaders of their profession are virtually driven to do research whether they want to or not.

While this observation of rewards in the academic profession was made over 60 years ago, it echoes all too true today. However, while research is considered the 'coin of the realm' in academe, there are many faculty in the United States and abroad who prefer teaching over other academic activities. Indeed, by a three-to-one majority, American academics have consistently reported their interests as focusing more on the teaching than on the research component of their role (Finkelstein, 1984). Thus, although teaching-oriented faculty are less likely to be productive researchers, they comprise a considerably large segment of the academic profession. Further, as many scholars have argued, it is through teaching (more than research) that faculty impact the lives of their students, and thus shape the future of their society. Certainly, a study which looks at how teaching-oriented faculty differ in perceptions and attitudes from their research-oriented colleagues can enhance our understanding of the academic profession.

The underlying theme throughout this discussion is based upon the author's belief in the relation between faculty preferences and teaching effectiveness, a belief that is supported by several research studies in which scholars have examined how faculty perceptions and attitudes affect the ways in which they approach their work. For example, Murray (et. al., 1990) found that the compatibility of instructors to courses is determined in part by personality characteristics. In another study, Sherman and Blackburn (1975) examined the degree of relationship between observed faculty personal characteristics and teaching effectiveness (as assessed by student evaluations). Their findings led these authors to suggest that "improvement of teaching effectiveness may depend more on changes related to personality factors than on those involving classroom procedures." Indeed, as Kember and Gow (1994) observed, students do tend to respond better to teaching-oriented faculty than to others.

Although teaching is the essence of academic work, since it is the nearest thing to a common activity that nearly all professors do, research is what distinguishes professors within their own disciplines and play a substantial role in forming hierarchies within institutions (see Bourdieu, 1988; Lewis, 1995). As described in Chapter 2, the modern academic profession in the U.S. and in many countries has dramatically changed over the centuries with the rise of the German-origin research university. The Ph.D.—a credential which signifies competence in research—has become the gold standard for entry into the profession, and publications have widely become the dominant measure of productivity used for tenure and promotion review committees. Yet, many would agree that it is through teaching future generations of leaders that higher education serves its most important function in society.

How a professor views their role as classroom instructor is particularly salient in today's world of increased accountability and concerns over the future of higher education. A small, but growing collection of scholars have begun calling for real changes in the assumptions held throughout the academic profession about teaching and learning in higher education. For example, Shulman (1993) described a new way of looking at teaching as community property. He observed that current institutional support for improving teaching "tends to reside in a universitywide center for teaching and learning . . . That's a perfectly reasonable idea. But notice the message it conveys—that teaching is generic, technical, and a matter of performance;

that it's not part of the community that means so much to most faculty, the disciplinary, inter-disciplinary, or professional community." Arguably, that which "means so much to most faculty" plays a crucial role in achieving his goal of changing how we view college teaching and learning. These and other studies illustrate the need to understand differences in how teaching-oriented and research-oriented faculty perceive their teaching activities, and what influences these perceptions.

This volume examines the issue of identity within the academic profession through the eyes of faculty who identify themselves as teaching-oriented. More precisely, this study explores how faculty views and attitudes toward teaching relate to their perspectives toward other dimensions of academic work and life. The international dimension of this study is particularly important. While university and college teaching, and the assessment and reward of teaching are among the most important topics in higher education worldwide, surprisingly little has been done towards examining these issues cross-nationally. This book represents the first study to look at the impact of teaching orientation internationally. In doing so, this study contributes to one of the richest bases of knowledge we have about any profession, and provides a valuable resource for developing conceptual frameworks in complementary areas of research such as organizational and cultural analyses, in addition to future comparative and international studies of higher education.

This study also provides a bridge between several existing bodies of research, including demographic studies of faculty, research on teaching methods and policies for the assessment of instruction, and comparative studies in higher education. As academe worldwide faces unprecedented challenges, the international dimension of this study presents a unique and timely opportunity to expand our understanding of the academic profession in many ways. Insight concerning how academics around the world cope with new challenges of today's fiscally-driven higher education environment has broad policy implications. This is particularly true for those faculty who would rather teach than research, and thus do not receive the same recognition and rewards as their research-oriented colleagues. While there are several noteworthy national and regional studies of faculty (cf., Finkelstein, 1984), the lack of comparative research in this area provides a compelling theme for this book. "Comparative studies have relevance to pragmatic national issues as well as providing a broader overview concerning higher education" (Altbach, 1979: 4).

Indeed, there is ample cause for developing an international and comparative perspective in research on the academic profession. Our world is rapidly become more interdependent and inextricably linked. Due to the increased globalization of scholarly work and communication, an international community of scholars has developed, and the distribution of information and knowledge has achieved dimensions never previously conceived. As Kerr (1990) and others have observed, we live in a world where the worldwide advancement of learning has become the single most influential factor affecting the human condition. Our understanding of how faculty approach the academic responsibility of teaching needs to encompass an international dimension, in order for our students—and our professors—to adequately address the demands of this increasing global interdependence. This study is thus concerned with illuminating common beliefs and perspectives held by faculty worldwide, and seeks to advance our understanding of teaching and learning in higher education.

The main point of inquiry in this study is the nature of faculty preference towards teaching or research—an important dimension of faculty identity. Throughout the volume, the terms "teaching preference" and "teaching orientation" are used interchangeably. The chapters of this book each tell a unique story about what it means to be oriented towards teaching in a diverse variety of countries. Together, they help form the beginning of a comprehensive picture of who teaching-oriented faculty are and how they see the world of academe differently than their research-oriented colleagues. By exploring perspectives shared among academics throughout the world, the study seeks to provide an understanding of how teaching preference may or may not be an important influence in how faculty view their work and careers. The study highlights generalizations about teaching-oriented faculty, and tests the validity of these generalizations by conducting a series of regression and correlation analyses of nearly 20,000 responses to an international survey of faculty. This is the first collection and analysis of faculty data to look at the impact of teaching orientation internationally. With the results of this study—the first of its kind—it is possible to more fully understand both similarities and differences among academics around the world, and particularly what it means for faculty to be teaching-oriented.

There are a number of questions that can be asked about the phenomenon of teaching orientation. In what ways are teaching-oriented faculty different from research-oriented faculty? Do teaching-oriented faculty have much in common, such as age, rank, gender, or institutional setting? If so, are these commonalities shared by faculty across international or disciplinary borders? What are the implications of teaching preference for how faculty work should be assessed? Do teaching-oriented faculty differ from their research-oriented colleagues in how they view higher education's role in society? A recent international survey of the academic profession conducted by the Carnegie Foundation for the Advancement of Teaching provides the first opportunity to address these and other related questions on a global scale.

INTERNATIONAL DATA ON THE ACADEMIC PROFESSION

Early in 1991, the Carnegie Foundation for the Advancement of Teaching initiated the first international study of college and university faculty, using a survey instrument based upon earlier surveys created and used by the Foundation for national studies of faculty in the United States. The architects of the study were "convinced that an international perspective is central to an understanding of key problems in education, and that we can learn much from the experiences and insights of other countries" (Boyer, 1996: xv). Fifteen nations collaborated in the survey: Australia, Brazil, Chile, Egypt, Germany, Hong Kong, Israel, Japan, Korea, Mexico, The Netherlands, Russia, Sweden, the United Kingdom, and the United States.[1] The questionnaire included more than two hundred items, capturing faculty opinions and information about many of the issues and trends most crucial to higher education: student access and excellence; professional activities including teaching, research, and service; basic demographic information concerning the professoriate; working conditions; institutional governance issues; the role of higher education in society; and international connections. The resulting international collection of data provides a unique and powerful source of information for our understanding of academics. These data show that "there is indeed an international academic profession with common perspectives and concerns, common problems and challenges" (Boyer, 1996: xv).

However, few scholars have utilized the potential of this resource. This international collection of faculty survey data provides a key research tool on a variety of issues related to teaching orientation, yet there has not yet been any research on why some faculty prefer teaching more than others, and what this preference means in relation to how they responded to other questions on the Carnegie survey. The analysis of the Carnegie data provided in these chapters represents the first exploration of these issues, and is the first study of teaching preference with such an international scope.

This study explores the Carnegie survey data on faculty orientation toward teaching or research, to determine whether any significant international trends exist. A sole question (q40) on the survey provides the focal point for this analysis. This question asked respondents to indicate whether their preferences lay "primarily in teaching", "leaning toward teaching", "leaning toward research", or "primarily in research." In essence, the structure of this question on the Carnegie survey forced faculty to choose between one of two directions: either toward teaching, or toward research. Teaching-oriented faculty were thus defined basically by a method of self-selection. Faculty who indicated on the Carnegie survey that their interests "lean toward teaching" or "lie primarily in teaching" were considered teaching-oriented, and those who responded that their interests "lean toward research" or "lie primarily in research" were considered research-oriented.

Overall, the Carnegie survey revealed that there are considerably more research-oriented faculty than teaching-oriented faculty worldwide. Naturally, there are national variations. Commitment to teaching dominates in five of the fourteen countries—Brazil, Chile, Mexico, Russia and the United States—while faculty interests lean toward research in the rest of the countries surveyed (see Table 1.1).

TABLE 1.1

Regarding your own preferences, do your interests lie primarily in teaching or in research (q40)?

	(N)	Primarily in Teaching	Leaning to Teaching	Leaning to Research	Primarily in Research
Australia	(1,420)	13%	35%	43%	9%
Brazil	(989)	20	45	36	3
Chile	(1,071)	18	49	28	5
England	(1,946)	12	32	40	15
Germany	(2,801)	8	27	47	19
Hong Kong	(471)	11	35	46	8
Israel	(502)	11	27	48	14
Japan	(1,889)	4	24	55	17
Korea	(903)	5	40	50	6
Mexico	(1,027)	22	43	31	4
The Netherlands	(1,364)	7	18	46	30
Russia	(438)	18	50	29	3
Sweden	(1,122)	12	21	44	23
United States	(3,529)	27	36	30	7

Source: Boyer, Altbach and Whitelaw, *The Academic Profession: International Perspectives.* Carnegie Foundation for the Advancement of Teaching (Princeton, NJ: 1994).

Faculty preference for teaching varies considerably between and within the countries surveyed, with Brazil, Chile and Mexico showing the strongest orientation towards teaching as compared to research. The primary focus of this analysis is on faculty who indicated on the Carnegie survey that their preferences were either "primarily in teaching" or "leaning to teaching," in terms of how they differ from faculty who indicated that their preferences were either "leaning to research" or "primarily in research." While defining faculty as either teaching-oriented or research-oriented may appear to construct a seemingly false dichotomy—since most faculty engage to some degree in both teaching and research activities—other studies of the Carnegie data have found significant relationships between faculty preferences and the kinds of work in which faculty engage. That is, faculty who responded that their interests lie primarily in teaching were significantly more likely to engage in teaching than research activities. Gottlieb and Keith (1996) found "a significant difference between faculty with different teaching or research orientations" (p.17) along several dimensions. Their study identified a "research cadre" and a "teaching cadre," as defined by the time spent on certain activities, and found that faculty interested in teaching spent more hours per week on teaching activities than faculty interested in research, while those interested in research spend an average 9 more hours per week on research than teaching faculty. Altbach and Lewis (1996) also found that "those who prefer teaching over research spend somewhat more time on local or campus-related activities (teaching, service, and administration) than do those who prefer research over teaching." (p.21)

Table 1.1 shows that faculty in Brazil, Chile and Mexico are relatively more interested in teaching than in the other countries surveyed. The Carnegie data also show that faculty in these three countries indicated that their institution is "very important" to them, while a large majority of faculty in every other country surveyed say this about their academic discipline. Altbach and Lewis (1996) observed that the professoriate in these countries stand out as having "the lowest commitment to research of any country surveyed, defined by faculty indications of interest in research overall, time spent in research activities, books and articles published, and the level of funding received for research" (p. 24). Clearly, there are significant relationships between faculty interests and the kinds of work in which faculty choose to engage.

"At the heart of this matter is the commitment faculty feel toward their discipline, on the one hand, and toward their institution on the other" (Boyer, Altbach & Whitelaw, 1994: 11). Orientation towards research or towards teaching reflects an important professional dilemma for most faculty, caught between the pull of research—in the discipline—and teaching, for which students enroll in their institutions. Faculty responses to the Carnegie survey contribute an important international dimension to our understanding of these issues. Overall, it seems quite clear that "the orientation of the academy is more cosmopolitan than local: *professional* loyalty is stronger than *campus* loyalty" (Boyer, Altbach & Whitelaw, 1994: 11). However, case studies of the Carnegie data in a few of the countries found considerable differences between faculty based on whether their interests lie more in teaching or research. For example, "German academics leaning toward, or even those whose prime focus is on, research feel the least committed to the department" (Enders & Teichler, 1996: 485).

This study is based on the belief that there are several key differences between faculty who comprise their country's "research cadre" and those who prefer to engage in teaching. As described earlier, Gouldner (1957) and other scholars of higher education have repeatedly suggested that this is an important distinction to make when studying issues of faculty preference and work. Thus, an initial correlation analysis was run to check the correlation between teaching orientation and faculty indications of importance of academic discipline, institution, and department.[2] As Table 1.2 demonstrates, orientation towards teaching or research was found to be correlated in most countries with how faculty rate the importance of their academic discipline, institution, or department.

TABLE 1.2

Correlations between orientation toward teaching or research (q40) and level of importance of academic discipline, institution, and department (q17a,b,c)*

IMPORTANCE OF MY ACADEMIC DISCIPLINE (Q17A)

POSITIVE Correlation	NEGATIVE Correlation		No Signif. Relationship
	Australia	r= -.12	Brazil
	England	r= -.10	Chile
	Hong Kong	r= -.17	Germany
	Israel	r= -.21	Russia
	Japan	r= -.20	
	Korea	r= -.15	
	Mexico	r= -.12	
	Sweden	r= -.15	
	United States	r= -.05	

IMPORTANCE OF MY INSTITUTION (Q17B)

POSITIVE Correlation		NEGATIVE Correlation	No Signif. Relationship
Chile	r= .02		Australia
Germany	r= .16		Brazil
Israel	r= .15		England
Japan	r= .16		Hong Kong
Mexico	r= .01		Korea
Sweden	r= .12		Russia
United States	r= .19		

IMPORTANCE OF MY DEPARTMENT (Q17C)

POSITIVE Correlation		NEGATIVE Correlation		No Signif. Relationship
Australia	r= .10	Mexico	r= -.03	Brazil
Chile	r= .11			Hong Kong
England	r= .07			Korea
Germany	r= .09			Russia
Israel	r= .12			
Sweden	r= .08			
United States	r= .14			

NOTE: All correlations presented were significant at the .05 level. *Also, note that Survey items #17a-c were omitted from the data released to the Carnegie Foundation from the Netherlands. Item #17c was omitted from the survey administered in Japan.

Variables

q17a-c: 1 = very important   4 = not at all important

q40: 1 = high teaching orientation/low research orientation;   4 = low teaching orientation/high research orientation

The analysis of the Carnegie data presented in Table 1.2 indicates that, with few exceptions, teaching-oriented faculty are less likely than their research-oriented colleagues to indicate that their academic discipline is important, and were considerably more likely than their colleagues to indicate that their institution and department are important. This distinction is most frequently noticeable among faculty responses from Israel, Sweden and the

United States, where negative correlations were observed between teaching orientation and views toward the importance of academic discipline, and positive correlations were observed between teaching orientation and views toward the importance of institution and department.

There are a few anomalies in Table 1.2 that should be mentioned. No significant relationships were found among faculty responses in Brazil or Russia. In Hong Kong and Korea, teaching-oriented faculty were significantly less likely than their research-oriented colleagues to rate their academic discipline as important, but were no different from their colleagues in indicating the importance of their institution or department. The opposite trend was observed among responses from Chile and Germany, where no significant relationship was found between teaching orientation and survey responses regarding the importance of a respondent's academic discipline. Overall, Table 1.2 indicates that internationally, orientation towards teaching or research has a relationship with how faculty responded to the Carnegie survey.

It is also interesting to note that the correlations presented in Table 1.2 are remarkably similar cross-nationally—that is, with few exceptions, teaching orientation has the same relationship in every country where a significant correlation was found. In no country were teaching-oriented faculty *more likely* than their research-oriented colleagues to indicate that their academic disciplines were very important, nor were they *less likely* to indicate that their institutions were very important. With the exception of Mexico, teaching-oriented faculty were not *less likely* than their research-oriented colleagues to indicate that their department was very important to them. The more countries in which this trend is found, the more international the trend. Clearly, the question of orientation towards teaching or research clearly provides an important and useful way of looking at the Carnegie data.

Overall, the Carnegie data appear to support Gouldner's (1957) cosmopolitan/local dichotomy described earlier in this chapter, and the international nature of this finding provides a compelling basis for further research. Perhaps teaching-oriented faculty worldwide are what Gouldner would consider "local", while research-oriented faculty are more likely "cosmopolitan"? This question is addressed throughout the book. While there are various conceptual frameworks for how to conduct and present research on faculty, this study adopts the view that the more countries in which a trend in the Carnegie data exists, the more international that trend is. The significance of this study's international scope cannot be overestimated. Cross-cultural trends in faculty preference for teaching are an important area of study, and can bring the discussion of teaching and learning in higher education to a new, global level.

THE INTERNATIONAL DIMENSION OF THIS STUDY

It is envisioned that this study will be particularly useful for informing our understanding of the perspectives and ideas toward teaching and learning that are shared by academics across cultures and nations. The international dimension of this study addresses a number of important issues—including cultural differences in teaching styles and academic norms—which enhance our understanding of higher education. Differences exist everywhere—for example, student access to the institution, resources available for the institution, or political or cultural expectations or (or restrictions on) the institution and its members. In Iran, there are limitations on who may teach at a university, including ethnic background or gender. A professor in an industrialized country has far greater access to research grants than their colleagues in the developing world. Teaching at a hands-on technical college in North Korea varies significantly from the large lecture halls of a German research university. However, there are also many similarities found among faculty worldwide. For example, when you ask a professor in virtually any nation about the issue of academic freedom, they know what you are talking about—that is, they understand the term, or at least the concept, of academic freedom—regardless of the political or social conditions of their geographic location.

For this discussion, the perspective is adopted that cross-national similarities inform more of our understanding of the academic profession than do cross-national differences. Additionally, "cross-national similarities lend themselves readily to sociological interpretation, while cross-national differences are much more difficult to interpret" (Kohn, 1987: 31). Looking at cross-national consistencies in the data helps to reduce complex levels to meaningful comparisons—such as culture, language and geography—and gain a collective understanding of issues shared by faculty across the major regions of the world. Thus, national differences are largely set aside in this study, in looking for an internationally shared phenomenon. Put another way, national differences are largely "washed out" in this analysis, in favor of discovering international trends in how teaching orientation is related to faculty responses to the Carnegie survey. In this sense, "the diffusion of cultural characteristics and the sharing of historical experiences constitute so many disturbing elements in the design of the sample of societies, and do not constitute criteria for the limitation of comparisons" (Rokkan, 1976: 18).

An internationally-shared phenomenon could include a relationship observed in the data from all countries between teaching-oriented faculty and responses to a particular item on the survey (such as exemplified in Table 1.2 of this chapter). However, this discussion also takes the view that the *lack of a relationship found in the data can also be an internationally significant trend*. That is, if teaching orientation does not play a role *anywhere* in how faculty responded to a particular survey item, this too can be considered an internationally-shared phenomenon, in that it emphasizes the lack of importance teaching orientation may have worldwide in how faculty view a certain dimension of academic life.

The international approach in studies such as this can only be made possible by the existence of data collected from a group of subjects within which reasonable comparisons can be made. "All the countries selected to participate in the Carnegie Foundation's survey have relatively well-developed systems of higher education and represent geographically diverse regions" (Boyer, Altbach & Whitelaw, 1994: 25). All the countries can be meaningfully thought to have class structures and systems of social stratification, within which higher education plays some role. Each country's sample resembles the national profile to a close degree, in terms of institutional type, gender, age of the professoriate, and so forth. In the United States, data were collected from faculty at both two-year and four-year institutions. However, for the purposes of the analyses provided here, only responses from faculty at four-year institutions are used. Faculty at two-year colleges are less likely to engage in research activities, and thus the paradigm of choice (between teaching and research) which is the core phenomenon of interest in this study would not apply in a manner comparable to faculty at four-year institutions.

In essence, this study is primarily interested in "testing the generality of findings and interpretations about certain aspects of a phenomenon across multiple settings" (Rokkan, 1976: 18). The phenomenon of teaching orientation, as recognized in each of the countries surveyed, is the focus of the analysis presented in this volume. However, there are several considerations in using this research agenda. To begin with, there must be data from each countries that is similar in form and substance, focused on the same topics, and collected in the same manner, in order for valid comparisons to be made. The Carnegie survey provides a great deal of data for this purpose, but it is not without flaws. Each country's data collection procedures were slightly different. Some country's survey administrators omitted certain questions from the survey, others re-worded survey questions to be more in line with local contexts. Survey data from several countries needed to be re-coded after collection so that the same ordinal construct would help establish consistency in the data, a consistency which is crucial for valid data comparisons across country data sets. Further details on the Carnegie survey, including issues of sampling and data collection, are provided in Chapter 3.

Overall, the Carnegie survey administrators accomplished their complex endeavor with admirable success, and the resulting possibilities for cross-national comparisons are promising. The survey data they collected indicates that faculty worldwide appear to have a great deal in common in how they feel about many dimensions of academic work. Professors around the world report intellectual satisfaction in their work, but feel that better ways are needed to evaluate their teaching. Further, "a majority of faculty worldwide indicated that they have a professional obligation to apply their knowledge to problems of society" (Boyer, Altbach & Whitelaw, 1994: 14). This rare collection of data allows for the first ever analysis of faculty teaching orientation worldwide, the results of which are provided in the remaining chapters of this volume.

LOGIC AND ORGANIZATION OF THE CHAPTERS

The central theme of this discussion concerns the nature of faculty preference towards teaching or research. Teaching orientation is viewed in this study as an intervening variable—one that is affected by some variables which and affects other variables. Thus, the study looks Diagram 1.1 provides a visual representation of the framework used in this study of the Carnegie survey data.

Diagram 1.1: Framework of the Data Analysis

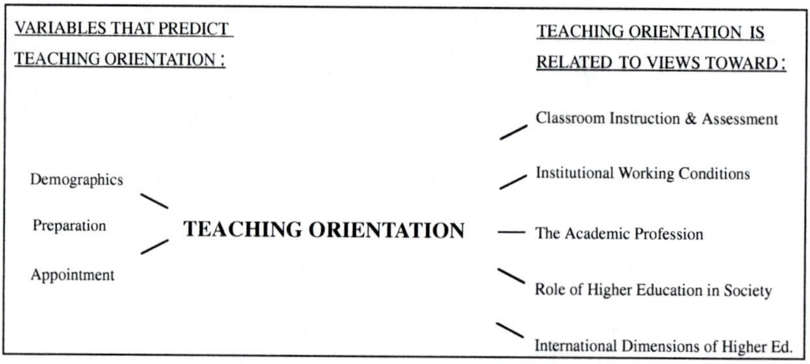

Diagram 1.1 represents a framework for exploring the Carnegie data in order to determine predictors and outcomes of teaching orientation. Chapter 4 provides the findings of the analysis that addresses the issues in the left side of the diagram, exploring the Carnegie data to determine what teaching-oriented faculty have in common in terms of demographic background, professional preparation, and other variables which might predict teaching orientation. For example, as female professors are found to be more teaching-oriented than their male colleagues, one could say that gender is a predictor of teaching orientation. This analysis helps to identify who teaching-oriented faculty are. Chapters 5 through 9 address each of the issues on the right side of the diagram, exploring the data to determine the relationship of teaching orientation with how faculty responded to several topical areas of the Carnegie survey.

The organization of these latter five chapters can be represented by a set of concentric circles, involving a micro-to-macro kind of topical organization. Imagine a camera zoom lens—we begin with a close-up, and then move farther away, allowing for the lens to capture an increasingly wider landscape. In chapter 5, we look at a relatively small arena—the classroom, specifically focused on classroom instruction and the assessment of teaching. The next three chapters each focus on increasingly wider arenas, that of the institution, the academic profession, and society at large. And finally, in chapter 9, we look at the international dimensions of higher education. Diagram 1.2 provides a visual representation of the organizational logic for these data analysis chapters.

Diagram 1.2: A Visual Representation of the Data Analysis Chapter Organization

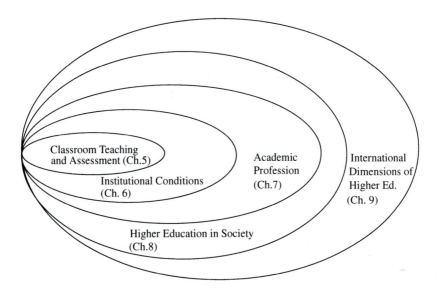

Diagram 1.2 represents an intuitive organization for how each chapter explores the differences teaching-oriented faculty and their research-oriented colleagues and their views toward various dimensions of academic life and work. The primary theme which connects all these chapters is faculty orientation towards teaching or research, and how this orientation relates to faculty responses to survey items within each of these dimensions. The final chapter of the book brings together the implications of the findings presented in the data analysis chapters. Overall, the significance of this study is that it shows how teaching orientation plays an important role in the lives of faculty worldwide. It is thus a useful means for looking at the academic profession in future research to determine more fully the impact of teaching orientation on the choices and decisions faculty make in their daily and professional lives.

CONCLUSION

"A survey is a strategy for uncovering causal relationships" (Denizen, 1989: 140). Several correlation and regression analyses of the Carnegie survey data were conducted in this study, in search of meaningful relationships between teaching orientation and responses to a wide variety of other items on the survey. These relationships in the data provide opportunities to enhance our understanding of the academic profession. To understand the academic profession, we must come to terms with the multiple interpretations that exist about it (Tierney & Bensimon, 1996). This is the first collection and analysis of faculty data to look at the impact of teaching orientation internationally. Through this study, we can gain a more thorough understanding of both the academic profession and what it means for faculty to be teaching-oriented. One of the overall implications of this study is that, as teaching orientation is correlated internationally with how faculty answered survey items within each of these themes, teaching orientation becomes a useful way of looking at the academic profession internationally. Further research is thus worthwhile to determine more fully the impact of teaching orientation on the choices and decisions faculty make in their daily and professional lives.

This study seeks to explore a number of questions about faculty perspectives and attitudes toward teaching, with the goal of informing new policies and methods for evaluating teaching. It is not irresponsible to suggest that current "top-down" approaches to improving accountability and assessment in teaching are ill-suited to the entrepreneurial environment of academia. However, before we can address the issue of how to develop "faculty-friendly" teaching assessment methods and policies, we must first develop a sound understanding of who faculty are, where they come from, what are the trends in their preferences and dispositions, and where they see the most encouragement (or discouragement) in their role as teacher. While the literature on teaching and learning is growing in terms of variety, comprehensiveness, and depth, unfortunately little of it incorporates existing demographic research on the academic profession, particularly that which informs our understanding of who academics are, and what they value in their careers.

Issues of compatibility and personality traits—for example, orientation towards teaching—are central to the discussion presented in later chapters of this volume. In exploring reasons for the failure of organizational change, Arthur Levine (1980) refers to compatibility—defined as the degree of congruence between the norms, values and goals of an innovation and its host—as a major component. In the same sense, scholars and policy-makers calling for the improvement of college teaching should consider whether the policy changes they are calling for and attempting to implement will be compatible with the academics whose activities they hope to change. Thus, an understanding of faculty attitudes and orientations toward teaching becomes crucial for determining the compatibility of innovative teaching reforms with the members of the organization at which these efforts are aimed. McKeachie (1990) and others have argued convincingly that faculty teaching can be improved with consultation. I would add to these observations that consultation which addresses specific personality traits and attitudes of academics will certainly be more successful than other forms of teaching assessment and improvement efforts. Thus, this analysis has implications for the management of academic staff as well as the study of academic organizations.

The chapters of this study address several important dimension of faculty identity, first by determining similarities among teaching-oriented faculty which distinguish them from their research-oriented colleagues, and then by identifying significant relationships between teaching orientation and faculty perspectives on a wide variety of issues and activities that impact their professional work and lives. Overall, the research questions and analyses described in these chapters seek to provide an understanding of what it means for a faculty member to prefer to teach. This preference is an important item to study, in that it can impact the quality of one's teaching. The implications of this study can inform research on higher education organizations, academic culture, and the assessment and improvement of instruction. Additionally, an understanding of factors which influence faculty preferences, particularly their preferences for doing those activities in which they see the most personal reward, has broad policy implications.

In analyzing the correlations in the Carnegie data related to teaching preference, this research provides a new and interesting dimension to current discussions and policymaking efforts on teaching assessment and faculty productivity in higher education. Further, this study can be useful for informing strategies for evaluating teaching performance across disciplinary and geographic boundaries. The continuing tension between classroom instruction and research persists, not only in the United States, but elsewhere, too. "Clearly, the challenge is to move beyond the teaching *versus* research debate and give to scholarship a broader, more efficacious meaning, one that not only promotes the scholarship of *discovering* knowledge, but also the scholarship of *transmitting* knowledge in the classroom" (Boyer, Altbach & Whitelaw, 1994: 22).

The existing research on the academic profession provides one of the richest bases of knowledge we have about any profession. However, as described in this chapter, there exists within this body of research a need for several bridges between areas of study, including demographic studies of faculty, and research on teaching methods and policies for the assessment of instruction. One reason why connections between these bodies of literature are rare is that the former often uses a sociological approach in discussing cultures, norms, rituals, and organizational behaviors, while the latter uses psychological terminology in exploring cognitive development, aptitudes, and responses to stimuli. Indeed, any association between these two fields of study is rare. Forming stronger connections between these areas of research is a crucial step towards forming a new understanding about the complexities of college teaching and higher learning. As suggested in the following chapter, demographic research reports—indicators of faculty attitudes and preferences—can be combined with other areas of research on the academic profession to inform our understanding of how faculty approach their work.

The discussion provided in this book represents an opportunity to build these kinds of bridges within the literature, by studying the relationship between faculty orientation towards teaching and perspectives toward other issues addressed by the Carnegie international survey of the academic profession. This study moves this discussion to a global level, by analyzing the contribution of approximately 20,000 perspectives on this topic from faculty worldwide. The research questions and analyses described in these chapters seek to provide an understanding of what it means for a faculty member to prefer to teach. This preference is an important item to study, in that it can impact the quality of one's teaching. An understanding of factors which influence faculty preferences, particularly their preferences for doing those activities in which they see the most personal reward, can inform new innovations in the assessment of teaching in higher education. The following chapter provides an extensive review of the literature on the academic profession which provides a theoretical grounding for the presentation and analyses of the data analyses presented throughout the remaining chapters of the volume.

NOTES

1 Responses indicated by "Germany" and "Korea" were in fact only collected from faculty in West Germany and South Korea. Also, Egypt did not provide complete data results of their survey to the Carnegie Foundation, and have thus been excluded from any comparative analyses of the data.

2 However, these were not considered "predictive" variables of teaching orientation, in that the reverse was possible—that is, teaching orientation could impact how faculty responded to these survey items. Variables like gender, age, rank, and so forth, cannot reasonably be impacted by teaching orientation, and thus any correlation found could be assumed predictive. In the case of importance, the correlation is noted, but not as predictive, but merely as informative. More discussion on this issue is provided in Chapter 3.

CHAPTER 2

Research on the Academic Profession: An Overview

INTRODUCTION

This book provides connections between several existing bodies of research, including demographic studies of faculty, organizational and cultural analyses, research on teaching methods and policies for the assessment of instruction. This chapter explores the existing literature within each of these categories, and identifies the relationship between them and the focus of this analysis. Research studies in these categories combine to form a comprehensive look at who academics are, what they do, and the social and cultural contexts in which they do it. In summarizing these studies, it is observed that an international perspective is particularly absent from existing literature on teaching and learning in higher education. This study is thus intended to help fill the void left by the lack of a cross-national or cross-cultural perspective on this important topic.

Categorization of the Literature

To begin, this chapter makes use of categories to define a framework within which the analysis of the literature is presented. Among the many themes of research on the academic profession, the following categories inform the focus of this study:

- **Demographic portraits of faculty** explore the nature of who academics are and what they do—from their socioeconomic backgrounds to their disciplinary affiliations, work preferences and habits, and research interests—which help us understand the levels of complexity surrounding academic careers. Borrowing a term from Finkelstein (1984), I have given these kinds of research the term "demographic portraits."

- **Research on teaching and faculty assessment** covers a wide range of issues, including teaching methods, student cognitive development, policies for the assessment of instruction and learning, academic reward structures, and efforts to improve teaching and learning in higher education.

- **Organizational and cultural analyses of the profession** incorporate themes of individual and group identity, the power of symbolism and imitation in making choices, issues of gender, race and sexual preference in the profession, the interaction between the academic profession and society in general, and the importance of understanding the values and beliefs of the profession which demographic research studies offer.

- **Comparative or international analyses of faculty** are relatively new, and present unique and complex challenges to the researcher. However, those that do exist provide excellent examples of how identifying cross-national similarities and differences can inform our understanding of the academic profession.

This analysis of the literature begins with a broad overview of each of the first three categories, and considers examples of integration between them—for example, research in which scholars refer to demographic research in developing organizational or cultural frameworks for describing certain activities within the academic profession. Within each of these categories, recent trends in the literature identify new challenges faced by the profession, covering a broad range of topics including alternatives to tenure, the growth of a part-time labor force, accountability, retrenchment, academic freedom, and the internationalization of scholarly work. The final category of relevant literature—comparative and international studies of higher education—is identified as a relatively new field of research which contributes significantly to our understanding of the academic profession in all three of the areas described here.

Most comparative studies of higher education have been published within the last two decades. Cross-national studies of the academic profession are even newer (and thus fewer in number), while international studies of the teaching and learning aspects of academic work are virtually non-existent. While there are several noteworthy national and regional studies of faculty (cf., Finkelstein, 1984), the lack of comparative research in this area provides a compelling theme for this discussion. The final portion of this chapter addresses the need for further research on faculty attitudes toward teaching and learning, as well as comparative studies on the academic profession. "Comparative studies have relevance to pragmatic national issues as well as providing a broader overview concerning higher education" (Altbach, 1979: 4). Certainly, a comparative approach to this hot topic would fill a substantial gap in the literature, and would be useful for informing our understanding of the perspectives and ideas toward teaching and learning that are shared by academics across cultures and nations.

DEMOGRAPHIC PORTRAITS

"Because the academic profession is at the heart of the academic enterprise, the views of scholars and scientists must be carefully considered" (Boyer, 1996: xvi). A significant body of literature on the academic profession is concerned with describing who the members of the profession are. Some researchers have focused their work on collecting and reporting data on elements such as the number of part-time and full-time faculty, at various ranks, and what their salaries are. Other studies—particularly those conducted by the American Association of University Professors (AAUP), the National Center for Education Statistics (NCES) and the Carnegie Foundation for the Advancement of Teaching—have attempted more in-depth analyses, exploring the socioeconomic backgrounds of academics, their attitudes and perspectives toward their work, and what kinds of work they do. For example, a recent study by the National Center on Postsecondary Teaching, Learning and Assessment (1995) found that "faculty with the least amount of student contact hours earn the highest salaries," and that "the more refereed publications a faculty member publishes, the higher their salary."

This study's focus on the issue of faculty preferences toward teaching builds upon existing research conducted largely in the United States. The attention paid to exploring and understanding the attitudes and work preferences of academics has grown considerably over the past three decades. Beginning in the late 1960s, faculty attitudes and belief systems have been increasingly studied in opinion surveys. Examples include Astin (1991), Bayer (1973), Ladd (1973, 1975, 1976), the National Center for Postsecondary Teaching, Learning and Assessment (NCPTLA) (1995), and Noll and Rossi (1966). The Carnegie Foundation for the Advancement of Teaching has studied the academic profession for years, producing vast databases of increasing scope and depth. Most recently, this organization conducted the first international survey of the academic profession, the results of which reflect a number of interestingly similar perspectives among faculty members in various corners of the world. For example, this study found that professors in all the countries surveyed are generally satisfied with their intellectual lives, with the courses they teach, and their relationships with colleagues (Boyer, Altbach & Whitelaw, 1994: Tables 38-40). Topic-specific survey research on issues such as attitudes toward industrial research on campus (Nora and Olivas, 1988) and the intersection of teacher personality traits with student instructional ratings (Murray, et. al., 1990) have also shed a good deal of new light on the work preferences of faculty.

A related and substantial body of literature on the academic profession focuses, not surprisingly, on what professors do—or are expected to do and be—in their various roles as teacher, researcher, and community citizen. This varies considerably for faculty, often in relation to their academic discipline or the kind of institution at which they are employed. For example, faculty in applied economics, environmental science, or nuclear physics are likely to be called upon for expertise more often than faculty in Shakespearean literature or Greek philosophy. There are also a variety of differences in higher education's role in society between private and public institutions of higher education, and there are differences between countries based upon the level of governmental involvement in their nation's higher education systems.

Faculty at American universities, especially research universities, have consistently been shown to teach less (Wilson, 1942; Parsons and Platt, 1968; Bayer, 1973; Ladd, 1979), and they are especially less likely to be found at the high end of the teaching load continuum (Finkelstein, 1984). Faculty at research universities usually publish, while faculty elsewhere typically do not, or at least are not strongly expected to. Fulton and Trow (1974) also found that at research universities in the United States, active researchers tend to teach as much as non-researchers, while at other institutions, research-oriented faculty taught less and researched more, and teaching-oriented faculty taught more and rarely published anything. The Carnegie international survey, described throughout this book, found that "those who prefer teaching over research spend somewhat more time on local or campus-related activities (teaching, service, and administration) than do those who prefer research over teaching." (Altbach & Lewis, 1996: 21)

A good deal of empirical research has served to defeat false assumptions of the nature of academic work. While conventional wisdom—according to the national media—would have us believe that faculty are by and large lazy, elderly, over-privileged white males, research has shown that this is indeed a false impression of the academic profession. Elaine El-Khawas' (1992) recent study on senior academic's preferences towards teaching contradicted yet another stereotype of the academic profession. Contrary to what much of the popular media would have us believe, El-Khawas found that most senior faculty are productive, contributing members of the academic professions, who are particularly active and interested in teaching undergraduates. These and other findings have particular implications for present discussions on the nature of (and direction of resources for) teaching and research in higher education.

Recent Trends

The connection between research and policy is a topic of increasing concern for many scholars and practitioners in higher education. However, while some researchers (Altbach, 1995; Fairweather, 1994; El-Khawas, 1994) have drawn on demographic portrait research to recommend important changes in the course of higher education, it seems that few connections have been made between policymaking and demographic research on the academic profession. Recent decades have seen a rise in politically-motivated research—both for and against tenure, affirmative action, religious or political advocacy in the classroom, and other aspects of academic life— often funded by politically- or ideologically-oriented associations, such as the Heritage Foundation or the Christian Coalition. Additionally an increasing number of reports which speak to "improving faculty productivity" are generated by a wide variety of sources, including policy "think tanks" and higher education governing boards. Much of this research is targeted not towards academic audiences, but more towards policymakers and the mainstream press, and thus have had a notable impact on our society's views towards faculty in recent years.

Newspapers and other periodicals of the mainstream press have focused increasing attention on the merits (or questions thereof) for continuing the tenure system. Notably, very little mention is currently made in the mainstream press of the difficulties faced by academics, while a number of articles have inadvertently lent support to the image of the professor as an upper middle class white male, relatively lazy, and out of touch with reality. This is indeed a problem for the profession—academics must find ways to enter their defense into the public debate over the nature of their work.

Often, research on current policy issues in higher education lead to startling predictions and unsettling realizations for academics. For example, Slaughter (1985) suggests that changing managerial role expectations for faculty may simply result in greater managerial control of the university. Such a prediction not only appalls devotees to the traditional guild authority of the academic profession, but also points an uncomforting spotlight on the ideological views that many academics share about institutional governance, academic autonomy and job security. As the academic work environment changes, faculty perspectives toward their work undoubtedly change. Tracking the changes of faculty responses to their environment help us strengthen and deepen our understanding of this important profession.

While some demographic portrait studies contribute much to the debate about the prospects for post-industrial society, (cf. Lipset, 1974) others seek to explore common themes among academics throughout the world. A significant amount of current research of this nature offers a wide range of descriptions for what it means to be a professor in today's society. Most recently, the literature on academic life has covered issues such as academic autonomy and accountability, economic stress, job mobility, concerns over the growth of a part-time labor force, institutional retrenchment, the changing size and demographic composition of today's classrooms, and the internationalization of scholarly work. Research on the attitudes and beliefs of the professoriate can and should help inform strategies for developing and implementing new methods of improving and evaluating teaching performance.

RESEARCH ON TEACHING AND FACULTY ASSESSMENT

Research on teaching and learning in higher education has, for the most part, ignored the demographic portraits which have informed other analyses of the academic profession. Rather than draw connections between these kinds of studies for analyses of faculty teaching preferences, researchers in this field have developed their own distinct body of literature. For more than 50 years, research on teaching has involved teacher observations, rating scales, questionnaires, and personality inventories—while attempting to systematize this research into categories such as teacher styles, behaviors, characteristics, competencies and methods (Ornstein, 1995). While the methodologies and findings of several of these studies are related somewhat with the demographic portrait studies described earlier, there are several noticeable differences. For the most part, the results of many of these studies—sometimes written in the form of recommendations or rules for teachers to follow—tended to focus on isolated teacher behaviors and methods, and held little regard for what those behaviors or methods meant in relation to the realities of the classroom (Ornstein, 1995).

Classroom instruction is a hot topic in the current research on higher education, and covers a broad enough area to justify a sub-categorization. For the purposes of this analysis, these studies can be grouped under the following sub-topics:

- teaching methods and environments;
- student cognitive development;
- teacher personality and teacher effectiveness;
- policies and methods for the assessment of instruction and learning;
- academic reward structures; and
- efforts to improve teaching and learning in higher education.

For the purposes of this discussion, I will focus mostly on research which is primarily concerned with how faculty approach teaching. While a good deal of compelling research on student cognitive development informs our understanding of college teaching, this discussion provides only cursory attention to this topic in relation to its relevance to a study of the academic profession.

Teaching Methods and Environments

According to McKeachie (1990), the question of whether small classes are more effective than large classes was probably the first major question that research on college teaching tried to answer. Among the first investigators of class size were Edmondson and Mulder (1924), whose comparison of students in two classes (one large, the other small) found relatively equal performance on learning assessments, although students reported a preference for small classes. Further studies—such as Macomber and Siegel's (1957, 1960) experiments at Miami University—determined that the effect of class size on learning depends on what the teacher does in that classroom. Glass and Smith's (1979) meta-analysis of class size research, which takes into account more basic outcomes of retention, problem solving, and attitude differentiation as criteria for learning, shows that small classes are indeed more favorable.

Another important body of research on teaching methods centers on the uses of lectures versus discussion. Bane's (1925) pioneering work on comparing lectures and discussions introduced a measure of 'delayed recall' to determine long-term learning. Bane's work showed clearly that, while there was little difference between his groups on the tests immediately following the course, there was a considerable superiority for students in the discussion group on the measure of delayed recall. Research on "student-centered" or "group-centered" teaching and learning, drawing on the "group dynamics" research of cognitive psychologists, added a new dimension to this discussion—more intelligent students achieved more with a higher proportion of discussion and interaction, whereas less intelligent students profited from a larger proportion of time in lecture halls (McKeachie, 1990). From the constructivist perspective (e.g., Halpern, 1994) lecturing does an adequate job of providing information to students, but is questionably efficient in helping foster the creation of knowledge (i.e., learning). "In experiments involving measures of retention of information after the end of a course, measures of transfer of knowledge to new situations, or measures of problem solving, thinking, or attitude change, or motivation for further learning, the results tend to show differences favoring discussion methods over lecture" (McKeachie, Pintrich, Lin, Smith, & Sharma, 1990: 12).

Recent research on college teaching has explored alternatives such as collaborative learning (cf. Panitz & Panitz, 1998) or group teaching, experiential learning, and the uses of technology for instruction. This latter point bears particular mention, given the rising interest throughout higher education in the promise of distance learning and the Internet. While absolutely under-researched, the uses of technology for expanding both access to and presentation of knowledge offer vast new opportunities—and equally vast challenges—to the future of the academic profession.

In general, a large body of research on college teaching focuses on the collection of accepted routines college professors rely on in the classroom.

Such routines include issues of method, time, physical space and tools, and evaluation procedures. Issues of method refer broadly to the type of instruction preferred by the teacher, whether it be lecture, group discussions, laboratory assignments, or whatever. There are a limited a number of these methodological routines, many of which have struggled to gain legitimacy within the academic profession. There are some methods which, based largely on ideological grounds, a number of academics hold strong criticism for, such as the extensive use of drama and humor in the classroom. Issues of time include the predictable nature of today's courses. They meet a certain number of hours each week, at the same time and on the same day of the week, in the same classroom, etc. As well, time-related routines in college teaching include how a professor begins and ends class periods. Overall, a professor's use of time in the classroom is considered throughout the academic profession as under the full authority of the instructor. Issues of physical space and tools include the size and layout of the classroom, the chairs, blackboard, pens, reading and homework assignments, exams, door, and wall clock.

In conclusion, teaching methods—or routines—have not changed since the first institutions of higher education at Bologna and Paris, perhaps a reflection of the organizational theory that where there might be uncertainty, individuals choose imitation. Recent questions raised over teaching behaviors and methods in terms of student cognition have generated interest, but mostly have not been well-received by most faculty members, the majority of whom are comfortably secure in their chosen routines of classroom activity. Using routines almost seems necessary to make ambiguity in teaching and learning understandable and manageable. A fair amount of the current literature on teaching and learning in higher education seems mostly directed towards developing new routines, adding to the collection of teaching routines a teacher may chose from, without questioning the underlying presumptions of the uses of routines in college teaching. Very recently, technology and distance learning have begun to change the direction—albeit slightly—of the teaching paradigms and routines within the higher education enterprise, the first real challenge to these established routines in centuries. How faculty respond to the challenges and opportunities of new technologies will most likely determine the course of higher education in the next decade.

Student Cognitive Development

Student cognitive development is of primary concern to any conscientious classroom instructor, thus the literature on this topic is increasingly incorporated into journals and edited volumes on teaching in higher education. Recent research in the professional field of student affairs—as reflected in the increasing variety and comprehensiveness of journals and books on these subject—has generated increased attention toward student personal and intellectual development. In general, cognitive theorists focus on how students reason, and the ways in which they think, act and make decisions. These theorists look at shifts in perceptions toward moral issues, perceptions and reasoning about the world, and encourage students to move toward advanced levels of cognitive development, sometimes by challenging them with alternative points of view. Perry (1970) stated that structures which offer challenge and support are necessary for cognitive development. Further, different students need different challenges and supports, as the same situation will not be equally challenging or supportive for all students. These and other models of development introduced by student cognitive theorists present a wealth of complexities for the classroom practitioner.

Curriculum and pedagogy are informed by knowing first where students are, and then affected by targeting appropriate cognitive levels and ways of knowing (Schmidt & Davidson, 1983). Effective teachers push students to achieve a level of reasoning just above, but not too far above, their current level. These theories contribute a great deal to our understanding of the teaching and learning activities in higher education. Critical thinking skills—the ability to evaluate different points of view and to look at evidence—are a key component to the success of students both during and beyond their higher education experiences, and as Kitchener and King's (1984) model of reflective judgment illustrates, a student's learning environment can (and, they argue, should) be constructed to challenge absolutistic assumptions and hold up the validity of alternative perspectives. In sum, student cognitive theories can and do inform effective policies and methods for improving college teaching and the assessment of teaching performance, and thus contribute a great deal to the changing expectations of how faculty perform in their role as classroom teacher.

Teacher Personality and Teaching Effectiveness

Certainly, demographic portraits can be applicable for research which seeks to enhance our understanding and methods of teaching and learning in higher education. The most promising work towards integrating demographic knowledge of the professoriate with theories for how this knowledge is useful comes from the field of educational psychology, particularly those studies which emphasize the relationship between faculty personality traits and teaching effectiveness. Despite a growing number of research efforts, very little is known for certain about the relation between teacher personality and teacher effectiveness. Some scholars have explored personality traits of academics to determine whether personal values and beliefs impact a professor's teaching abilities. In one study (Murray, et al., 1990), 29 personality traits of 46 psychology instructors were systematically compared with the instructor's teaching effectiveness ratings in six different courses. Personality traits were significantly related to teaching effectiveness, and specific traits were differentially effective, depending on the course. In addition, role flexibility—arguably a personality trait as well—

was shown to play an important role in an instructor's teaching perform-ance. Perhaps most striking, however, was their finding that "the compati-bility of instructors to courses is determined in part by personality charac-teristics." (Murray, 1990: 3)

Feldman (1986) reviewed the research that relates the perceived effec-tiveness of teachers with their personality traits, as the latter are deter-mined by teachers' own responses, gained primarily from self-reported per-sonality inventories and related means of obtaining self-descriptions. He found "no studies in which perceived teaching effectiveness was compared with teachers' general values or general interests. According to Feldman, "those who contend that college teachers' effectiveness (at least as per-ceived by their students) is associated with, and presumably even deter-mined by, the personality characteristics of these teachers do not receive a great deal of support from research in which personality traits are measured using self-reported personality inventories, direct self-description by teach-ers, and related means of assessing personality traits."

In another study, Sherman and Blackburn (1975) determined the degree of relationship between observed faculty personal characteristics and teaching effectiveness (as assessed by student evaluations). Their findings led these authors to suggest that improvement of teaching effectiveness may depend more on changes related to personality factors than on those involving classroom procedures. Clearly, as the somewhat contradictory findings of these studies reflect, there is no clear agreement on the rela-tionship between teacher personality and teaching effectiveness. As stated previously, demographic portrait research can offer a great resource for these studies, but the connection is mostly absent. A number of demo-graphic studies of the academic profession have shed light on how faculty feel about the current environment of increasing accountability. However, no scholar has yet convincingly shown how demographic indicators of fac-ulty attitudes can inform effective strategies for changing teaching prac-tices, or conversely, changing public perceptions of academic work. These issues are becoming increasingly important in today's higher education environment, where heightened concern over the effectiveness of teaching and learning has introduced new pressures and challenges to members of the academic profession.

Policies and Methods for the Assessment of Instruction and Learning

Anyone who carries out research on teaching effectiveness quickly runs into the problem of evaluating the outcomes of teaching (McKeachie, 1990). How do classroom processes affect learning outcomes? Students react dif-ferently to the same teacher, and yet the overwhelming majority of current teaching assessment methods throughout the world rely on student evalu-ations (Altbach, Boyer & Whitelaw, 1994). McKeachie (1990) observed that "despite faculty doubts about the ability of students to appreciate good teaching, the research evidence indicates that students are generally good judges—surprisingly so, in view of the fact that most research on student evaluation has been carried out in introductory classes, in which one would expect the students to be less able to evaluate them than in more advanced classes" (p.21). In general, methods of assessing teaching performance have changed very little over the last several decades. However, as mentioned previously, the evaluation of teaching has become an increasingly hot—and troublesome—topic of public debate and policymaking.

The measurement of student learning is another somewhat controversial area of research on college teaching. We do not yet know to what extent examinations reflect what has been taught. Some scholars have even claimed that examinations should challenge students to go beyond what has been taught. To add an additional layer of complexity to the issue, there is little agreement as to what it is we want students to retain (and thus, what types of learning we should attempt to assess). While some scholars maintain the superiority of key conceptual knowledge, others promote the necessity of learning and retaining factual knowledge, while still others call for ensuring that students develop the ability to solve problems. Of course, the lack of consensus over evaluation criteria *across disciplines* adds a dimension of complexity which make the acceptance of new evaluation theories and practices almost impossible. Overall, student evaluations have earned acceptance, however reluctantly in some quarters, as useful tools for assessing teaching performance, particularly when measuring characteristics such as intellectual challenge, knowledge of material, enthusiasm for subject, stimulation of discussion, sensitivity to class level and progress, and the ability to explain clearly. However, Angelo (1993) and other researchers are quick to remind us that our assessment of a teacher's performance should not rely on student evaluations alone. As many thoughtful researchers have noted, the most important indicator of quality teaching is in student learning—a topic which has its own Pandora's box of confusion and problems.

Challenges notwithstanding, quality research on student learning has been conducted and made available. A recent report of the National Center on Postsecondary Teaching, Learning and Assessment (NCPTLA, 1995)— the results of a longitudinal survey of 4,000 undergraduates over three years of college—found that, among many other things:

- The most influential experiences in noncontent learning for students involve human interaction: students encounters with new and different ideas and people via student-faculty and student-student contacts.
- Active student involvement in their own learning—collaborative learning, internships, meaningful work-study—brings students greater learning effectiveness

- A positive association exists between high student ratings of teacher organization and preparation and students reading comprehension, mathematics, and critical thinking achievements.
- Students learn more from a coherent and developmental sequence of courses

In general, the NCPTLA report states that faculty are the key to improving undergraduate education. While this seems rather intuitive, this research promises to inform the development of new policies which, it is hoped, will make academic work both more effective and rewarding.

New approaches to measuring student learning and teaching effectiveness have been introduced in recent decades. Portfolios are gaining increasing acceptance for use in assessing student learning as well as student effort (Smith, 1998). While student evaluations of teaching are the most common worldwide (Boyer, Altbach & Whitelaw, 1994: Table 27), many faculty have their teaching assessed by their departmental peers, administrators, and in some cases, consultants from outside the institution. Certainly, while there is widespread concern over ways in which faculty assess and improve student learning, the policies and methods adopted by an institution for the evaluation of faculty teaching are affected by current academic reward structures and the tenure system.

Structures for Identifying and Rewarding Effective Teaching

The evaluation of teaching bears particular relevance for the development of policies and procedures which identify and reward effective teaching. Academic reward structures in the post-war years increasingly favored sponsored research over teaching, and scholars rose to the pinnacle of their professions primarily by means of their research and not necessarily by their teaching prowess. Beginning in the 1970s, institutions began focusing their hiring criteria to obtain "star faculty" who "exemplify the research imperative" (Gumport, 1991: 27). Quality in research was shown to be much easier to assess than quality in teaching. How can you measure the effectiveness of a teacher in fostering inquisitiveness, or of the effectiveness of a minister in increasing faith? (Stuart and Whetten, 1985) Presented with the difficulty of quantifying the long term impact of a teacher on a student, several researchers have made assumptions about the maximum number of students a professor can effectively instruct, and then treated faculty/student ratios as indicators of the quality of education (Stuart and Whetten, 1984).

Another critical body of literature in this area focuses on whether structures or programs to reward effective teaching are appropriate or useful. For example, Australian scholars Anwyl and McNaught (1993) undertook a longitudinal study in Australia to determine what effects, if any, institutional teaching award programs might show in overall improvements in college teaching. The authors found that recognizing and rewarding excellent teachers does not equate with recognizing and rewarding *excellent teaching*. The authors also found that the criteria used to reward excellent teachers varied between institutions in their study, thus undermining the usefulness of these teaching award programs across a wide array of institutions.

In general, research on how to identify and reward effective teaching provides a framework for further discussion. Despite what is sometimes represented in the popular media, academics are conscientious about their teaching, and throughout the world faculty feel that better ways are needed to evaluate teaching performance (Boyer, Altbach and Whitelaw, 1994: Table 28). A significant area in which knowledge in this field can and should be pushed further is in research-based development of new ways of identifying and rewarding effective teaching. While effective teaching may be hard to qualify or identify, a fairly substantial body of literature offers us guides by which to develop a framework for discussion.

Efforts at Improving Teaching and Learning in Higher Education

During the past two decades, an increasing amount of attention has been directed towards improving teaching and learning in higher education. Notable examples include Wilbert McKeachie's (1994) *Teaching Tips*, Diane Halpern's (1994) *Changing College Classrooms: New Teaching and Learning Strategies for an Increasingly Complex World*, and several new journals such as Carfax Publishing's *Teaching in Higher Education*. Chickering and Gamson (1978) summarized years of study on effective college teaching in "Seven Principles for Good Practice in Undergraduate Education," which has set the standard for research and discussion on this topic for the past two decades. They concluded that good teaching:

1. Encourages contacts between students and faculty
2. Develops reciprocity and cooperation among students
3. Uses active learning techniques
4. Gives prompt feedback
5. Emphasized time on task
6. Communicates high expectations
7. Respects diverse talents and ways of learning

Within eighteen months of its original publication, 150,000 copies of the article (in the form of a special section of the *Wingspread Journal*) had been distributed by the Johnson Foundation, which had supported its development, and "Seven Principles Resource Center" has been developed at Winona State University (Creed, 1993). Without doubt, this has become the most popular article on the subject to date. However, as Angelo (1993) and others have suggested, these principles are inherently limited, and useful only as companions to other approaches to evaluating good teaching.

Evaluation instruments tend to favor teachers adept in observable or measurable teaching behaviors, while teachers who stress abstract or divergent thinking often do not fare well on such evaluations. These and other issues often confound the usefulness of the relationship between evaluation and reward of effective teaching. However, as McKeachie, Pintrich, Lin, and Smith (1986) have pointed out, most research of this sort does not result in the discovery of new teaching strategies, or the one "best" method of instruction, or a magic elixir for fostering student learning and motivation, but it can help college faculty conceptualize teaching and learning in useful ways.

Recent Trends

In the current higher education environment, there is a growing chorus of voices calling for change in the way academics fulfill the teaching function of their profession. While a good deal of research on college teaching centers primarily around issues of methods or policies, new reports on topics such as "improving faculty productivity" and "faculty renewal" are appearing on the scene with increasing frequency. State legislative mandates for productivity standards and performance measures pose new challenges to faculty autonomy, while attempts to measure the quality of academic work are forcing a nationwide debate over core elements of faculty life, such as the tenure system.

A driving force behind a good deal of research on the academic profession is the goal of enhancing or improving the daily work lives of faculty members, and perhaps help them become more effective in their roles and responsibilities. At the same time, an increasing amount of attention is being focused on what faculty do in the classroom. Indeed, there are efforts to redefine the role of the professor and to place more emphasis on teaching and less on research (Altbach, 1995). Recent trends in the field of pedagogical research include the development of constructivist learning theories, collaborative teaching methods, and exploration into the promises of distance education. However, a growing amount of institutional-based research on faculty is conducted for the purposes of identifying institutional or systemwide savings, and for developing policies to "improve faculty productivity."

The rising demands for teacher accountability in higher education have mirrored an increasing focus in the literature on the assessment and evaluation of quality teaching. Conference presentations, articles in research journals, and edited volumes are bringing an increasing number of voices to bear on the topic, while policymakers and administrators struggle to find middle grounds between collective bargaining agreements, legislative or trustee mandates, academic autonomy, and constituents growing more and more disenchanted with rising tuition and fees throughout the higher education landscape. Faculty are expected to teach students more efficiently and effectively, to increase their sponsored research dollar support and research output, and to regenerate the economy through service to the wider society, most particularly the business sector (Slaughter, 1985). The evaluation of academic work overall has captured new significance in public debate, and demographic research on the academic profession can be useful for meeting these challenges. Although the connections between demographic research and pedagogical research are rare, they must be fostered. Demographic portraits of the academic profession contribute to one of the richest bases of knowledge we have about any profession, and provide a valuable resource for developing conceptual frameworks in several complimentary areas of research, including organizational and cultural analyses.

ORGANIZATIONAL AND CULTURAL ANALYSES

Over the last 50 or so years, two competing theories about organizations have developed (Peterson, 1985). The first theory is oriented toward the traditional paradigm that considers organizational reality as objective facts. The other theory exists within a cultural paradigm that emphasizes an organization's ability to socially construct its reality (Chafee & Tierney, 1988). Clearly, the intersection of cultural and organizational perspectives has generated "an interest in the strain between fragmentation and integration [of the academic profession]" (Clark, 1987: 260). These two contextual themes provide assistance towards organizing and reviewing a relatively large category of literature on the academic profession. One subcategory of organizational and cultural analyses of the academic profession takes an 'environment-central' approach—which looks at how faculty interact and respond to changes in their environment—while another set of authors describe how members of the academic profession affect change among their colleagues and within their institutions. In both areas of literature, demographic portrait research often informs the framework in which these scholars develop their analyses.

Organizational Environments and Contexts of the Academic Profession

Some of the finest minds in academe have grappled with the definition of the academic profession. James Bess (1981) argued that the academic profession is comprised of a number of "subprofessions," and "what unites them is not so much a 'professional' culture but the university/research culture with its set of norms and symbols, methods for recruiting new members, and patterns of exchanging and disseminating knowledge through publication and consulting" (p.7). Other authors have observed a form of faculty "institution-dependency", noting that

> . . . academic professionals, unlike other professional groups, are very
> dependent on the institutions they serve for development of their
> careers. Doctors, lawyers, and the clergy, for example, are not bound to
> hospitals, the system of courts, or to churches alone to meet their
> career goals. Professors, however, cannot profess without the benefit of
> the college or university (Simpson, 1990).

Indeed, universities and colleges do shape the careers of academics and
obviously determine to a great extent what is meant by the "academic profession." While some may argue that the spread of distance education
methods and technologies may present opportunities for less faculty
reliance on the institution, the current costs involved currently prohibit a
large number of institutions from pursuing these forms of innovative communication with students, much less faculty.

In contrast to this group of "institutionalist" scholars, Burton Clark (1987)
observed that the institutional context is but one of several—including the
contexts of nation and discipline—that are important to faculty. The organizational perspective of faculty reliance on their employing institution for
many aspects of what defines their profession is certainly disconcerting,
particularly when demographic portrait research shows that many colleges
and universities do a relatively poor job in paying attention to the human
needs of their instructional staff (Schuster and Bowen, 1985). Indeed, as
Gumport (1992) and others have pointed out, the department in which a
faculty member works can make "a formidable statement about the importance of organizational contexts in shaping academic identities, especially
in terms of what and who is perceived as dispensable in a budget crisis" (p.
284).

A number of scholars on the academic profession focus on the disciplinary environment in which faculty work, and often rely on demographic portraits of the profession to construct the framework of their analyses. As
Ruscio (1987) observes, while "the role of academics—their tasks and attitudes and behaviors, their sense of professionalism and sense of being part
of a larger academic community—are functions of the institutions to which
they are attached, the discipline also exerts a powerful influence" (p. 331).
Perkin (1987) describes the academic profession as the only one in which
members look outside for their primary identity. In a nutshell, Perkin suggests that academics look to their occupation for their identity as teachers,
but outside it for their identity as a subject specialist. The content knowledge required for effectively filling the expectations which our society holds
for professors requires specialization—immersion—in a particular subject
area. As well, the work of Tony Becher (1989) and others on the cultures of
individual disciplines have shown that bodies of knowledge variously determine the behavior of individuals and departments. Demographic portrait
research informs several analyses of faculty culture, and suggests new and
potential directions for further research in this area.

Organizational Cultures of the Academic Profession

Cultural analyses of the academic profession are also useful for defining what makes academics part of a profession. As Furniss (1981) explains, the academic profession is an excellent example of a "one life, one career" profession. For those going into the professoriate, there is a vague but nonetheless real understanding that an academic career is a calling as well as a job (Shils, 1983). Like other professions such as law, medicine, or the clergy, faculty are conditioned to believe they are committing themselves for a lifetime to a discipline (Simpson, 1990). Cultural analyses of the academic profession refer to intangible, yet very salient, aspects to academic work, such as intrinsic motivation, civic virtue, and professional control. It is generally accepted that "the multiplicity of cultures that shape faculty identities—the culture of the profession, the cultures of the disciplines, the culture of the institution and department, and the cultures of institutional types (Austin, 1990)—make it impossible to conceive of a generalizable faculty essence" (Bensimon, 1996: 38). Nevertheless, it is common to view academics in terms of a generalized class of professionals.

Damrosch's (1995) call for intellectual collaboration among academics raises a number of questions about the nature of academic work, much of which is conducted in isolation. With the exception of some fields in science, where collaboration is an important rule, certain aspects of academic culture seem to prohibit faculty members from working together, which arguably can produce research of higher quality and broader scope. Decisions of tenure and promotion review committees reflect this aspect by their emphasis on singly-authored publications as having more "weight" than co-authored works. Within the arena of social analyses of the academic profession lies a subunit of research on the socialization of new faculty members. Van Maanen's (1976) work on socialization, Tierney's (1988) work on the culture of academic departments and institutions, and particularly Boice's (1989, 1991, 1992) work on the experiences of new faculty members brings another layer to the cultural dimension of our understanding of the academic profession.

A fair amount of literature on the academic profession combines both organizational and cultural perspectives in their analyses. Some studies take into account the interchange of culture and personality systems, which revolves around the cultural patterning of modes of personal identity or style—in essence, the social environment of the institution becomes internalized as part of the individual personality (Parsons and Platt, 1973). Other scholars have explored the intersection of multiple cultures within an academic organization, and the tensions which this intersection generates. For example, Newton (1992) looks at the nexus of both culture and organization, by exploring how conflicts encountered between the "corporate community" culture of administrators and the "community of scholars" academic culture affect organizational change.

As Clark (1983) observed, "how to divide work and authority and still have the parts interrelated is the central problem of formal organizations and professions" (p.17). Chaffee & Tierney (1988) offer one of the clearest examples of the complex interaction between culture and organization in the academic profession. In observing the "challenges a cultural view of organizations presents to organizational leaders," these scholars present a multi-layered diagram to help the reader conceptualize the various dimensions of culture, and explain how congruence between all these dimensions is necessary to achieve real organizational change (see Diagram 2.1).

Diagram 2.1: A Cultural View of Organizations

Organizational Culture

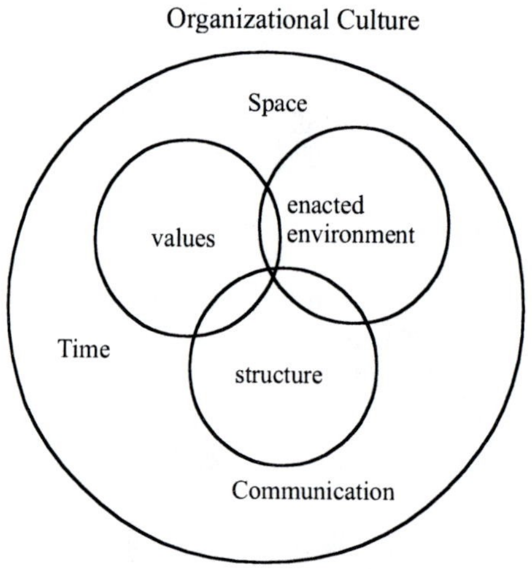

"Dynamic Equlibrium in Organizational Culture," model
developed by Ellen Chaffee and William Tierney (1988)

According to these and other cultural and organizational analyses of the academic profession, values held by members of an organization—in this case, academics—are an important factor to understanding the challenges to leadership and organizational change (Chaffee & Tierney, 1988). As well, in exploring ways to provide organizational support for faculty-, institutional-, and organizational-development activities, Gaff (1975) notes the importance of taking into account the interests and talents of the academic staff. In an early study of this kind, Gouldner (1957) proposed a distinction between two kinds of professional, the "cosmopolitans" who are high in commitment to specialist skills and in orientation to outside, discipline-based reference groups but who are low in institutional loyalty, and the "locals" who are opposite in each respect. In his study of faculty at a small liberal arts college in the United States, Gouldner suggested that the further an individual's contribution moves from research toward teaching, the more that individual is likely to pursue local loyalties and to identify with his or her institution. He concluded that there is tension between an organization's bureaucratic need for expertise and its social system need for loyalty. Other scholars have echoed Gouldner's observations that, overall, there is at least some tendency for organizational members who are committed to their profession psychologically to face outwards rather than to stress their local organizational loyalty (Hughes, 1979).

However, there are also some studies of the academic profession which have suggested that the cosmopolitan/local dichotomy is an oversimplification. It has become clear that a simple division of personnel into cosmopolitans and locals cannot satisfactorily be achieved (Grimes and Berger, 1970). Many faculty are both locals and cosmopolitans in the sense that they manage to combine loyalty to the organization and to their profession. The contrast is not an either/or distinction, as Toomey and Child (1971) have commented, but rather a more fragmented organization of attitudes. However, as observed in Chapter 1, the Carnegie international survey data provide some support for making Gouldner's distinction between faculty based upon where their primary interests lie. As shown in Table 1.2 of the previous chapter, teaching-oriented faculty are significantly more likely to indicate affiliation with their institution and department, while research-oriented faculty are significantly more likely to indicate that their discipline is most important to them. Thus, this analysis of the Carnegie data suggests that perhaps teaching-oriented faculty are more "local" and research-oriented faculty are "cosmopolitan" in their views toward higher education.

Empirical data in this area are scarce, and there is clearly scope for research to be undertaken from differing viewpoints. A significant aspect of this distinction is the perception of the situation held by the participants themselves, the ways in which they construct their own reality (Greenfield, 1975). For example, does a particular faculty member introduce herself as a Biologist or as a professor at Eastern State University? Clearly, demographic portrait research on faculty can provide an invaluable resource in enhancing our understanding of—and decision-making within—academic organizations.

Recent Trends

According to organizational identity theory, organizations that are eminently successful in pursuing a single identity enter a second domain of activity because of their success in the first (Stuart and Whetten, 1985). Although higher education in the United States has been a continuing story of unprecedented successes, the singular organizational identity of the academic profession is experiencing new dimensions of diversity (both in terms of population and mission of academe) which undermines prospects for continuing along with a "business as usual" attitude. New attention towards autonomy and accountability of academic institutions and faculty performance, depleted funding resources, rising demand for higher education, new technologies, and a politicized "PC" learning environment all pose new challenges for the members of the academic profession.

Recent themes in this literature include: faculty stress and the pressure to publish; cultural conflict within departments and institutions; and the challenges of integrating non-traditional faculty—in general, women, minorities, gays and lesbians—into the profession. Although data have been collected on the social origins of academics, almost nothing is known about the precise influence of their backgrounds on their careers (Lewis, 1977). Research on faculty exclusion and inclusion issues provide useful windows through which to view the changing population of academics. The work of Gumport (1993) and other authors on faculty responses to institutional retrenchment and financial exigencies provide new opportunities to enhance our understanding of academic life and its inhabitants. Tierney's (1993, 1996) work on enhancing the acceptance of diversity in academic culture contributes an important perspective to the discussion on the future of the academic profession. While little is known about the impact this research has had on organizational change, this is one area in which knowledge in this field can and should be pushed further.

INTERNATIONAL AND COMPARATIVE STUDIES OF THE ACADEMIC PROFESSION

As Altbach (1992) observed, "universities worldwide share a common culture and reality. In many basic ways, there is a convergence of institutional models and norms" (p.3). "Since the establishment of the Western university model in the medieval period, there has been an international community of scholars, with professors frequently teaching abroad, usually in Latin, the international language of academe in the medieval period" (Altbach & Lewis, 1996: 3). In the modern period, "with the evolution of the international academic labor market and scientific community, along with more efficient travel and communications, the international community of scholars and scientists has become much stronger and more professionally connected" (Ibid., p.3). However, international and comparative studies of the academic profession are rare, perhaps due in part by the immense complexities involved in this kind of research. Geographic distances, language and cultural differences, costs of travel and communication, and differences in the structure and function of higher education all present considerable challenges to the comparative researcher. Research of this nature must also take into account the context and climate of professional academic life for each region studied.

Despite these challenges, there is ample cause for developing an international and comparative perspective in research on the academic profession. "Perspectives from other countries can at least suggest ways of approaching problems that might lead to solutions" (Altbach, 1979: 92). Our world is rapidly become more interdependent and inextricably linked. Due to the increased globalization of scholarly work and communication, an international community of scholars has developed, and the distribution of information and knowledge has achieved dimensions never previously conceived. Comparative and international studies expand our understanding of the academic profession in many ways. Insight concerning how academics around the world cope with new challenges of today's fiscally-driven higher education environment has broad policy implications. "Comparative studies have relevance to pragmatic national issues as well as providing a broader overview concerning higher education" (Ibid., p. 4).

Some of the earliest efforts at comparative analyses of higher education include C.F. Thwing's (1911) description of European universities during his travels there, and Abraham Flexner's analysis of German universities, stimulated in part by problems perceived in the American university of the twenties (Altbach, 1979). Recent decades have seen increased attention to providing an international scope to the study of higher education. Journals such as *Higher Education* and *Prospects* reflect a growing interest in comparative and international research, and the field of study overall is gaining significant recognition. Certainly, "the work of higher learning has always crossed national boundaries" (Altbach & Lewis, 1996: 3). Within each category of research identified in this chapter, there are small but growing collections of international and comparative studies.

Demographic Portraits: International Perspectives

As Brown (1992) observes, "the inheritance of all the main scholarly traditions—Asian, Judaeo-Christian, Islamic—is that knowledge is for sharing trans-nationally, at least among the community of scholars" (p. 1). Cross-national studies of the academic profession are increasingly useful for "recognizing both the common challenges facing the academy worldwide and the increasing international connections of the professoriate" (Altbach and Lewis, 1996: 3). As mentioned previously, a recent international study by the Carnegie Foundation for the Advancement of Teaching—the first of its kind—reported how some 20,000 academics in 14 countries evaluate their lives and careers. As Altbach and Lewis (1996) observe, this study provides us with the opportunity to study the similarities and contrasts among academics in different countries, "to examine how the organization of academic systems, specific crises, or distinctive emphases may affect the attitudes and the roles of the academic profession" (p. 5). While there are certainly many differences in teaching environments and cultures across national and geographic boundaries, there are also a great deal of similarities shared by faculty around the globe. The researchers found that "most academics worldwide are full-time, middle-aged, middle class males, generally dissatisfied with their salaries, classrooms, laboratories, research equipment, libraries, and with the technology available for teaching" (Ibid., p. 11-13).

The Carnegie study also found that most academics are generally satisfied with what they teach, with their collegial relationships, and with their freedom to pursue research of interest to them (Boyer, Altbach & Whitelaw, 1994: Tables 38-40).

While studies such as the Carnegie survey or Burton Clark's (1990) social history of the profession address a wide range of research issues, other studies have focused on singular topics within the academic profession. Goodwin and Nacht (1991) studied how academics have become more mobile, seeking employment or following their research interests to various corners of the world, or perhaps pursuing a better life in another country. Altbach (1994) observed how the politics of the academic community has had a remarkable impact on society in many parts of the world. Other comparative studies of faculty consist largely of case studies in a few countries or within a particular region, such as Pelczar's (1977) essay on academics in Latin America, Neave's (1983) work on Western European faculty, and Miller's (1992) comparison of the academic profession in Australia and the United Kingdom. In general, comparative and international studies of the academic profession are relatively new, but the field is growing in breadth and depth, and certainly provides a valuable perspective for our understanding of faculty worldwide.

Comparative Research on Teaching and Faculty Assessment

While journals such as *Higher Education, Studies in Higher Education, International Journal of Teaching in Higher Education*, and others publish articles—and sometimes whole issues—on college teaching from various corners of the world, a majority of these are case studies rooted in a specific region. Case studies are indeed useful—Australian approaches to current issues of accountability, instructional technology, or teaching assessment and improvement can inform the approaches to these issues in Canada, while approaches to multiculturalism in South African higher education can inform discussions on this topic in the United States. However, for the most part, cross-national studies on college teaching and student learning are noticeably absent, and their value and need are surely underestimated.

Concern over teaching in the university is a truly international phenomenon, in dimensions beyond those related to the academic profession. Indeed, as British scholar W.H. Taylor (1993) observes, "the young need to be educated to realize how much of their lives will be determined by transnational forces" (p.439). A recent volume, *University Teaching: International Perspectives* (Forest, ed., 1998), provides the first cross-national collection of comparative essays and research studies on the subject of teaching, learning and assessment in higher education. Clearly, there are many important dimensions within this area of research. A Confucian approach to teaching and learning is significantly different from a traditional Western modernist approach. Students in Malaysia have significantly different approaches to classroom interaction and individual learning than their counterparts in

North America, and thus require markedly different approaches to classroom interaction. A lecture in Germany is not quite the same—and does not mean the same to its audience—as a lecture in Argentina. These and other issues underly the complexities of teaching and learning in both local and international contexts, and reflect a clear need for extensive comparative and international research in the coming years.

Organizational and Cultural Analyses: International Perspectives

Two decades ago, Joseph Ben-David (1977) published what has become a classic in the field of comparative higher education. In his comparative analysis of higher education in Britain, France, Germany, and the United States, Ben-David explores how similarities in history, structure, and educational reform have had surprisingly different consequences in each country's higher education system. Burton Clark (1978) examined four modes academic organization: the European, the British, the American, and the Japanese. His comparative perspective has provided a useful framework for many subsequent research activities on the culture and organization of universities worldwide. Scholars such as Lesley Wilson (1993) and Guy Neave (1993, 1994) have provided a good deal of comprehensive and comparative analyses on the changing nature of academic organization in Europe, while William Tierney (1993) and others have developed salient cross-national discussions on academic culture.

The international perspective is an important one in this context, as the challenges posed to academic organizational and cultural traditions are pervasive throughout the world. Altbach's (1984) international analysis of the management of universities in an environment of sustained institutional dependence on state, federal, and corporate funding sources provides another example of the usefulness of the comparative perspective. The international dimension of the Carnegie international survey of the profession informs several recent analyses of academic culture, and creates the potential for a great deal more research in this area. Our understanding of who academics are in various countries can be combined with a comparative analysis of the cultural and social contexts in which they work to provide a rich and useful discussion on the academic profession.

ANALYSIS AND IMPLICATIONS FOR FURTHER RESEARCH

In modern societies, the elements of rationalized formal structure are deeply ingrained in, and reflect, widespread understandings of social reality (Meyer and Rowan, 1978). Demographic studies of the profession help us to understand how academics, in the broadest sense, view the social reality of their work—their responsibilities to their professions, to society and to themselves. According to the current review of the literature, most of the scholarship on the academic profession ends at this level—that is, achieving understanding of this social reality, which in itself is not an altogether meaningless achievement. Yet, little has been done to present strategies for translating this understanding into practice, further research, and particularly policymaking, regarding teaching and learning in higher education.

Many scholars on this topic agree that organizations look for marginal change, rather than explore new worlds, new languages, or new establishments. Change in higher education comes about extremely slowly. Places like Bennington College are made all the more distinctive through their departure from this dominant paradigm—the exceptions reinforce the rule. Members of the academic profession are generally slow to change, reluctant to examine or modify their own behaviors, but willing nonetheless to respond to society's demands for improvement in the way higher education does business. Academics are intelligent, rational decision-makers. A good number of them would be willing to change their approach to teaching if they believed it would benefit their students and themselves. Academics are also largely autonomous, and are usually rewarded only for their work as independent researchers or teachers, as opposed to collaborative research or teaching. When members of an organization—or, in this case, a profession—are autonomous and independent social actors, the most likely form of organizational change will be slow and incremental.

However, incremental change in teaching and learning unfortunately does not satisfy the current demands of many higher education policymakers, state legislatures, benefactors and particularly the media. In the current political and social environment, policymakers—and to a large degree the popular press—judge faculty performance on perceived outcomes. They demand change in routines to improve outcomes, rather than encouraging a re-thinking of common presumptions about those routines. As teaching routines become more important for promotion and tenure, we will more likely see less—instead of more—willingness to question the presumptions upon which we base our use of these routines, and the presumptions upon which we base our evaluation of effective use of these routines. Academics may not explore new ideas for teaching and learning in higher education—by the same logic as their aversion to controversial or "illegitimate" research topics—when the decisions they make about their teaching may undermine their career goals and job security.

A number of demographic research projects have collected extensive data on academics' views towards their role as a teacher, including the levels of support from their discipline, institution and society for teaching, as well as their preparation for college teaching. These and other indicators of faculty attitudes and preferences can be used to identify a group of academics with which reform-minded policy-makers in higher education would be wise to coordinate their efforts. The introduction of new methods for evaluating teaching performance would certainly be better served, and most likely more successful, when they are targeted towards an audience more willing to participate in teaching reform. Demographic studies can be combined with research on teaching and assessment in higher education, as well as cultural and organizational analyses of the academic profession, to improve college teaching and the assessment of teaching performance. Overall, there is clearly scope for research from differing viewpoints, particularly from an international perspective.

As Tiernery and Bensimon (1996) observed, "the beliefs one holds about the academy inevitably frames how one acts in a postsecondary institution" (p. 5). This study seeks to address these issues by exploring various perspectives of faculty who identify themselves as teaching-oriented. As Stanley Hauerwaus (1988) points out, "teaching is a way to enhance our society through knowledge and wisdom. The moral authority of the teacher derives from this commitment and is the reason why the society as a whole feels betrayed when it is not honored" (p.12). Demographic portrait data results can be used to inform a wide variety of important and current research topics on teaching and learning in higher education, including:

- the relationship between a college teacher's intents and course outcomes;
- preferred teaching strategies and the criteria of effective teaching;
- the kinds of teaching organization and structure that affect learning;
- the quantity and quality of interactions between professors and students;
- the role and responsibility of the university as a system in organizing and providing assistance in teaching;
- the effects of university teaching policies; and
- the role of administrators in efforts to improve classroom instruction.

Further, the underlying paradigms for how academics perceive their role and responsibilities as classroom teacher need serious exploration. As Boyer (1990) argued, scholarship is multidimensional, and the application, integration and teaching of knowledge are part of its expanded definition. We must broaden our conception of structural barriers to organizational change in college teaching from beyond routines, standard procedures, and expectations of style and format to include ideological barriers within the academic profession. An understanding of what influences faculty attitudes toward teaching and learning can facilitate the development of a framework within which to approach this complex issue in a manner acceptable to faculty in all corners of the world.

In exploring reasons for the failure of organizational change, Arthur Levine (1980) refers to compatibility—defined as the degree of congruence between the norms, values and goals of an innovation and its host—as a major component. In the same sense, scholars and policy-makers calling for the improvement of college teaching should consider whether the policy changes they are calling for and attempting to implement will be compatible with the academics whose activities they hope to change. Thus, an understanding of faculty attitudes becomes crucial for determining the compatibility of innovative teaching reforms with the members of the organization at which these efforts are aimed. McKeachie (1990) and others have argued convincingly that faculty teaching can be improved with consultation. I would add to these observations that consultation which addresses specific personality traits and attitudes of academics will certainly be more successful than other forms of teaching assessment and improvement efforts.

Faculty perspectives toward the evaluation of their work also provide an important contribution to this discussion. According to a report by the Carnegie Foundation for the Advancement of Teaching, regarding their recent international study of the academic profession:

> How to evaluate academic work is of high interest internationally. At least two-thirds of the professors in all nations [surveyed], except Germany and Japan, note that teaching is evaluated regularly. . . Still, we found widespread dissatisfaction with faculty evaluation. Replies from all countries overwhelmingly indicate that better ways are needed to evaluate teaching performance. (Boyer, Altbach and Whitelaw, 1994: 12)

An understanding of factors which influence faculty preferences, particularly their preferences for doing that in which they see the most personal reward, thus becomes almost paramount for any true adoption within the profession of many proposed innovations in teaching and learning in higher education. In sum, the literature on teaching and learning has by and large neglected to incorporate many important aspects of demographic portrait research on the academic profession. The link between these two bodies of literature is necessary to inform a more complete and useful discussion on how to develop new policies and methods for teaching and the evaluation of teaching in higher education. Further, as discussed earlier, comparative and international research on this topic would undoubtedly be useful for broadening our understanding of teaching and learning in higher education.

Studies of a comparative or international nature are needed in order to more fully understand the perspectives and ideas toward teaching and learning that are shared by academics across cultures and nations. The Carnegie Foundation for the Advancement of Teaching has collected a considerable amount of international data on this topic, but it has not yet been analyzed comprehensively. Kerr's (1990) notion of "the internationalization of learning" reflects the need for developing the international and comparative perspective. We are no longer afforded the luxury of swimming alone—our world is rapidly become more interdependent and inextricably linked. "Due to the increased globalization of scholarly work, coupled with increased travel and worldwide communications, an international community of scholars has developed" (Altbach & Lewis, 1996: 41). Additionally, the distribution of information of knowledge has achieved dimensions never previously conceived. As Kerr (1990) observes, "we live in a world where . . . the worldwide advancement of learning has become the single most influential factor affecting the human condition" (p. 5). Our understanding of the academic responsibility of teaching needs to encompass an international dimension, in order for our students—and our colleagues—to adequately address the demands of this increasing global interdependence.

CONCLUSION

The existing research on the academic profession provides one of the richest bases of knowledge we have about any profession. However, as described in this chapter, there exists within this body of research a need for several bridges between areas of study, including demographic studies of faculty, and research on teaching methods and policies for the assessment of instruction. The discussion contained in this volume attempts to build these kinds of bridges within the literature, by studying the relationship between faculty orientation towards teaching and perspectives toward other issues addressed by the Carnegie international survey of the academic profession. Forming stronger connections between these areas of research is a crucial step towards forming a new understanding about the complexities of college teaching and higher learning.

The chapters of this study address several important dimensions of faculty identity, first by determining similarities among teaching-oriented faculty which distinguish them from their research-oriented colleagues, and then by identifying significant relationships between teaching orientation and faculty perspectives on a wide variety of issues and activities that impact their professional work and lives. Overall, the research questions and analyses described in this book seek to provide an analysis of what it means for a faculty member to prefer to teach. This preference is an important item to study, in that it can impact the quality of one's teaching. The implications of this study can inform research on higher education organizations, academic culture, and the assessment and improvement of instruction. Additionally, an understanding of factors which influence faculty preferences, particularly their preferences for doing those activities in which they see the most personal reward, has broad policy implications.

CHAPTER 3

Comments on the Data and Methods of Analysis

INTRODUCTION

To provide a linkage between the categories of literature on the academic profession described in the previous chapter, this study relies on data collected by an international survey of faculty conducted in 1991-93 by the Carnegie Foundation for the Advancement of Teaching. This chapter provides an overview of several important issues regarding the Carnegie data, particularly those concerning data collection and comparability. Following this discussion, the chapter describes the methods of analysis which produced the findings reported throughout this study. The main purpose of this chapter is to enable the reader to statistically reproduce the findings in the Carnegie data that are described in the remaining chapters of this book.

SAMPLING AND COLLECTION ISSUES
CONCERNING THE CARNEGIE SURVEY DATA[1]

The Carnegie Foundation for the Advancement of Teaching conducted an international survey of faculty during 1991-93 (see Appendix A). Nearly 20,000 faculty from around the world responded to this survey, providing the first ever data collection of this kind. The data provide a unique and powerful source of information for our understanding of academics, in showing that "there is indeed an international academic profession with common perspectives and concerns, common problems and challenges" (Boyer, 1996: xv). However, few scholars have utilized the potential of this resource. This international collection of faculty survey data provides a key research tool on a variety of issues related to teaching orientation, yet there has not yet been any research on why some faculty prefer teaching more than others, and what this preference means in relation to how they responded to other questions on the Carnegie survey. The analysis of the Carnegie data provided in this volume is the first exploration of these issues, and is the first study of teaching preference with such an international scope.

For the purposes of their international study of the academic profession, the Carnegie Foundation for the Advancement of Teaching developed a twelve page questionnaire that included over two hundred and fifty items. After several stages of development, in coordination with the research directors from each country, the final survey instrument reflected the Carnegie's interests in academic career patterns, general working conditions, professional activities, attitudes toward teaching and research, university governance, international dimensions of academic life, and a wide range of social and educational issues.

Because of differences in language, culture, and institutional structures, the Carnegie Foundation undertook a complex process of checking each survey for accuracy and comparability. The final questionnaire first was translated into the languages of each country (Arabic, Dutch, German, Hebrew, Japanese, Korean, Portuguese, Russian, and Spanish; an English version was used in Australia, Hong Kong, Sweden, the United Kingdom and the United States). Then each country's survey was returned to the Carnegie Foundation for backtranslation to standard U.S. English and comparison to the initial version. The backtranslators—scholars who were experts in both language and higher education—suggested alternative wording and other useful comments for the research directors in each country, who then made the final decisions on appropriate changes and proceeded with printing and distributing the questionnaire.

To facilitate the survey, scholars in the field of comparative international higher education were selected in each participating country. The research directors were involved in all aspects of the project, including preparing the questionnaire for distribution, sampling and administration of the study in their own country, and sending completed questionnaires to the Carnegie Foundation. The design of the sample in the Carnegie study involved two stages. In the first stage, all public and private institutions of higher education which award a baccalaureate degree (or its equivalent) or higher were included in the population from which the sample was drawn. Institutions were separated into two categories, when possible. The "first tier" of institutions included major research universities; the "second tier" included all remaining institutions in the population. Institutions were randomly selected from each of the two categories using a standardized process.

In the second stage, academics were randomly selected from lists of faculty at each of the institutions in the sample. The universe from which the sample was drawn included all academics who have a significant commitment to an academic career. Individuals could be full- or part-time or could have research, administrative, or other non-teaching roles as part of their career responsibilities. The specific choices concerning academic ranks to be selected, full-time or part-time status, and other variables were to be made by the research directors in the context of the broad commitment indicated above. Most countries planned to select enough faculty members so that they would obtain a minimum of 1,000 usable responses.

Throughout the survey, a sample of public and private institutions that award a baccalaureate degree (or its equivalent) was chosen. However, some countries elected to sample additional groups of institutions. For example, The Netherlands administered questionnaires to the Dutch-HBO institutions (which are comparable to the British Polytechnics and the German *Fachhochschulen* institutions) in addition to the Dutch universities. In the United States, questionnaires were administered to faculty at all types of institutions of higher learning including research and doctoral universities, master's-level institutions, baccalaureate colleges, and community, junior and technical colleges. These additional groups of institutions were not included in the international comparative analyses presented in this book.

Problems With the Carnegie Survey Data

"Because the survey method requires data collection in widely varying situations among dissimilar persons at different points in time, factors intrinsic to the process of data collection cannot be ignored" (Denizen, 1989: 140). Without question, any cross-cultural analysis of the kind described in this study must incorporate a certain level of caution. As Mary Jean Whitelaw, the technical director for the Carnegie survey, notes, "While every effort was made to enforce similar sampling procedures, cultural variation and country-specific techniques result in some methodological differences among countries" (Whitelaw, 1996: 677). The Carnegie survey provides a great deal of data for the purposes of this research exploration, but it is not without flaws. To begin with, the possibilities for cross-national comparisons are in places limited by a lack of complete or comparable data. Each country's data collection procedures were slightly different. Some country's survey administrators omitted certain questions from the survey, others re-worded survey questions to be more in line with local contexts. Survey data from several countries needed to be re-coded after collection so that the same ordinal construct would help establish consistency in the data, a consistency which is crucial for valid data comparisons across country data sets.

"Any comparative analysis of the Carnegie international data set must also take into account differences in the structure and function of higher education, and in the context and climate of professional academic life" (Whitelaw, 1996: 670). For example, in some countries college teaching is sometimes a "second" job, "in some countries faculty may be reluctant to answer questions that are subject to a political interpretation, and in some countries faculty will complete a questionnaire only if it comes through personal contacts" (Ibid., p. 670). In Germany, "only 28% of faculty returned completed questionnaires, indicative that in general, most German academics are not very supportive of surveys of this kind" (Enders & Teichler, 1996: p. 445). In Russia, the survey response was almost half that of Germany—only 438 faculty returned useable surveys, a response rate of only 15%. Further, as Levin-Stankevich and Savelyev (1996) observe, the Russian survey was carried out mainly in the Moscow region, and "does not necessarily reflect the perspectives of academics throughout the country" (p. 567). At the time the Carnegie survey was conducted (1992), post-Soviet Russia was in state of enormous transition, witnessing the fall of Gorbachev, the rise of Yeltsin, the fall of the Berlin wall, and social turmoil. Certainly, this may have had some impact on both faculty who responded, and those who did not.

The elimination of the binary system in Australia, as well as the incorporation of many institutions, surely had some impact on faculty responses in that country. In Israel, at the time this survey was administered, a nationwide strike of professors was taking place. As this strike was called to protest low salaries and deteriorating working conditions, one can expect that Israeli faculty had some particularly strong opinions about these items on the Carnegie survey. Survey responses from faculty in Hong Kong may have been somewhat impacted by anticipation of the 1997 return to Chinese rule. And in England, relatively recent changes in the higher education system, reflective of the increasingly centralized role of state involvement in the determination of several aspects of education and academic life (Hyland, 1998), no doubt affected the views of the academics responding to the Carnegie survey.

There are certainly a variety of obvious limitations to any analysis of an international collection of data, and the Carnegie survey is no different. However, the advantages of exploring this data far outweigh the disadvantages. This is the first collection of data resulting from a common survey and compatible research designs concerning the academic profession. Relatively similar data collection procedures were followed, comparable sets of data were collected, and response rates fell within a range considered acceptable for questionnaire surveys. Overall, the Carnegie survey administrators completed their complex endeavor with admirable accuracy and success, and the resulting possibilities for cross-national comparisons are promising.

RESEARCH FRAMEWORK

The main point of inquiry in this study is the nature of faculty preference towards teaching or research. This research explores common perspectives among academics throughout the world, to provide an understanding of how teaching preference may or may not be an important influence in how faculty view their work and careers. The study highlights generalizations about teaching-oriented faculty, and tests the validity of these generalizations by conducting a series of regression and correlation analyses of the Carnegie international survey data. This is the first study of the Carnegie data to look at the impact of teaching orientation internationally. With the results of this study—the first of its kind—it is possible to more fully understand both similarities and differences among academics around the world, and particularly what it means for faculty to be teaching-oriented.

There are a number of questions that can be asked about the phenomenon of teaching orientation. In what ways are teaching-oriented faculty different from research-oriented faculty? Do teaching-oriented faculty have much in common, such as age, rank, gender, or institutional setting? If so, are these commonalities shared by faculty across international or disciplinary borders? What are the implications of teaching preference for how faculty work should be assessed? The research methods employed for this study involve correlation and regression analysis techniques to determine relationships in the survey responses with how faculty responded to a single question (q40) on the Carnegie survey which asked respondents to indicate whether their preferences lay "primarily in teaching", "leaning toward teaching", "leaning toward research", or "primarily in research."

In essence, the structure of this question on the Carnegie survey forced faculty to choose between one of two directions: one toward teaching, and the other toward research. The importance of these two activities at opposite ends of a spectrum emphasizes the image of the academic caught between the pull of research—in the discipline—and teaching, for which students enroll in their institutions. As observed earlier in this discussion, the Carnegie survey data on orientation reflect this pull in showing significant correlation with how faculty responded to questions regarding the importance of their academic discipline, institution or department (see Chapter 1, Table 1.2). According to this analysis, teaching-oriented faculty worldwide were more likely to indicate that their institution or department is very important, while research-oriented faculty were more likely to indicate that their academic discipline was high important. Also, several related analyses of the Carnegie data have found that faculty who prefer to teach do in fact teach more than their research-oriented colleagues (cf. Gottleib & Keith, 1996; Altbach & Lewis, 1996). Thus, orientation towards teaching or research provides a useful lens through which an analysis of the Carnegie data can be conducted.

It is often assumed that teaching-oriented faculty are a considerably different species of academics than research-oriented faculty. This study tests the validity of this assumption, by using regression and correlation analysis techniques to examine the relation of teaching orientation with many other responses to the Carnegie survey. Teaching orientation is viewed in this study as an intervening variable—one that is affected by some variables and that affects other variables. First, this study explores background data collected by the Carnegie survey to determine what variables seem to influence how faculty responded to the survey question on orientation towards teaching. For example, as female professors are found to be more teaching-oriented than their male colleagues, one can say that gender is a predictor of teaching orientation. This study then explores the relationship of teaching orientation with faculty responses to survey questions on: (1) teaching and the assessment of teaching; (2) institutional working conditions; (3) life in the academic profession; (4) the role of higher education in society; and (5) the international dimension of higher education.

Thus, this study looks for both predictors and outcomes of teaching orientation. Diagram 3.1 provides a visual representation of the framework used in this study of the Carnegie survey data.

Diagram 3.1: Framework of the Data Analysis

VARIABLES THAT PREDICT TEACHING ORIENTATION :		TEACHING ORIENTATION IS RELATED TO VIEWS TOWARD :
		Classroom Instruction & Assessment
Demographics		Institutional Working Conditions
Preparation	**TEACHING ORIENTATION**	The Academic Profession
Appointment		Role of Higher Education in Society
		International Dimensions of Higher Ed

Diagram 3.1 shows how this study explores the Carnegie data in order to determine predictors and outcomes of teaching orientation. Chapter 4 provides the findings of the analysis that addresses the issues in the left side of the diagram, exploring the Carnegie data to determine what teaching-oriented faculty have in common in terms of demographic background, professional preparation, and other variables which might predict teaching orientation. This helps to identify who teaching-oriented faculty are. Chapters 5 through 9 address each of the issues on the right side of the diagram, exploring the data to determine the relationship of teaching orientation with how faculty responded to several topical areas of the Carnegie survey, as described later in this chapter.

The final chapter of the volume brings together the implications of the findings presented in the data analysis chapters. Overall, the significance of this study is that it shows how teaching orientation plays an important role in how faculty worldwide view academic work and life. It is thus a useful means for looking at the academic profession in future research to determine more fully the impact of teaching orientation on the choices and decisions faculty make in their daily and professional lives. The remainder of this methodology chapter is organized in two parts, much the same as Diagram 3.1. First, the research and analysis methods for Chapter 4—predictors of teaching orientation—is presented, including issues of regression analyses and variable re-coding. This discussion is followed by a description of the research and analysis methods used for Chapters 5 through 9, "outcomes of teaching orientation." The SPSS syntax and output, including regression tables, crosstabs and frequencies, are all available from the author.

METHODOLOGY PART 1: PREDICTORS OF TEACHING ORIENTATION

In developing this analysis of the data, the first research question concerns the prediction of teaching orientation—that is, do teaching-oriented faculty differ from research-oriented faculty, and if so, how? The hypothesis generated from this research question is:

- Faculty who prefer teaching over research are significantly different from faculty who prefer research over teaching.

Multiple regression analysis techniques—measuring the degree of association between a set of independent variables and one dependent variable—were employed to identify influences on faculty teaching orientation worldwide. Chapter 4 reports the results of a multiple hierarchical regression analysis for each country surveyed, and makes comparisons between countries. In all cases, the multiple regression syntax included gender and age as the first two steps (entered listwise), because these are the most basic elements of any respondent. The remaining variables were chosen for the hierarchical regression by the computer in order of their importance (in terms of their impact on the variance in responses to q40).

The multiple regression was conducted for 13 potential predictive variables, to find their impact on faculty indications of preference toward teaching or research (q40). In statistical terms, this regression analysis sought to determine how much of the variance in response to q40 can be explained by these variables. The resulting output of this regression analysis for each country are provided in Appendix B. However, it is important to pay close attention to the variables used for these analyses. As indicated in this example, several of the variables required statistical re-coding (represented by the nomenclature "-new", as in "q11anew") in order to effectively perform a meaningful comparative analysis. All correlations reported were significant at the .05 level.

Summary of Methodology Part 1

The first data analysis presented in this volume (Chapter 4) consists of an exploration into the Carnegie survey data to determine whether variables such as gender, age, rank, credentials, and other data related to demographic background, professional preparation, or academic appointment might provide useful predictions for strong faculty orientation towards teaching. Certainly, several other variables collected by the Carnegie Foundation survey would be interesting to explore in terms of their relation to teaching orientation. For example, academic discipline, institution of employment, or academic department may play a role in a faculty member's orientation toward teaching. However, ranking these kinds of dichotomous variables is inappropriate. As well, a respondent's views toward the quality of one's students, or satisfaction with their salary, institutional resources, or discipline could feasibly impact their orientation towards teaching. The number and kinds of courses they are assigned, or the number of students they teach could also be a useful predictor of teaching orientation. However, in cases such as these the reverse relationship is possible—that is, teaching orientation may play a role in how the faculty member responded to these survey questions. For the purposes of this analysis, only one-way relationships were sought. Thus, only variables which could not reasonably be affected by teaching orientation were chosen for this portion of the study, in order to adequately determine where influences on teaching orientation might be found. Also, the variables that were chosen for this analysis are ones which almost every country's survey administrator included in the final data collection and analysis, thus allowing for a more complete cross-national study of the data. In analyzing and presenting the data relationships found in this study, it is assumed that the more countries in which a trend in the Carnegie data exists, the more international that trend is.

While the first portion of the data analyses presented in this chapter focus on predictors of teaching orientation, the second data analysis section of this volume looks at the opposite end of the spectrum—outcomes of teaching orientation.

METHODOLOGY PART 2: OUTCOMES OF TEACHING ORIENTATION

Another primary research question addressed in this study is how, if at all, teaching orientation significantly impacts faculty views and approaches to other aspects of the academic profession. As stated earlier, the research question that frames this analysis of the Carnegie survey data is whether or not teaching orientation impacts faculty perspectives toward other areas of their professional lives. To effectively organize the immense amount of data collected by the Carnegie survey in useful ways for this analysis, certain categories of information were chosen, based on issues of data comparability and personal research interests. Thus, the second research question generated the following hypotheses:

• Teaching-oriented faculty view classroom instruction and the assessment of teaching differently than do research-oriented faculty.
• Teaching-oriented faculty have different feelings about the institutional working conditions than their research-oriented colleagues do.
• Teaching-oriented faculty have different feelings about life in the academic profession than their research-oriented colleagues do.
• Teaching-oriented faculty have different views than research-oriented faculty about the role higher education should play in society.
• Teaching-oriented faculty have different views than research-oriented faculty about whether international dimensions of higher education are important in their work.

The organization of these chapters involves a micro-to-macro kind of view. Imagine a camera zoom lens—we begin with a close-up, and then move farther away, allowing for the lens to capture an increasingly wider landscape. In chapter 5, we look at a relatively small arena—the classroom. Here, the study explores how teaching orientation is related with how faculty view classroom instruction and the assessment of teaching. The next three chapters each focus on increasingly wider arenas, that of the institution, the academic profession, and society at large. And finally, chapter 9 looks at the international dimensions of higher education (see Diagram 1.2 for a visual representation of the data chapter organization). The primary theme which connects all these chapters is faculty orientation towards teaching or research, and how this orientation relates to faculty responses to survey items within each of these dimensions. For uncovering potential correlations with teaching orientation—in this case, the independent variable—correlation analysis methods were used to determine whether statistically significant data relationships existed (at the $p < .05$ level of significance), and if so, the direction of the influence of teaching orientation on the dependent variables.

CONCLUSION

"The survey can be employed as a method of determining the stable and routinized patterns of interaction that exist in social groups." (Denizen, 1989: 154). As described in earlier chapters of this book, the Carnegie international survey of the academic profession can help illuminate many of the patterns of interaction that exist in higher education institutions around the world, particularly between faculty and their students, as well as each other. The primary focus of this study revolves around issues of faculty identity and perspectives, which are particularly useful for understanding the intellectual context of faculty work. This study takes the position that a faculty member's preference for teaching over research is an intervening variable, a determinant of varying importance for faculty responses to other portions of the Carnegie survey. The methodology of this study largely involves several basic forms of descriptive and bivariate statistical analyses. There are three primary goals of these data analyses: (1) to determine if there are professional activities, institutional contexts, demographic variables or educational background experiences which are related to a faculty member's views toward teaching in meaningful ways; (2) to determine how a faculty member's preference for teaching relates to his or her views toward other aspects of academic work; and (3) whether these relationships hold true across national and cultural contexts.

This study thus sets out to examine the validity of three general research hypotheses (H_1) and their related null hypotheses (H_0):

H_1: Teaching-oriented faculty internationally share similar demographic profiles, academic rank, or other background variables that distinguish them from their research-oriented colleagues.

H_0: There is no difference between teaching-oriented faculty and research-oriented faculty in terms of demographic profiles, academic rank, or other background variables.

H_1: Teaching-oriented faculty reflect different views than their research-oriented colleagues toward: (1) teaching and the assessment of teaching; (2) institutional working conditions; (3) life in the academic profession; (4) the role of higher education in society; and (5) the international dimension of higher education.

H_0: There is no difference between teaching-oriented faculty and research-oriented faculty regarding their views toward these issues of academic work and life.

H_1: There are meaningful international trends in how teaching-oriented faculty differ from research-oriented faculty in responding to the Carnegie survey.

H_0: There are no international trends in how teaching-oriented faculty differ from research-oriented faculty in responding to the Carnegie survey.

Through these research questions and hypotheses, the study helps define teaching orientation as a meaningful way of looking at faculty internationally. Where the results of this analysis produced a significant statistical result (at the $p<.05$ level of significance), this means there is at least a 95% probability that we can reject the null hypothesis, which states there is no significant difference in responses to q40, based on the predictive variable.

Faculty orientation towards teaching is an important item to study, in that it can impact the quality of one's teaching. The implications of this study can inform research on higher education organizations, academic culture, and the assessment and improvement of instruction. Additionally, an understanding of factors which influence faculty preferences, particularly their preferences for doing those activities in which they see the most personal reward, has broad policy implications. It must be remembered here that where teaching orientation plays a significant role in how faculty responded to the Carnegie survey, so must its opposite—orientation towards research. Stronger research orientation is correlated in the opposite manner that stronger teaching orientation is. For example, where teaching-oriented faculty are significantly less likely to indicate that their academic discipline is important to them, the reverse is true for research-oriented faculty. It is envisioned that this study will be particularly useful for informing our understanding of many perspectives shared by academics across cultures and nations.

The comparative analyses provide an important cross-cultural perspective on these issues. It is believed that, while faculty worldwide come from similar academic traditions—particularly regarding one's preference for teaching or research—there are a number of demographic and institutional variables that may influence these preferences in different ways. Further, it is believed that a faculty member's preference for teaching in one part of the world—say, Japan—has a considerably different impact on their views toward other aspects of academic work and life than in the United States. However, if the reverse proves true, and meaningful cross-cultural similarities are discovered, these would certainly be a compelling topic for further studies of the academic profession.

On the whole, the comparative perspective of this study provides a new and interesting perspective for our understanding of the academic profession. The remaining chapters of this book explore the international data collected by the Carnegie data, testing the validity of certain assumptions about the relationship between teaching orientation and faculty perspectives toward other dimensions of their lives. Each chapter presents the results of a commonly accepted statistical methodology, in table and narrative form, with the goal of collectively presenting a more comprehensive understanding of who teaching-oriented faculty are, as well as illuminating the common beliefs and perspectives held by teaching-oriented faculty worldwide.

NOTES

[1] Much of the description of the Carnegie data provided here is borrowed by permission from chapters of a recent publication, Altbach, Philip G., ed., *The Academic Profession: An International Perspective*. The Carnegie Foundation for the Advancement of Teaching (Princeton, NJ: 1996). The chapters are: "Introduction," by Philip G. Altbach, and "The International Study of the Academic Profession: Methodological Note," by Mary Jean Whitelaw.

CHAPTER 4

Professors Who Prefer Teaching

INTRODUCTION

This chapter represents the first of six data analysis chapters of this book. As described in the previous chapter, this study explores the relationship between a faculty member's orientation toward teaching and their views towards other dimensions of academic life and work. However, before this can be done properly one must first come to terms with an understanding of who teaching-oriented faculty are. Thus, this chapter presents the findings of a multiple regression analysis of the Carnegie international survey of faculty, conducted in order to determine meaningful predictors of strong faculty preference for teaching. The chapter describes the relationship between teaching orientation and demographic background, professional preparation, and academic appointment among faculty data collected by the Carnegie survey.

As observed in the previous chapter, there are certainly other data collected by the Carnegie survey which might provide useful insights on faculty who prefer teaching over research. However, for the purposes of this analysis, only one-way relationships were sought. That is, only variables which could not reasonably be affected by teaching orientation were chosen for this portion of the study, in order to adequately determine where influences on teaching orientation might be found. Also, the variables that were chosen for this analysis are ones which almost every country's survey administrator included in the final data collection and analysis, thus allowing for a more complete cross-national study of the data. The findings of this chapter conclude that there are indeed significant differences between teaching-oriented and research-oriented faculty, and that these differences exist in virtually every country surveyed.

To understand the academic profession, we must come to terms with the multiple interpretations that exist about it (Tierney & Bensimon, 1996). It is

generally accepted that "the multiplicity of cultures that shape faculty identities—the culture of the profession, the cultures of the disciplines, the culture of the institution and department, and the cultures of institutional
types (Austin, 1990)—make it impossible to conceive of a generalizable faculty essence" (Bensimon, 1996: 38). Nevertheless, it is common to view academics in terms of a generalized class of professionals, and distinctions are
often made between those academics who are research scholars and those
who have never published anything. As this study explores the usefulness
of drawing distinctions between teaching-oriented and research-oriented
faculty, it is first important to determine generalizable aspects to the identity of teaching-oriented faculty.

Particularly, as observed earlier in this discussion, the research-based
distinction proposed by Gouldner (1957) has some support from the
Carnegie international survey. Gouldner suggested that there are significant
differences between faculty based upon whether their primary affiliations lie
with their academic discipline (cosmopolitan) or with their institution
(local). As described in Chapter 1, this analysis found that teaching-oriented faculty are more likely to indicate strong affiliation with their institution,
while research-oriented faculty are more likely to indicate strong affiliation
with their academic discipline. The international nature of this finding provides a compelling basis for further research.

As noted in the Chapter 2, studies of the American academic profession
have collected data on demographic variables such as age, gender, salary,
and ethnicity. Several of these studies have sought relationships between
these variables, for example gender and salary (Fairweather, 1993), while
others have focused on the relationship between demographic variables
and faculty productivity (cf. El-Khawas, 1992). The research presented in
this chapter complements these studies, in seeking to determine demographic patterns for certain phenomena in the academic profession—
specifically, the strength of a faculty member's teaching orientation. This
chapter tests the validity of the following hypothesis:

> Teaching-oriented faculty around the world share similar demo-
> graphic profiles, academic rank, or other background variables
> that distinguish them from their research-oriented colleagues.

Generally speaking, most faculty have some preference for (and are usually required to engage in) both teaching and research, but each to different
degrees. Indeed, as faculty combine loyalty to their institution and to their
profession, the contrast is not an either/or distinction but rather a more
fragmented organization of attitudes (Toomey & Child, 1971). However, as
described in the previous chapter, the wording of the Carnegie survey forced
faculty to choose one or the other, by asking them to indicate whether their
primary interests lay more towards research or towards teaching. According
to the initial Carnegie survey data report, a majority of faculty in five coun-

tries—Brazil, Chile, Mexico, Russia and the United States—indicated a preference toward teaching, while a majority of faculty in all other countries indicated a preference toward research (Boyer, Altbach & Whitelaw, 1994: Table 17). This chapter was thus initially conceptualized as a research study that would explain why faculty in these particular countries appear to have a higher degree of preference for teaching than their colleagues elsewhere. For this reason, the design of the research sought to identify significant patterns and linear relationships within the Carnegie survey data. However, as described further in the chapter, the findings of this analysis provide no conclusive reason for the different levels of strength in faculty orientation towards teaching found between each country's sample. Rather, this study yielded findings that appear to hold true for most faculty regardless of the country in which they work.

Using multiple regression analyses, this study found that despite diverse regional, cultural, systemic, and other differences between faculty responding to the survey, descriptive information can be used to predict their orientation towards teaching or research to a certain degree. For example, this analysis of the data found that in 9 of the 14 countries surveyed, gender is a significant predictor of teaching orientation—in these countries, female faculty were more likely than males to indicate a preference for teaching. Age was also found to be a predictor of teaching orientation in many of the countries surveyed—the older the professor, the more likely he or she indicated a preference for teaching on the Carnegie survey. These and several other findings are presented in detail throughout this chapter, coupled with abbreviated explorations into the implications of the patterns found in the data.

Overall, the most important international predictor of teaching orientation found in this study of the Carnegie data is a faculty member's professional training. This analysis found that in virtually every country surveyed:

- higher academic credentials are negatively correlated to teaching orientation—that is, holding a doctoral degree was found to be a significant predictor of lower preference for teaching.
- faculty who felt more positive about their training for teaching were significantly more likely to indicate a preference for teaching.
- faculty who felt more positive about their training for research were significantly less likely to indicate a preference for teaching.

As discussed later in this chapter, these findings raise questions about the research focus of typical doctoral degree programs, particularly in an era which has seen rising demands for improving teaching in postsecondary education. Indeed, there are efforts to redefine the role of the professor and to place more emphasis on teaching and less on research (Altbach, 1995; Boyer, 1990). Further, this study echoes several concerns raised by Boyer

(1990), Eble (1972) and others about current approaches to graduate training while adding a new international dimension to these issues. The findings presented in this study provide the groundwork for future international explorations into faculty culture, academic reward systems, and organizational change. In analyzing and presenting the data relationships found in this study, it is assumed that the more countries in which a trend in the Carnegie data exists, the more international that trend is.

In looking at cross-national consistencies in the Carnegie data, we can form a broader, international understanding of the academic profession. As Altbach and Lewis (1996) observe, cross-national studies of the academic profession are increasingly useful for "recognizing both the common challenges facing the academy worldwide and the increasing international connections of the professoriate" (p.3). This research study thus looks for statistical regularities, seeking not differences but similarities in the data. The results of this data exploration demonstrate a number of commonalities shared by faculty across many part of the world, allowing us even more incentive for further research on the academic profession from an international or comparative perspective.

This chapter explores some potential explanations for the different levels of teaching orientation found among the national data samples of faculty, by determining what types of useful (and cross-nationally comparable) information collected by the Carnegie survey may predict stronger orientation towards teaching. Technically speaking, this chapter presents the results of a form of aggregate data analysis, which seeks to "separate a signal from noise" (Deutsch, 1978) by determining to what extent the variances within particular data relationships can explain a larger event, in this case orientation towards teaching shared by faculty internationally. The results of this analysis are organized around relationships between teaching orientation and three general themes:

- each survey respondent's demographic background (age, gender, years in the profession);
- their preparation for the academic profession; and
- the nature of the respondent's academic appointment.

The reasons behind having chosen these three general themes include issues of comparability—that is, data within each of these categories were collected from faculty in all the countries participating in the survey—as well as personal research interests. The underlying theme throughout this discussion is based on the author's belief in the relation between faculty orientation and teaching effectiveness, a belief that is supported by several research studies. For years, scholars have explored personality traits of academics to determine whether personal values and beliefs impact a professor's teaching abilities. For example, Murray (et. al., 1990) found that the compatibility of instructors to courses is determined in part by personality characteristics. In another study, Sherman and Blackburn (1975) determined the degree of relationship between observed faculty personal characteristics and teaching effectiveness (as assessed by student evaluations). Their findings led these authors to suggest that "improvement of teaching effectiveness may depend more on changes related to personality factors than on those involving classroom procedures" (p. 129). Indeed, as Kember and Gow (1994) observed, students do tend to respond better to teaching-oriented faculty than to others.

Earlier studies of the Carnegie data have indicated that there are significant differences between faculty with different teaching or research orientations. For example, Gottlieb and Keith (1996) describe a positively correlated relationship in their findings between faculty orientation and faculty work activity—that is, faculty who prefer to teach do in fact teach more, and those who prefer research engage in more research activities than their colleagues. Altbach and Lewis (1996) found that throughout all countries surveyed, "those who prefer teaching over research spend somewhat more time on local or campus-related activities (teaching, service, and administration) than do those who prefer research over teaching." (p.21)

Naturally, this relationship between orientation and work activity varies by country—for example, faculty in Australia and Chile spend considerably more time on teaching than on research, but while faculty in Chile are predominantly teaching-oriented, their Australian colleagues are considerably more oriented towards research. Enders and Teichler (1996) found that "for each hour of teaching, German university professors who are strongly research-oriented spend about 1½ hours on teaching-related activities, while those who are strongly oriented toward teaching spend almost 4 hours" (p. 460). These studies provide an important backdrop for the analysis presented here, and are woven into this discussion where possible. If teaching-oriented faculty teach significantly more than their colleagues, and if students learn more effectively from teaching-oriented faculty, then a study of what predicts teaching orientation around the world seems warranted.

The first portion of this chapter concerns issues of age and gender in the academic profession, particularly how these dimensions of demographic background relate to the strength of a faculty member's preference for teaching. "It is widely recognized that the international professoriate is both male and aging" (Welch, 1998: 8). Thus, the research presented here offers a timely exploration into whether faculty of different ages or genders are significantly different in terms of their orientation towards teaching or research. If such differences do indeed exist, they would have implications for our understanding of both the academic profession and the future of higher education.

DEMOGRAPHIC BACKGROUND AS PREDICTOR OF TEACHING ORIENTATION

For years, the collection of demographic information has played an important role in research on the academic profession. In the United States, beginning in the late 1960s, studies—particularly those conducted by the American Association of University Professors (AAUP), the National Center for Education Statistics (NCES), and the Carnegie Foundation for the Advancement of Teaching—have collected data on the socioeconomic backgrounds of academics, their attitudes and perspectives toward their work, and what kinds of work they do. The results of these studies have informed a variety of perspectives on the academic profession. For example, several researchers have pointed to a relationship between teaching orientation and gender or age. In looking at the U.S. data collected by the Carnegie international survey, Gottlieb and Keith (1996) found that more females than males are oriented towards teaching. The analysis of the Carnegie data presented in this discussion contributes an international dimension to these studies, by showing that in most of the countries surveyed, women are more teaching-oriented than men. There is also some indication in the data that older faculty are more teaching-oriented than their younger colleagues. These findings and their implications provide an important cross-national perspective to our understanding of the academic profession.

Gender

Gender plays an important role in most any society—indeed, perhaps there is nothing more fundamental to social organization than gender (Schlegel, 1996). While certainly there are culturally-specific concepts and norms for how gender impacts social interaction and structures, it may generally be said that diverse backgrounds and perspectives have always had some influence on classroom teaching and learning experiences. The issue of gender is particularly important in the academic profession, as recent decades have seen increases in the percentage of female faculty worldwide. In the Carnegie data used for this study, the percentage of female academics ranged from 8% in Japan to 39% in Brazil. The issue of gender in the academic profession is particularly salient when discussing teaching orientation. In the United States, where considerable research exists on the role of gender in academic professionals' experiences, it has been found that women tend to have a stronger teaching orientation than their male counterparts (Olsen, Maple & Stage, 1995) and that female faculty have generally higher amounts of student contact hours than male faculty (National Center on Postsecondary Teaching, Learning and Assessment, 1995).

This analysis of the Carnegie data sought to answer the following question: Is gender related to teaching orientation? Certainly, there are more female faculty in some countries than others. Perhaps there are larger percentages of female faculty in those countries where teaching orientation is proportionally higher? A cursory glance at the data might suggest so: in rank order, the countries with the highest percentage of female faculty are (1st) Brazil, (2nd) Mexico, (3rd) Australia, (4th) Chile, and (5th) the United States. Four of these countries are also those in which faculty indicated a relatively stronger orientation towards teaching.

However, this is not true for Australia, ranked 3rd in terms of women faculty percentage, but whose faculty indicated a stronger preference for research than for teaching. Further, while the Carnegie data show that gender is indeed a modestly significant predictor of teaching orientation in most countries surveyed, this is not true for responses from Brazil or Mexico, two countries in which teaching orientation is quite strong (see Table 4.1).

TABLE 4.1
Gender as a predictor of teaching orientation

Country	(% females)	Beta	R^2	F	P
Australia	(35%)	-.13	.02	13.31	.0003
Chile	(33%)	-.18	.03	12.55	.0004
England	(23%)	-.11	.01	17.74	.0000
Hong Kong	(25%)	-.26	.07	23.0	.0000
Israel	(28%)	-.27	.07	11.34	.0010
Japan	(8%)	-.07	.01	4.09	.0436
Russia	(26%)	-.25	.06	19.31	.0000
Sweden	(26%)	-.10	.01	5.91	.0153
United States	(30%)	-.13	.02	38.37	.0000
Countries where gender was not a significant predictor of teaching orientation					
Brazil	(39%)	-.06	.00	1.52	.2184
Germany	(17%)	.01	.00	.05	.8236
Korea	(13%)	-.03	.00	.41	.5216
Mexico	(36%)	.06	.00	1.48	.2244
The Netherlands	(22%)	.04	.00	1.58	.2084

NOTE: The number in the R^2 column indicates the amount of variance in teaching orientation accounted for by gender (at the $p<.05$ level of significance). The data on gender were coded as 1=female, 2=male, so negative correlations in Table 4.1 reflect stronger teaching orientation among female faculty. Complete tables for each country are available from the author. Please refer to Chapter 3 for more information.

Rather than finding conclusive reasons why a majority of faculty in some countries are more teaching-oriented than in others, this analysis found a more striking pattern in the data—in most of the countries surveyed, women are more likely to indicate a stronger orientation towards teaching than the male participants of the survey. Specifically, in 9 of the 14 countries surveyed, gender contributes significantly to predictions of teaching orientation. The significance of the relationship between gender and teaching orientation varied across countries, from 7% of the variance in Israel to 0.5% in Japan. However, national variations do not yield a clear explanation for the variation in the relationships between gender and teaching orientation. That is, there are few if any social-structural arrangements shared by the countries where the relationship between gender and teaching orientation exists. Latin American countries line up on both sides of the table; so do Asian countries. As well, the academic systems and cultures of the five "teaching-oriented" countries do not appear to have much in common that is not shared with the others in the Carnegie survey where gender was found to play a significant role in predicting teaching orientation. There also does not appear to be a relationship between gender as a predictor of teaching orientation and the percentage of female academics responding to the survey in each country.

The strongest relationship between gender and teaching orientation was found in Israel and Hong Kong (7% of the variance). While strong, cultural-ly-defined gender roles can be identified in both countries, there are few things in common here—Hong Kong's roots include a mixture of Confucianism and Western capitalism, while Israel's predominantly Jewish faculty view the world in considerably different ways. The weakest relation-ships of significance between gender and teaching orientation were found in England, Japan and Sweden (1% of the variance). While these three coun-tries share some academic traditions, few would propose that a female pro-fessor in a Japanese university faces similar challenges as a female profes-sor in Sweden—for one thing, only 8% of Japanese academics are female, compared to 26% in Sweden.

Thus, the question that emerges is why gender is important in some countries and not important in others in terms of predicting teaching ori-entation. Further research in this area would certainly be useful, but is largely non-existent, particularly from a cross-national perspective. There are, however, several studies on females in the U.S. academic profession which might help inform this discussion. For example, in a recent qualita-tive study of junior faculty in the United States, Tierney and Bensimon (1996) speak of "doing 'mom work,'" a term used by an assistant professor [in their study] to describe the imposition of nurturing and caretaking roles on women" (p.85). The female faculty interviewed by these scholars generally felt that gender played a definite role in their academic experiences. As one of their study's participants observed, "We are expected to be good teach-ers, and when a man does a good job teaching he gets complimented. When a man in the department is a nurturing father, he is seen as caring, and when a woman runs around taking care of her kids, it's seen as that she's simply doing her role . . ." (p.86). In another U.S. study, Goodwin and Stevens' (1993) suggest that female professors might place greater value or impor-tance on, or be more interested in, enhancing students' self-esteem and in encouraging student interaction and participation in class than their male colleagues. In general, the Carnegie data collected on U.S. faculty support these and other research studies in showing that women faculty approach their teaching duties differently than their male colleagues. This analysis of the Carnegie data thus demonstrates the pertinence of examining gender in the academic profession from a cross-national perspective, perhaps expanding upon existing research in the U.S.

Several studies of women in academe (see for example, Aisenberg & Harrington, 1988; Turner & Thompson, 1993; Clark & Corcoran, 1986) have found that across disciplinary contexts, institutional types, or cultural or national settings, women faculty have markedly different experiences in the academy than their male colleagues. To begin with, certain academic disciplines have more women faculty than others. Women faculty can be found largely in fields such as nursing, education, and social work, but rarely in the hard sciences, where many of the government-funded, high profile research laboratories are located, and often where less teaching in general takes place. Women are also most commonly found in the lower ranks of their department, in positions that are associated with heavy teaching loads. These are all important considerations which may certainly impact the relatively higher teaching-orientation reflected by female faculty in the Carnegie data.

While recent decades have seen a significant rise in the number of women and minority faculty in U.S. higher education classrooms, there are many challenges in the academic profession that women face. To begin with, these faculty are in high demand by the increasing numbers of female and minority students, who seek them out as mentors and role models. The extra pressures and workload which accompanies the responsibilities of role modeling and mentoring are rarely recognized or rewarded by academic departments. Further, as many institutions strive to be more inclusive in their administrative structures and proceedings, women and minority faculty are asked to sit on several departmental committees. However, as they are often the only women or minority faculty, they find themselves sitting on considerably more institutional committees than their white male counterparts, particularly at institutions with a commitment to diversity in staffing and governance. Additionally, there are likely to be few mentors of the same gender or ethnicity in their department who can to show them "the ropes." In looking at female faculty in the U.S., Tierney and Bensimon (1996) described a "hidden workload" that women and minority faculty must bear, undoubtedly affecting their experiences in the academic workload, and in many places contributing to their diminished presence within the faculty ranks. Unfortunately, research studies in the U.S. have indicated that minority faculty are less likely to be tenured than Caucasian female faculty who, in turn, are less likely to be tenured than Caucasian males (Carter & Wilson, 1992).

In light of the findings presented here and elsewhere, which indicate a stronger preference for teaching among women faculty worldwide, the academy must strive more diligently to retain women and minorities, and must focus more attention to what these faculty must do in order to survive (Johnsrud & Des Jarlais, 1994). In *Lifting a Ton of Feathers: A Woman's Guide to Surviving in the Academic World*, Paula Caplan (1993) suggests several coping mechanisms for women faculty to consider in successfully navigating the male-dominated world of academe. The author's suggestions include net-working, handling sexist comments, and looking for mentors, all of which could make a woman academic's job less stressful and increase her chances for success. Lynne Welch's edited volume, *Perspectives on Minority Women in Higher Education* (1992), also offers a wide range of observations and useful recommendations for both faculty and administrators to work together in improving the academic work conditions of women and minority faculty. More research along these lines will undoubtedly be useful in improving the experiences of women and minority faculty, which translates directly into higher percentages of them remaining in the academic profession—and, perhaps, aiding the academy in renewing its commitment to teaching.

In sum, while gender does appear to be a significant predictor of teach-ing orientation in most of the countries surveyed by the Carnegie study, there is practically nothing in terms of social-structural arrangements or academic history that explains why. Perhaps one goal for future research would be to conduct studies, similar to the U.S. research described above, on how female academics in these countries feel about being a female aca-demic. Specifically, Tierney and Bensimon's (1996) work on the responsibil-ities and expectations of female faculty might generate useful information for addressing this question. If that fails to flesh out any meaningful expla-nations for why gender is a predictor of stronger teaching orientation in these countries, perhaps research on the role gender plays in professional careers in each country would be useful. Overall, identifying a relationship between gender and teaching orientation is only the beginning of a much larger discussion, one which hopefully will attract the attention of future scholars.

Age

Teaching can be an exhausting activity. The preparation involved, the challenges of making the topic relevant and stimulating to an increasingly large number of diverse students, the painstaking effort that goes into read-ing and commenting on each paper and examination—after years of this, one might expect professors to get a bit worn out. However, while Sykes (1988) and others—including at times the mass media—would have us believe that senior faculty are by and large tired, elderly, over-privileged white males, research has shown that this is indeed a false impression. Elaine El-Khawas' (1992) recent study on senior academic's preferences towards teaching contradicted this stereotype, finding that most senior fac-ulty are productive, contributing members of the academic profession, who are particularly active and interested in teaching undergraduates.

The issue of age is generally an important one, given the relatively aging academic profession worldwide—in 9 of the 14 countries surveyed by the Carnegie Foundation, the average age of all faculty members was 45 or more. In several of the countries surveyed, older faculty hold positions that are significantly different in terms of responsibilities and expectations than newer, younger faculty. It is thus relevant to look at whether older faculty tend to be more or less teaching-oriented than their younger counterparts, and if so, whether this is true cross-nationally.

According to the Carnegie survey, age does indeed have a positively correlated relationship with orientation towards teaching, and this relationship is international in scope. In all but two countries surveyed, older faculty are significantly more likely to indicate a stronger preference for teaching than for research. The significance of the relationship between age and teaching orientation varied across countries, from 7% in Chile and England to 2% in Australia and Russia, as indicated in Table 4.2.

TABLE 4.2
Age as a predictor of teaching orientation

Country (Mean age)		Beta	R^2	F	P
Australia	(45)	.14	.02	15.45	.0001
Brazil	(43)	.20	.04	16.99	.0000
Chile	(47)	.27	.07	30.93	.0000
England	(45)	.26	.07	96.36	.0000
Germany	(41)	.24	.06	27.66	.0000
Israel	(51)	.18	.03	4.87	.0290
Japan	(51)	.24	.06	50.31	.0000
Korea	(45)	.25	.06	42.65	.0000
Russia	(51)	.13	.02	5.01	.0259
Sweden	(47)	.18	.03	19.01	.0000
the Netherlands	(42)	.20	.04	33.16	.0000
United States	(48)	.18	.03	79.47	.0000
Countries where age was not a significant predictor of teaching orientation					
Hong Kong	(42)	.07	.01	2.04	.1539
Mexico	(39)	-85	.00	.00	.9874

NOTE: The number in the R^2 column indicates the amount of variance accounted for in terms of responses to the (q40) survey question on orientation towards teaching or research.

The two exceptions to this international trend are found among faculty responses from Mexico and Hong Kong. In Mexico, the average age of faculty is 39—the youngest average faculty age of all the countries surveyed by the Carnegie study. Thus, perhaps the lack of a significant cohort of elderly faculty as found elsewhere has some impact on the absence of the trend indicated here. In Hong Kong, the mean age of faculty is only slightly higher (42), indicating that perhaps the same trend may exist to some degree as in Mexico. However, it may also be that because "Hong Kong's institutions of higher education were largely teaching institutions until the mid-1980's"

(Postiglione, 1996: 206), research orientation has not developed as firm a hold on the academic profession there as in the other countries surveyed.

Interestingly, the strongest relationship between age and teaching orientation was found in countries with the highest percentages of male faculty—particularly Japan (92%), Korea (87%), Germany (83%), England (77%) and Chile (67%). Thus, perhaps there exists a relationship within some combination of age and gender in terms of teaching orientation. Do older men prefer teaching less than older women? Do younger women prefer teaching less then younger men? Perhaps there are significantly more younger female professors than older ones worldwide, indicating how recently women have gained a significant foothold in the academic profession. As indicated earlier, research in the U.S. has found that women faculty approach their professorial duties differently than their male colleagues, and often do not share the same challenges and experiences. However, perhaps these differences are diminished as one ages in the academic profession. More research in this area beyond the scope of the Carnegie data may prove useful for determining the role of organizational socialization—in addition to cultural and social norms—in determining how aging faculty of each gender may grow more or less teaching-oriented.

In general, this analysis of the Carnegie data supports El-Khawas' findings of senior faculty productivity and commitment. In almost every country surveyed, older faculty are more likely to indicate a stronger preference for teaching over research. The reasons for the relationship between age and teaching orientation could exist in any number of sources. Perhaps some explanations are related to research on human developmental models, several of which indicate a peak of professional interest and productive activity in the middle of one's lifespan—somewhere between the ages of 40 and 55. Or maybe as professors age, they become less interested in making a name for themselves through research, and become more concerned with passing their accumulated knowledge on to future generations. Yet another possible explanation for this widespread relationship between age and teaching preference might be rooted in traditional academic reward structures that are shared among all the higher education systems surveyed. The older the professor, the less likely he or she will be striving to achieve tenure (the assumption being that they already have it), and therefore they have fewer pressures for research productivity. Also, as the academic job market has become more competitive over the last few decades, the research standards in many departments may have led to higher expectations for the scholarly productivity of younger faculty. While any of these suggested explanations are possible, there are currently no research studies available that have addressed these issues.

This study thus generates several questions and topics for further research. One suggestion for exploring this topic further might be to develop a survey on potential reasons for teaching preference, collecting responses from a large population of academics worldwide, and then drawing distinctions in the data collected along gender and age variables. As noted earlier, most members of the academic profession throughout the world are over 45 years old. One might speculate on whether, given the relationship between age and teaching orientation, the higher education enterprise in general will move naturally toward a more teaching focus as the academic profession grows older. Overall, more research into the potential reasons for this association between age and teaching preference will certainly yield valuable insights into the academic profession.

Other Variables of Interest

In addition to gender and age, three other demographic background variables of interest to this study were chosen:

- how long the survey respondent has been employed in higher education;
- how long the respondent has been employed at their current institution; and
- how long the respondent has been employed outside of academeme.

These variables were chosen for this analysis to determine simply whether they might provide interesting insights into the importance of work experiences—both in and outside of academe—in influencing faculty preference for teaching or research. These variables are also related somewhat to the discussion provided earlier concerning how older faculty in virtually all countries surveyed indicate a stronger preference for teaching over research.

Based on the relationship between faculty age and teaching orientation, one might expect that longevity in the academic profession impacts faculty preference for teaching. However, the data indicate that the length of time one stays in academe generally does not have an impact on one's teaching orientation. In only three countries—Australia, Japan and Korea—was there found a significant relationship between teaching orientation and years employed in higher education. Further, in all three of these countries the relationships observed in the data were only *slightly* significant at the $p<.05$ level, indicating a rather weak value of prediction. Thus, this analysis suggests that faculty fresh from graduate school have no more or less preference for teaching than faculty who have been in their positions for many years. This finding should be incorporated in any discussion of organizational socialization within the academic profession, as the Carnegie data indicate that experience within academe do not seem to significantly impact preference for teaching.

This analysis of the Carnegie data also sought to find some predictive value for teaching orientation in how long the faculty member has been employed at their institution. It may be generally believed that staying at an institution for longer periods of time helps develop a certain sense of loyalty and affiliation with that institution, which in turn leads to more preference for teaching (an institutional activity) as opposed to research (an activity which reflects a strong interest in the faculty member's academic discipline). As described in an earlier chapter, this study found that throughout the Carnegie survey, teaching-oriented faculty are less likely than their research-oriented colleagues to indicate that their academic discipline is important, and were considerably more likely than their colleagues to indicate that their institution and department are important. One would also expect longevity in an institution to correlate with teaching preference, because faculty who stay put are more likely to be focused on their institutional and students' needs, rather than adhering to the call of high-profile research projects which could propel them to a higher status in their discipline (and potentially lead to better job offers elsewhere).

However, in only 6 countries—England, Hong Kong, Japan, Mexico, Sweden, and the U.S.—was a relationship found between longevity at one's current institution and orientation towards teaching. In these countries, the longer a faculty member stays at one institution, the more likely he or she is to indicate a stronger preference for teaching over research. However, in all cases the relationship was only slightly significant at the $p<.05$ level, thus explaining only very little of the variance in survey responses to the item on teaching orientation. Thus, longevity at an institution and the strength of faculty affiliation with that institution may not necessarily be related. Both of these findings have implications for a conversation on issues such as faculty burnout, as well as organizational socialization within academe.

So, if time spent inside the academy or at one's institution does not seem to either reduce or enhance the level of one's teaching orientation, is there anything to be said for time spent outside academic life? Perhaps accumulating significant experience in the world of work leads to a stronger passion for passing on the lessons one has learned to future generations. For example, a retired diplomat may be more interested in sharing his or her experiences in the classroom than doing research, while an academic may prefer to dig through archival data and publish scholarly works about the intricacies of diplomacy. However, this nuance—if it does indeed exist at all—is only reflected in the data from the United States. Here, faculty who spent considerable number of years outside the academy were more likely than others surveyed to indicate a stronger interest in teaching than in research. Further, this relationship was also only slightly significant at the $p<.05$ level, thus explaining very little of the variance in survey responses to the item on orientation towards teaching or research.

Given these findings in the Carnegie data, one may indeed wonder what it is about age that provides a predictive value for teaching orientation. If neither experience within nor outside the academic profession significantly impacts a faculty member's preference for teaching, perhaps there is something about growing old in general that leads to greater teaching orientation. Certainly, in all countries surveyed, there are cultural and social norms associated with respect for elders as bearers of knowledge, and perhaps there are some expectations embedded in these norms for passing on knowledge to younger generations. This analysis of the Carnegie data thus generates an interesting area for further research—particularly in the United States, but elsewhere as well—where the percentage of elderly persons in the population is rapidly increasing. Should older faculty be given special duties or responsibilities different from their younger colleagues? Will we see the emergence over time of younger faculty engaging almost exclusively in research, while older faculty take on the lion's share of teaching responsibilities? What are the pros and cons of such an age-based distribution of activity within the academic profession? Further research addressing these and other questions will certainly generate a more clear understanding of how the future of the profession—and higher education in general—is likely to evolve.

ACADEMIC PREPARATION AS PREDICTOR OF TEACHING ORIENTATION

Preparation for the academic profession has historically involved advanced degree programs which focus almost entirely on developing research skills and a competent knowledge base in a particular discipline. While no solid research exists on the topic, it is fairly safe to estimate that over 90% of all doctoral programs—regardless of discipline—involve practically no exposure to (or training in) pedagogical methods or theory. Further, while a significant number of doctoral students work as teaching assistants at large universities, they are rarely given any formal training for their classroom responsibilities. Yet, as observed by the Carnegie international survey—in addition to other research in the U.S. (cf. NCES, 1993; HERI, 1995)—the majority of most faculty member's working time is spent in activities related to teaching, whether this be office hours, classroom instruction, tutorials, or otherwise.

However, it has been largely assumed that this form of professional preparation adequately enables one to be a competent teacher—an assumption that has drawn a great deal of fire over the last few decades. Some observers have begun to argue that if we are to train future professors to be better classroom instructors, we must move away from the traditional doctoral training program which emphasizes research skills and largely neglects training in the methods and theories of teaching and learning. Indeed, there are efforts to redefine the role of the professor and to place more emphasis on teaching and less on research (Altbach, 1995; Boyer,

1990). These arguments have become more common, particularly in the United States, as increasing attention toward accountability in higher education has led to a growing concern for assessing and improving classroom instruction. Reflecting on the impact of teaching orientation on the effectiveness of teaching activities, this exploration of the Carnegie data sought to determine whether preparation for the academic profession significantly impacts a faculty member's orientation towards teaching or research. Specifically, three preparation-related variables were examined in terms of their relationship with stronger faculty preference towards teaching:

- highest academic degree earned by the survey respondent;
- the respondent's satisfaction with the quality of their training for teaching; and
- their satisfaction with the quality of their training for research.

This analysis of the Carnegie data yielded several key findings in the area of professional preparation. In 8 countries, all three of these preparation variables were found to have some impact on teaching orientation. In virtually all of the countries surveyed, at least two of the three were found to be statistically significant in predicting teaching orientation. Overall, according to this analysis of the Carnegie data, preparation for the academic profession has a considerable impact on orientation towards teaching or research. Further, the impact of professional preparation on teaching orientation was found to be significantly stronger than demographic background variables or the nature of a respondent's academic appointment.

Credentialing—The Doctoral Degree

A doctoral degree (including Ph.D., Ed.D., J.D., M.D., etc.), otherwise termed a 'terminal degree,' is widely considered the pinnacle of mastery in one's discipline. In general, the Ph.D. degree—often called 'a research degree'—is the stamp of approval required for classroom instruction in most academic disciplines. The main exception to this is found in the medical field, where proficiency in some area of specialization (for example, cardiovascular surgery) must accompany the terminal degree in order to teach future practitioners. Given the relative lack of training for teaching in most graduate education programs, it could be expected that Ph.D. recipients would naturally gravitate towards that for which they are trained—research. Thus, this study sought to determine whether faculty with a doctoral degree differ from faculty without a doctorate in terms of preference for teaching or research.

According to the Carnegie data, the possession of a doctoral degree is a statistically significant negative predictor of lower teaching preference in all but one of the 13 countries in which data on academic credentials were collected. That is, in virtually every country involved in the Carnegie survey, respondents with a doctoral degree were *significantly less likely* to indicate a stronger preference for teaching that for research. The strength of the statistical relationship between the doctoral degree and teaching orientation varied among countries, from 13% of the variance in England to 1% in Australia and the Netherlands (see Table 4.3).

TABLE 4.3
The doctoral degree as a predictor of teaching orientation

Country	(% with doctorate)	Beta	R^2	R^2 Change	F Change	P
Australia	(49%)	-.15	.26	.01	14.3	.0002
Chile	(18%)	-.24	.30	.05	26.3	.0000
England	(54%)	-.36	.20	.13	214.7	.0000
Germany	(62%)	-.18	.22	.03	12.4	.0005
Hong Kong	(54%)	-.23	.25	.04	16.5	.0001
Japan	(57%)	-.33	.17	.11	110.6	.0000
Korea	(78%)	-.09	.15	.01	5.4	.0202
Mexico	(8%)	-.20	.14	.03	13.9	.0002
Russia	(28%)	-.20	.21	.03	12.2	.0005
Sweden	(70%)	-.37	.17	.12	82.8	.0000
The Netherlands	(54%)	-.10	.10	.01	6.8	.0090
United States	(63%)	-.23	.19	.05	138.8	.0000
Countries where the doctoral degree was not a significant predictor of teaching orientation						
Israel	(85%)	-.16	.32	.02	3.84	.0522

NOTE: The number in the R^2 **Change** column indicates the amount of variance accounted for in terms of orientation towards teaching or research ($p < .05$). Also, note that this question was not asked on the survey in Brazil, thus they are omitted from Table 4.3. Almost all respondents with doctorates indicated that they held the Ph.D. degree, although a doctoral degree could be a Ph.D., Ed.D., or M.D.

Israel is the only country in which a significant relationship was not found between teaching orientation and credentials. Although a correlation was found among the Israeli responses, this was just outside the range of significance ($p < .05$) established for this analysis. In all the other countries, the significance of the data correlations is impressive. Further, it is important to note that in three of the countries—England (where the doctoral degree accounted for an astounding 13% of the variance in teaching orientation), Japan (11%), and Sweden (12%)—holding a doctoral degree was *the most significant* predictor found among *all* the variables included in this hierarchical regression analysis. In other words, this statistical procedure ranked all variables in terms of the strength of their predictive value for teaching orientation, and the doctoral degree was the *strongest* indicator in these three countries. Brazil did not include the item on credentials in their final survey, although we know that only roughly 25% of all faculty in Brazil hold doctoral degrees (Schwartzmann & Balbachevsky, 1996). Thus, Brazil's faculty responses could not be included in this analysis.

While the relationship between the doctoral degree and teaching orientation is an important one, the nature of graduate training—whether it be focused on research skills or on teaching—provides only part of the picture. For the most part, preparation for the doctoral degree incorporates far more emphasis on research than on teaching. Indeed, only a handful of doctoral programs incorporate more of a teacher training focus than others. However, the orientation of a program does not necessarily lead to a stronger teaching orientation among the program's graduates. Faculty perceptions concerning the *quality* of their graduate training may impact their teaching orientation. That is, faculty who feel they were well-prepared to teach may be more likely to prefer teaching than their colleagues. It is suggested here that regardless of the structure or course content of a graduate program, the perceived quality of a program plays an important role in determining orientation towards teaching. It may largely be assumed that if a faculty member feels inadequately prepared to teach effectively, this would affect their orientation towards teaching. Research in this area would surely have broad implications for current debates at several research universities on restructuring the graduate curriculum. Thus, in further exploring the issue of how graduate training impacts teaching orientation, this study's regression analysis included survey data on how faculty view the quality of their training for teaching and research, in relation to their orientation toward teaching or research.

Quality of Training for Teaching

"In most parts of the world, training of university and college faculty for teaching is likely to be inservice, voluntary, and left to local initiative" (Main, 1985: 2212). In some countries, attempts have been made to incorporate training programs or courses in teaching methods for graduate students and teaching assistants, such as the cross-disciplinary teaching practicum at Canada's York University. However, "teaching skill is not universally regarded as a major criterion for the selection and promotion of faculty members, and as a result training for teaching is not highly developed" (Ibid, p. 2212).

With the exception of England and the Netherlands (both of which excluded this question from their country's survey), respondents were asked to rate the quality of the training they received for their role as teacher. Granted, the wording of this question was largely subjective—by asking faculty to rate the "quality" of their training, faculty who were disillusioned with their department, their mentor, or their institution could easily register their dissatisfaction, regardless of the real quality of their training for teaching. Additionally, this survey question offered an opportunity for faculty to "blame" any current discomfort they were experiencing in their teaching on their training for the role of teacher. Nonetheless, the question does raise an important issue, particularly in today's academic environment of worldwide concern over the quality of teaching in postsecondary education. Further, exploring the correlation between teaching orientation and satisfaction with preparation for teaching provides an important perspective for these discussions.

In most countries, graduate training involves little if any preparation for teaching. Even at non-research-oriented institutions, preparation for the academic profession is almost always rooted in a focus on developing expertise within the discipline, with little attention paid towards how to make that expertise accessible to a diverse group of students. Thus, reflecting on the quality of training for teaching and how it may impact a faculty member's orientation towards teaching is useful for informing discussions on how graduate training might better address the widespread concern over teaching in postsecondary education.

In all of the countries in which data were collected on this topic, responses to this survey question were found to have a significant predictive impact on teaching orientation. Of all the data relationships included in this analysis, this one seems the most intuitive—that is, it could largely be expected that faculty who feel well prepared to engage in a certain activity would enjoy that activity more than their colleagues who feel less prepared. The same would arguably hold true for any number of professions. Much like the earlier discussion on doctoral degrees, this finding indicates that graduate training programs can play a prominent role in a faculty member's orientation towards teaching. Responses to the survey question on training for teaching accounted for different levels of variance in answers to the teaching orientation, from 1% (Brazil) to 6% (Israel), as shown in Table 4.4.

TABLE 4.4

Satisfaction with quality of training for teaching as a predictor of teaching orientation

Country	Beta	R^2	R^2 Change	F Change	P
Australia	.16	.25	**.02**	24.4	.0000
Brazil	.11	.19	**.01**	4.19	.0400
Chile	.27	.34	**.04**	21.33	.0000
Germany	.23	.18	**.05**	26.84	.0000
Israel	.24	.26	**.06**	10.70	.0014
Korea	.21	.14	**.03**	26.43	.0000
Mexico	.15	.22	**.02**	7.94	.0051
Russia	.15	.23	**.02**	7.10	.0081
Sweden	.13	.20	**.02**	9.77	.0019
United States	.13	.21	**.02**	47.73	.0000
Countries where training for teaching was not a significant predictor of teaching orientation					
Hong Kong	-.08	.01	**.01**	3.18	.0751
Japan	.02	.05	**.00**	0.46	.4961

NOTE: The data the number in the R^2 column indicates the amount of variance accounted for in terms of responses to the (q40) survey question on orientation towards teaching or research. Also, note that this question was not asked on the survey in England or the Netherlands, thus they are omitted from Table 4.4.

In most countries surveyed, the data indicate that faculty who are more satisfied with the quality of their training for teaching are more likely than their colleagues to indicate a stronger preference for teaching. The two exceptions to this are found among responses from Hong Kong and Japan. Generally speaking, faculty in non-Western cultures do seem to feel differently about teaching than their Western counterparts. For example, research in Japan (Hess & Azuma, 1991; Purdie, Hattie, & Douglas, 1996), Hong Kong and China (Kember, & Gow, 1991; Marton, Dall'Alba, & Tse, 1996; Watkins & Biggs, 1996) have collected data on a variety of approaches to teaching that are not shared by Western educators. Research on teachers both in Hong Kong and China (Gao, 1996; Lo & Siu, 1990) found the widespread belief that the ability of teachers to foster responsibility and good moral conduct in their students was seen as a sign of a good teacher. Further, many teachers in Asian societies today regard good teaching as involving not only educating students from the intellective or academic perspective, but also in terms of conduct and morality (Watkins, 1998). Thus, perhaps there exists a divergence between expectations of teachers in Asian academic settings and the kinds of academic training offered in Western universities. Certainly, following this line of reasoning, Asian faculty trained in the West would return to their societies relatively ill-prepared to meet the teaching expectations of their social surroundings.

Perhaps there are several other reasons for the differences found here among responses from faculty in Hong Kong and Japan which require more research. However, the real story here is the international similarities found in this analysis of the Carnegie survey responses. Across the wide range of diverse higher education systems and cultures, faculty preference for teaching is significantly correlated with their perspectives toward the quality of their training for teaching. As graduate training programs typically involve an emphasis on developing research skills rather than teaching skills, it is also useful here to look at how faculty feel about their training for research to determine any relationship with their preference or teaching.

Quality of Training for Research

In addition to the quality of teacher training, the Carnegie survey was interested in learning about faculty perceptions concerning the quality of their research training. With the exception of England (which declined to include this item on the survey), respondents were asked to rate the quality of the training they received for their role as researcher. Given the previous findings of this analysis with regard to the doctoral degree and preference for teaching, one might expect that faculty who indicate a high level of satisfaction with the quality of their training for research would be less likely to prefer teaching. Indeed, *in all countries surveyed*, responses to this question had a significant predictive impact on responses to the survey question on teaching orientation, as shown in Table 4.5.

TABLE 4.5					
Satisfaction with quality of training for research as a predictor of teaching orientation					
Country	Beta	R^2	R^2 Change	F Change	P
Australia	-.37	.17	**.14**	127.60	.0000
Brazil	-.32	.14	**.10**	50.16	.0000
Chile	-.39	.25	**.15**	73.57	.0000
Germany	-.27	.13	**.07**	37.87	.0000
Hong Kong	-.38	.21	**.14**	57.01	.0000
Israel	-.24	.30	**.04**	8.60	.0039
Japan	-.08	.18	**.01**	5.84	.0159
Korea	-.22	.11	**.05**	35.49	.0000
Mexico	-.32	.11	**.10**	40.17	.0000
Russia	-.33	.18	**.10**	35.90	.0000
Sweden	-.16	.19	**.02**	16.18	.0001
the Netherlands	-.21	.08	**.04**	41.67	.0000
United States	-.32	.15	**.10**	262.90	.0000

NOTE: The data the number in the R^2 column indicates the amount of variance accounted for in terms of responses to the (q40) survey question on orientation towards teaching or research. Also, note that this question was not asked on the survey in England, thus they are omitted from Table 4.5.

It is certainly important to note that this analysis found a correlation in the Carnegie survey data that holds true in virtually every country surveyed—an unusual rarity, given the multiple dimensions of variety between each country's academic culture, system, and data sample. Further, in 10 of these countries, training for research was statistically *the most significant predictor of teaching orientation.* That is, of all the data variables included in this analysis of predictions of teaching orientation, a faculty member's training for research was *the strongest predictive variable* in over 2/3 of the countries surveyed. Even more important, this is the only variable in this analysis of the Carnegie data that was found to be a statistically significant predictor of teaching orientation across *all* the countries surveyed.

In all cases, a negative correlation was observed—that is, a respondent who indicated higher quality in their training for research was significantly less likely to indicate an orientation towards teaching. Responses to the survey question on training for research accounted for different levels of variance in answers to the teaching orientation, from 2% (Sweden) to 15% (Chile). This finding—that a higher perceived quality of training for research contributes to a weaker orientation towards teaching—has several implications for further research. Further, when combined with the earlier finding that holding a doctoral degree significantly predicts a weaker orientation towards teaching, this analysis of the Carnegie data raises several timely and compelling questions about current training programs for future academics.

This analysis of the Carnegie data has implications for further examining today's doctoral programs, perhaps with an eye towards re-engineering them to develop a stronger teaching orientation among future faculty. Ernest Boyer's landmark *Scholarship Reconsidered* (1990) addresses this issue poignantly. Boyer suggests that "what's needed is a requirement that teacher training be incorporated into all graduate preparation" (p.71), and that "graduate study must be broadened, encompassing not only research, but integration, application, and teaching" (p. 74). The results of the Carnegie international survey indicate that Boyer's concerns apply not only to graduate training in the United States, but to doctoral degree programs worldwide. Thus, imaginative ideas and new approaches to how future faculty are prepared for the profession are strongly needed throughout academe.

Of course, there is a great deal of current research surrounding the preparation of academics to more effectively meet the challenges of new and diverse classroom environments and technologies. Recent scholarly journals and books focus on topics ranging from pedagogical methods and theory (cf., Prichard & Sawyer, 1994; Forest, 1998), classroom assessment, instructional technology, evaluating good teaching, and the impact of faculty reward systems—for example, the role that teaching plays in tenure and promotion committees (cf., Tierney & Bensimon, 1996; Lewis, 1996). However, as observers have noted, higher education in general has always been slow to change. Moving from research-based recommendations to practical implementation takes a considerable amount of time and patience. Clearly though, the development of future faculty must address the changing needs of higher education. The findings presented in this chapter thus provide a useful insight into this important issue of reforming graduate training programs worldwide.

Overall, this study found that certain preparatory variables (such as indicators of credentials and the quality of one's training for research or for teaching) are significant predictors of orientation towards teaching or research. In all countries where statistically significant relationships were found, three primary trends were found: (1) the doctoral degree was related to a *decreased* likelihood of teaching preference; (2) high satisfaction with the quality of one's training for research meant a considerably *decreased* likelihood of teaching preference; and (3) high satisfaction with the quality of one's training for teaching contributed to a slightly *increased* likelihood of teaching preference. These findings seem to reflect a considerable deficiency in the kinds of preparation that might otherwise lead to a significant interest towards teaching activities. Higher education—particularly graduate schools and programs—must address this deficiency immediately, in order to adequately prepare future members of the academic profession to meet the needs of society.

ACADEMIC APPOINTMENT AS PREDICTOR OF TEACHING ORIENTATION

Certainly, the nature of a faculty member's academic appointment influences their orientation towards teaching or research. For example, a professor of physics employed to work exclusively on a particle acceleration research project would certainly respond to the Carnegie survey much differently than a part-time lecturer in political science. As well, a faculty member's teaching orientation could surely be influenced by the kinds of institution they were employed at, with marked differences between community college faculty and those at research universities. Thus, the issue of academic appointment may play a prominent role in how faculty identify themselves as either teaching-oriented or research-oriented.

In most of the countries surveyed, the set of institutions chosen reflect the national composition of higher education institutions. That is, since research universities comprise only a small percentage of each nation's higher education system, only a representative sample of them were included in this survey. Thus, every attempt was made to avoid skewing a national sample's response due to an institution's focus on research or on teaching. However, it should be noted that in most every country surveyed, some kinds of institutions do not promote people for research, but rather primarily for teaching. Thus, an analysis of how institutional type effects teaching orientation would surely be useful.

Unfortunately, most of the countries participating in the Carnegie survey did not differentiate in their data collection by institution type. Only data from the U.S. ("classification"), Japan and the UK ("tier") provide an indication of what kind of institution each faculty response came from. For these countries, institution type was strongly correlated with faculty response to the question on teaching orientation. For example, as one might expect, faculty in the U.S. employed at a Liberal Arts II institution were significantly more likely to indicate a preference for teaching, while faculty employed at a Research I or II institutions were more likely to indicate a preference for research. However, while this is an important point to consider, the lack of cross-national comparability in the data collected by the Carnegie survey prevents any real comparative analysis for the purposes of this discussion. It should be noted, though, that U.S. community college faculty are not included in this analysis of the Carnegie data. Also, as Fairweather's (1993) study of U.S. faculty found that regardless of institutional type and prestige, faculty who do research earn salaries that are significantly higher than faculty who primarily teach, it may be that the relationship between faculty orientation and faculty rewards is more important than that between faculty orientation and institutional type.

To explore the relationship between academic appointment and teaching orientation, this analysis choose to look at data on rank, tenure status, and full-time or part-time status, as these data were made available by all countries in the survey. It was assumed, based on existing research, that reward structures embedded in the tenure system—which most often gives preference to research productivity over teaching effectiveness—may influence teaching orientation to some degree. In general, one's advancement in rank and tenure status is largely determined by that which one's departmental peers value, and thus a look at who achieves the higher levels of rank and status yields information on what those values are. In fact, a growing body of research exists on this very topic. For example, a recent study of the U.S. academic profession found that "faculty with the least amount of student contact hours earn the highest salaries," and that "the more refereed publications a faculty member publishes, the higher their salary" (NCPTLA, 1995: 11).

In general, several research studies have found a relationship between research productivity and higher rank, status and salary level. Thus, it would seem logical to assume that academics would naturally prefer to focus their interests on research than on their classroom activities, in order to advance up the academic career ladder. However, as indicated earlier, the Carnegie data show a majority of faculty in five countries—Brazil, Chile, Mexico, Russia and the United States—are more interested in teaching than in research. Thus, an exploration of the Carnegie data was conducted to determine what influence the nature of one's academic appointment (including academic rank, tenure status, and working time) has on orientation towards teaching.

The results of this analysis show that academic rank was a significant predictor of teaching orientation in slightly more than half of the countries surveyed, while tenure status was a predictor in only three countries. Further, in many of the countries surveyed by the Carnegie Foundation, full-time faculty were found to be only slightly different than their part-time colleagues in terms of interests toward teaching. Thus, in the majority of countries, the nature of one's academic appointment appears to have only a limited effect on one's preference for teaching or research.

Academic Rank

In all the countries surveyed by the Carnegie Foundation, the academic profession is relatively democratic in terms of hiring and evaluation. That is, faculty advance in rank and status based on what their colleagues view as attributes and productivity worth rewarding. Thus, based on many scholars' description of a research-biased academic reward structure, it is relatively easy to assume that most professors who have advanced to higher ranks are more focused on research (which plays a prominent role in their advancement in rank) than on teaching.

This analysis of the Carnegie data produced mixed results concerning the relationship between academic rank and preference for teaching. Negative correlations were found in Australia, Chile, Israel, Korea and the United States. In these countries, faculty at higher academic ranks were significantly less likely than their colleagues to indicate a strong teaching orientation. In several of these countries, the significance of these data relationships is quite small (1% or less of the variance, with relatively small betas). However, in two of these countries, the predictive value of academic rank was particularly strong—5% of the variance in teaching orientation in Australia, and 10% in Israel. Digging deeper into the Carnegie data yields some additional similarities among the faculty responses from these two countries. For example, faculty in Australia and Israel were more likely than their colleagues in other countries to indicate that "a strong record of successful research activity is important in faculty evaluation at this institution." Certainly, there is cause for further exploration into why there appears such a strong relationship between academic rank and preference for teaching in these countries.

On the other hand, an opposite trend was found among responses from England and Germany, where higher academic rank was positively correlated with stronger preference for teaching. This relationship in the data seemed more intuitive, given the finding presented earlier in this chapter that showed age was a significant predictor of teaching orientation. Certainly, one can expect to find older faculty among those of higher academic ranks, and younger faculty are usually of lower academic rank. However, this study found that while older faculty are typically more teaching oriented, in only two countries are faculty at higher ranks more teaching oriented than their colleagues. Perhaps there is a significantly strong preference for teaching among the older faculty who are still in the lower segment of their academic rank systems. Certainly, there is room for more in-depth research on this issue beyond the scope of the Carnegie data collection. For example, an analysis which incorporates more qualitative measures of attitudes and perspectives of faculty at all academic ranks in each country would provide a particularly rich resource for our understanding of these issues.

Throughout the rest of the countries surveyed, no significant relationships were found between academic rank and teaching orientation. The Hong Kong survey administrators encountered difficulty collecting data on academic rank, because "at the time of the survey, a reclassification of academic staff was being carried out" (see Postiglione, 1997: 722, endnote 22). Problems with the organization of the Dutch and Mexican academic professions prevented comparable data collection there as well. In Mexico, "the actual number of faculty and the kinds of their academic appointments remain unknown, since one person often holds several posts" (Antón, 1996: 314). The structure of academic appointments in the Netherlands is markedly different from other countries surveyed. In addition to the traditional ranks of full, associate and assistant professor, Dutch academics indicate their position as research associate or teaching associate, which is indicative of this country's efforts to separate these two primary functions of academe into two distinct career tracks. Thus, comparable data were not collected in several of the countries included in this survey.

Overall, no clear international—or even regional—trend emerged which would suggest that academic rank is a significant predictor of teaching orientation. National variations do not yield a clear explanation for the variation in the relationships between academic rank and teaching orientation in the Carnegie data. As observed earlier, faculty tend to focus their time more on activities which represent where their primary interests lie. However, faculty pursue advancement to higher academic ranks, they are more likely to be evaluated based on their performance in activities which the department values, regardless of the individual faculty member's interests. Previous chapters of this volume have outlined several issues related to academic rewards and the tenure system, most of which can be summarized by Boyer's (1990) observation that "most professors support the proposition that changes in faculty evaluation procedures are important and overdue" (p. 34). Thus, in addition to exploring the potential connections between academic rank and teaching orientation, this analysis also sought to discover whether tenured faculty are more or less teaching-oriented than their non-tenured colleagues.

Tenure

The academic tenure system has been a topic of recurring debate in higher education since its inception. The tenor of these debates has risen and fallen over the decades, but the current resurgence of attention towards academic tenure may in fact be leading us towards the development of something entirely new. Certainly, there is an increasing amount of agreement among faculty that "the promotion and tenure system as it exists in the late twentieth century is in need of dramatic overhaul" (Tierney & Bensimon, 1996, p. 125). While some scholars have proposed alternatives to the tenure system (cf. Chait & Ford, 1982), others have been less than diplomatic in their assessment of the tenure system, such as Sykes' (1988) *Profscam*, or Bloom's (1987) *The Closing of the American Mind*. One of the more pressing concerns of these debates is whether faculty with tenure are less likely to be concerned with their teaching activities than their colleagues. As described earlier in this discussion, many observers of higher education have argued that the reward structure associated with the tenure system compels faculty to focus on research projects—preferably those which bring external funding to the department—while teaching gets a second class ticket.

In a recent analysis of teaching and the academic labor market, Lewis (1996) suggested that the motivation to teach is often intrinsic, and not related to extrinsic rewards such as tenure or promotion. This study of the Carnegie data appears to support Lewis' observation. In only 3 of the countries surveyed by the Carnegie study—Brazil, Sweden, and the United States—was tenure status found to be a significant predictor for teaching orientation. In all three cases, the data were positively correlated in nature—that is, faculty with tenure were more likely than other respondents to indicate stronger teaching orientation. However, in all three cases this relationship was only slightly significant, explaining only 1% of the variance in responses to the survey question on preferences.

Interestingly, data from Brazil and Sweden showed no correlation between academic rank and teaching orientation, and yet they did show a correlation between tenure status and teaching orientation. While these findings may at first seem to be contradictory, it should be noted that there are many instances where tenure and academic rank are separate. For example, the Brazilian academic profession has a large percentage of part-time faculty, who may be awarded a high rank as a form of status, but without tenure. A judge who is invited to teach at a local law school would not likely accept the position at any rank lower than full professor, and yet he or she is not a member of the tenure system. Thus, there may be less of a relationship between tenure and academic rank here than elsewhere, which in turn would explain the differences in these variable's relationship with the teaching orientation variable in the Carnegie survey.

In the other countries surveyed, no significant difference was found between tenured and untenured faculty in terms of teaching orientation. The lack of any internationally-significant trend here has several implications. If tenure status does not appear to significantly impact one's orientation towards research, we might assume that tenure status also does not impact one's teaching effectiveness. Further research on these issues can inform current discussions over new and innovative approaches to academic employment (cf. Chait, 1997). Additionally, as higher education worldwide has seen a rise in part-time academic appointments, these issues affect our understanding of organizational culture, institutional management, and the intellectual concerns of faculty in their work.

Full-Time versus Part-Time Academic Appointments

The Carnegie survey development team sought to collect data on individuals holding regular academic appointments. Faculty were included in the universe from which samples were drawn if they had some teaching or research responsibilities at the institutions selected for the sample (Whitelaw, 1997). However, although the traditional academic career has involved both teaching and research responsibilities, the recent decade has seen a rise in the number of adjunct faculty in our college and university classrooms. Particularly in the United States, the academic profession has seen a considerable growth in part-time appointments, as institutions face significant reductions in resources to hire full-time staff. While this a relatively new trend in the U.S., part-time faculty have become quite common throughout Latin America (Altbach, 1995). These academics often do not have campus offices, and are not expected to perform research or service activities. Thus, given that their primary responsibility is to teach, it can be expected that they are more interested in teaching than their colleagues who must perform in all three arenas. However, this study found that in most of the countries surveyed by the Carnegie Foundation, full-time faculty are basically no different than their part-time colleagues in terms of interests toward teaching.

In only 5 of the countries surveyed—Brazil, Germany, Hong Kong, Japan, and the United States—were significant correlations found between data on working time and on teaching orientation. Brazil has an extraordinarily large percentage of part-time academics (44%), the highest of any country participating in the Carnegie survey. In contrast, only 1% of faculty respondents in Hong Kong and Japan indicated part-time employment. Thus, perhaps one reason that a correlation was found in these countries and not others is because these countries are at the extremes of the spectrum in terms of part-time faculty. However, it must be noted that throughout all the Latin American countries surveyed, part-time professors dominate the professoriate, and yet only in Brazil was a correlation found between data on working time and on teaching orientation.

In most of these cases, a negative direction of correlation was observed—that is, survey respondents who hold part-time positions at their institution were *more* likely to indicate stronger teaching orientation than their colleagues. There was one exception to this—the data collected from survey respondents in Germany indicate that part-time faculty are *less* likely to have a strong orientation towards teaching. Perhaps this is a reflection on the structure of the German academic profession, in which part-time researchers are more common than part-time classroom instructors. Overall, for each country in which a correlation was found between working time and teaching orientation, the statistical significance of the correlation was marginal at best. Thus, this analysis of the Carnegie data does not support the widespread assumption that full-time faculty differ significantly from their part-time colleagues in terms of teaching orientation.

Other Variables of Interest

Related to the discussion on full-time versus part-time work, a study of the relationship between holding other academic appointments and teaching orientation may be useful. The Carnegie survey sought to account for the potential of duplicity by soliciting information on academic appointments held *outside* one's current institution. The current analysis of this data sought to determine whether holding multiple academic positions—in most cases, teaching at multiple institutions—has an impact on one's teaching orientation. For the most part, it does not. Only data from faculty in the Netherlands indicate that holding other academic appointments influences one's inclination towards a stronger preference for teaching. Here, the data showed a positive correlation, albeit with only modest statistical significance. That is, faculty in the Netherlands who hold more than one academic appointment were slightly more likely to indicate stronger teaching orientation on the Carnegie survey. The lack of significance in this finding does not support further investigation.

This analysis of the data also sought to determine whether holding a non-academic appointment outside one's institution affects faculty preference for teaching. As Furniss (1981) explains, the academic profession is an excellent example of a "one life, one career" profession. Those going into the professoriate, like other professions such as law, medicine, or the clergy, are conditioned to believe they are committing themselves for a lifetime to a discipline (Simpson, 1990). However, a growing number of academics throughout the world—most notably in Latin America—are lawyers, doctors, or business leaders first, and professors second, usually going from work via taxi to the local college or university. As mentioned in the previous discussion on working time, these faculty are brought in almost exclusively to provide classroom instruction—no research or service responsibilities are usually attached to such positions. Thus, one might expect that these academics are naturally more teaching-oriented than their full-time colleagues.

However, the data collected by the Carnegie study found this to be true in only one country—Mexico. In the analysis of the Mexican data, holding non-academic appointments (in addition to their faculty appointment) accounted for a full 3% of the variance in faculty responses to the (q40) survey question on preferences toward teaching or research. The relationship observed was positively correlated—that is, Mexican faculty who held non-academic appointments were slightly more likely to indicate a stronger preference for teaching than their colleagues. Curiously, in all other countries surveyed, full-time faculty—laden with pressures of research productivity, service to their department and community, and teaching increasingly large classrooms—appear to be no different in terms of teaching orientation from their "taxicab" colleagues.

Perhaps one explanation for these findings lies in the ways faculty of all kinds of appointments view the role of the academic profession in society. According the Carnegie data, a majority of faculty in all countries surveyed believe that they have a professional obligation to promote intellectual inquiry and to apply their knowledge to problems of society. In virtually every country surveyed, this commitment to service likely influences a shared belief in the importance of teaching effectively. Thus, while some observers may suggest that full-time, tenured, higher ranking academics are less inclined to be concerned with their teaching than other faculty, the analysis presented here shows that these critiques of the academic profession are largely untrue. The data collected by the Carnegie survey indicate that tenure, working time, and academic rank—essential elements of a faculty member's academic appointment—play a minor role at best in influ-encing teaching orientation in the academic profession.

CONCLUSION

The research presented in this chapter tested the validity of a hypothesis which stated that teaching-oriented faculty around the world share similar demographic profiles, academic rank, or other background variables that distinguish them from their research-oriented colleagues. The opposite of this, the null hypothesis, states that there is no real difference between teaching-oriented faculty and research-oriented faculty in terms of demo-graphic profiles, academic rank, or other background variables. According to this analysis of the Carnegie, data, we can reject the null hypothesis—teaching-oriented faculty are significantly different from their research-ori-ented colleagues. In each country, the variables chosen for this analysis accounted for considerable amounts of the variance in responses to the survey question on orientation towards teaching or research, ranging from 35% in Chile to 11% in The Netherlands (see Appendix B).

In most cases, the regression analyses showed correlations that were either always positive or always negative across all countries' data samples. There are a few cases in which teaching orientation had a positive correla-tion in some countries, and a negative one in others, but overall the find-ings show that teaching orientation is correlated in much the same way throughout all the countries surveyed. Thus, these findings provide an inter-national insight into who teaching-oriented faculty are.

The study found that age and gender were found to be significant pre-dictors of teaching preference. This supports an existing body of literature that shows women and older professors are more inclined towards teaching activities than research. The significant relationship found between age and teaching orientation does not support assertions made by Sykes (1988) and others that tenure allows professors to sit back on their haunches and neg-lect their classrooms or avoid any future research productivity. As well, this analysis provides an important perspective for the ongoing debate about tenure and academic reward structures. "Faculty work for, and are socialized to, academic rewards that are located in a cultural system" (Tierney, 1997, p.8). The findings of this study do not support the notion that the tenure system—through an inordinate emphasis on rewarding research productiv-ity—is inhibiting efforts to change or improve classroom instruction and assessment activities. According to the Carnegie data, tenure or rank plays a significant role for predicting teaching orientation in less than half the countries surveyed, and only a statistically small significance was observed in those countries. Also, the data show that being part-time or holding more than one position may be a significant predictor of teaching orientation in only a handful of countries.

Overall, the most important predictor of teaching orientation found in this study is one's professional training. According to this study, a faculty member's professional preparation has a considerable impact on their orientation towards teaching, followed in importance by their demographic background and by the nature of their academic appointment. Survey respondents with a doctoral degree were significantly less likely in almost all of the countries surveyed to indicate a strong preference for teaching. Further, in all countries in which the survey collected data on professional preparation, this study found a strongly negative correlation between training for research and teaching orientation. In other words, throughout the entire survey, respondents who indicated a high level of quality in their training for research were significantly less likely to indicate a preference for teaching than their colleagues. Thus, one implication of this study is that there is a need throughout the academic profession for a stronger emphasis on the quality of graduate training for teaching.

This supports the argument made by Boyer and others that graduate training needs to incorporate a more 'teaching-friendly' focus. That is, without losing sight of the academic goal of creating knowledge through traditional research, future university and college faculty must be trained with an increased understanding of—and appreciation for—the importance of teaching. As Kenneth Eble (1972) observed, "upgrading the preparation of college teachers in graduate schools is fundamentally important not only to improving teaching but to refashioning higher education" (p. 180). Certainly, the research presented in this chapter echoes these and other scholars' concerns, and provides an international dimension to the importance of examining and developing new approaches to training future academics.

The attention paid to exploring and understanding the attitudes and work preferences of faculty has grown considerably over the past three decades, and the body of research on the academic profession as a sociological entity continues to expand. Faculty orientation towards teaching is of particular interest, as a growing number of individuals seek new ways to assess and improve teaching in higher education in today's environment of assessment and accountability measures. The underlying paradigms for how academics perceive their role and responsibilities as classroom teacher need serious exploration. As Boyer (1990) argued, scholarship is multidimensional, and the application, integration and teaching of knowledge are part of its expanded definition. We must broaden our conception of structural barriers to organizational change in college teaching from beyond routines, standard procedures, and expectations of style and format to include ideological barriers within the academic profession. An understanding of what influences faculty attitudes toward teaching and learning can facilitate the development of a framework within which to approach this complex issue in a manner acceptable to faculty in all corners of the world. The international dimension of the findings presented in this chapter bear particular importance for our understanding of the academic profession. Clearly,

"cross-national similarities greatly extends the scope of sociological knowledge" (Kohn, 1987: 31).

The findings of this chapter conclude that there are indeed significant
differences between teaching-oriented and research-oriented faculty, and
that these differences exist in virtually every country surveyed. However,
while it is important to understand what impacts teaching orientation, this
is but one of many possible units of analysis. An exploration of how teaching-oriented faculty view the world of academe differently than their
research-oriented colleagues is thus warranted. What does teaching orientation mean in terms of how academics approach other aspects of their professional lives? Surely, faculty who prefer teaching over research are likely to
differ from their research-oriented colleagues in other ways besides this
singular variable dichotomy. The remaining chapters of this volume explore
the effects of this orientation towards teaching on other survey items collected by the Carnegie study—specifically, those related to classroom
instruction, the assessment of teaching, institutional working conditions,
academic work and life, the role of higher education in society, and the
international dimension of higher education. The following chapters
address each of these issues in the order presented here, beginning with
faculty views toward classroom instruction and the assessment of teaching.

CHAPTER 5

Issues of Instruction and Assessment

INTRODUCTION

This chapter provides the first of four topic-based analyses of the Carnegie data to determine the significance of faculty teaching orientation in how faculty responded to the survey. As described earlier in this volume, the organization of these chapters follows a pattern of increasingly broader topics—beginning with the classroom, then to the institution, followed by the academic discipline, the academic profession, the role of higher education in society, and finally, the international dimensions of higher education. The analysis of the Carnegie data presented in this chapter seeks to determine whether orientation towards teaching has a significant relationship with how faculty approach classroom instruction and the assessment of teaching. The theoretical basis for this analysis is the belief that if teaching orientation were to be significantly related to anything at all on the Carnegie survey, this relationship would surely involve survey items that concern teaching and the assessment of teaching. The findings presented in this chapter are useful for informing our current discussions on the nature of academic work and assessment.

The Carnegie international survey paid special attention to faculty views toward these issues, based on a growing debate in many countries over how to properly assess and reward faculty productivity. "Respondents in all countries note that teaching is evaluated most often, with research coming second; service activities are seldom assessed" (Altbach & Lewis, 1996: 33). The survey results also show that teaching is evaluated similarly in almost all of the countries surveyed, yet there is strong agreement among faculty worldwide that better ways of evaluating their work are needed. Indeed, in an earlier study of U.S. faculty, Boyer (1990) observed that "most professors support the proposition that changes in faculty evaluation procedures are important and overdue" (p. 34). The exploration of the Carnegie survey data presented in this chapter contributes to our understanding of the academic profession by examining the relative importance of teaching orientation in how academics view teaching and the assessment of teaching, as well as providing a new, international dimension to the ongoing debate on these issues.

As observed earlier in this discussion, the existing research on the academic profession indicates that beliefs and attitudes of faculty influence the ways in which they fulfill their professional responsibilities. For years, scholars have explored personality traits of academics to determine whether personal values and beliefs impact a professor's teaching abilities. For example, Murray (et. al., 1990) found that the compatibility of instructors to courses is determined in part by personality characteristics. In another study, Sherman and Blackburn (1975) determined the degree of relationship between observed faculty personal characteristics and teaching effectiveness (as assessed by student evaluations). Their findings led these authors to suggest that "improvement of teaching effectiveness may depend more on changes related to personality factors than on those involving classroom procedures" (p. 22). Indeed, as Kember and Gow (1994) observed, students do tend to respond better to teaching-oriented faculty than to others.

This particular analysis is concerned with differences between teaching-oriented and research-oriented faculty regarding their views toward teaching and the assessment of teaching. The chapter tests the validity of the following hypothesis:

> Teaching-oriented faculty view teaching and the assessment of teaching differently than do research-oriented faculty.

Specifically, this data exploration sought to determine the relationship of teaching orientation with: (1) the percentage of undergraduate classroom time faculty spent on lectures, classroom discussions, and laboratory work; (2) views toward spending time with students outside of classrooms; (3) views toward current ways of assessing teaching effectiveness; (4) views toward student involvement in the assessment of teaching; and (5) views toward the use of teaching effectiveness for faculty hiring and promotion. The chapter is organized around these themes for reasons of data comparability—almost no country omitted any of these items from their survey—and personal research interests.

In analyzing and presenting the data relationships found in this study, it is assumed that the more countries in which a trend in the Carnegie data exists, the more international that trend is. The following internationally significant relationships were found in this analysis of the Carnegie survey data:

> • In virtually every country surveyed, teaching-oriented faculty were significantly more likely than their colleagues to indicate that "teaching effectiveness should be the primary criterion for the hiring and promotion of faculty."

- In a majority of countries surveyed, teaching orientation plays a role in whether faculty agreed with the statement, "student opinions should be used in evaluating teaching effectiveness." In most countries, teaching-oriented faculty indicated stronger support for this statement, Mexico being the only exception.
- In most countries, teaching orientation plays a role in whether faculty agreed with the statement, "better ways are needed for evaluating teaching effectiveness." In most countries, teaching-oriented faculty indicated stronger support for this statement, Mexico being the only exception.
- When looking at responses to the survey items addressed in this chapter, teaching orientation plays a significant role more often in faculty responses from Australia, Europe, Israel and the United States, and less often in responses from Asian and Latin American faculty.

There are intra-regional variations in how teaching orientation is related to faculty responses to these survey items, but overall, the findings presented in this chapter indicate that there are significant differences between teaching-oriented faculty and research-oriented faculty in how they view the assessment of teaching. Further, there is considerably strong support among teaching-oriented faculty worldwide for using teaching effectiveness as the primary criterion for the hiring and promotion of faculty. However, this study also found that teaching orientation does not appear to have a significant international relationship with how faculty approach their teaching duties. The international scope of these trends provides a valuable insight for our understanding of faculty worldwide.

DIMENSIONS OF CLASSROOM ACTIVITIES

Earlier studies of the Carnegie data have indicated that there are significant differences between faculty with different teaching or research orientations. For example, Gottlieb and Keith (1996) describe a positively correlated relationship in their findings between faculty orientation and faculty work activity—that is, faculty who prefer to teach do in fact teach more, and those who prefer research engage in more research activities than their colleagues. Altbach and Lewis (1996) found that throughout all countries surveyed, "those who prefer teaching over research spend somewhat more time on local or campus-related activities (teaching, service, and administration) than do those who prefer research over teaching." (p.21) Naturally, this relationship between orientation and work activity varies by country—for example, faculty in Australia and Chile spend considerably more time on teaching than on research, but while faculty in Chile are predominantly teaching-oriented, their Australian colleagues are considerably more oriented towards research. Enders and Teichler (1996) found that "for each hour of teaching, German university professors who are strongly research-oriented spend about 1 1/2 hours on teaching-related activities, while those who are strongly-oriented toward teaching spend almost 4 hours" (p.460).

The amount of faculty preference towards these "campus-related activities" warrants particular attention in today's environment of heightened scrutiny of higher education worldwide. A fair amount of recent criticism directed towards higher education is focused on the need to better prepare graduates with critical thinking and problem solving skills, while moving away from traditional focus on developing rote memorization skills. Thus, a look at the classroom activities preferred by faculty who indicated that their interests lie more in teaching than research can certainly yield valuable insights on the academic profession.

As observed earlier in this volume, studies have shown a correlation between teaching effectiveness and the teaching methods used. However, any correlation between teacher effectiveness and classroom method used varies from teacher to teacher, often based on the inter-meshing between teacher preference and method. For example, some teachers, because of their personality traits, can be excellent lecturers, but will never be effective facilitators of classroom discussions. Also, certain methods of instruction may not be appropriate for a particular classroom environment. For example, classroom discussions may be significantly ineffective in certain classroom environments in Asia, where the lecture method is so predominant that students may not know how to function effectively in any other learning environment. However, according to the Carnegie survey data, one method of instruction appears to pervade higher education worldwide—the lecture. "The majority of all faculty indicated that the traditional lecture is the primary means of communicating knowledge in introductory undergraduate courses, although class discussions are prominent in all of the countries surveyed except Japan" (Altbach & Lewis, 1996: 22). This question on the Carnegie survey (q35) was worded as follows:

> In your introductory undergraduate courses, what percentage of class time is usually devoted to each of the following activities? (Figures should add to 100 percent. Options are (a) Lectures; (b) Class discussion; (c) Laboratory work; and (d) Other.)

The wording of this question in a way forces respondents to rank order these activities on a scale of importance, defined by how much of their classroom time is spent on each. Thus, the data show that the lecture is the most important mode of classroom instruction for faculty worldwide.

However, scholars worldwide have observed that the lecture may not be the most effective means of instruction. As Ekeler (1995) observed, "of the basic teaching methods . . . it is the lecture that has come in for the greatest amount of criticism" (p. 27). Early research on the impact of lectures versus classroom discussions (cf. Bane, 1925; Solomon, et al., 1964) as well as more recent studies (cf. McKeachie, 1984) have consistently found that lectures tend to be at least equal to, and often more effective then, discussion for immediate recall of factual knowledge on a course examination, but discussion tends to be superior for long-term retention. From the constructivist perspective (e.g., Halpern, 1994) lecturing does an adequate job of providing information to students, but is questionably efficient in helping foster the creation of knowledge (i.e., learning). In experiments involving measures of retention of information after the end of a course, measures of transfer of knowledge to new situations, or measures of problem solving, thinking, or attitude change, or motivation for further learning, the results tend to show differences favoring discussion methods over lecture (McKeachie, Pintrich, Lin, Smith, and Sharma, 1990). It is thus reasonable to assume that teaching-oriented faculty, who can be expected to have a great deal of concern over the successful learning of their students, would be more inclined to adopt methods of classroom instruction other than the lecture. However, the Carnegie data generally do not show this to be the case (see Table 5.1).

The most important finding reflected in Table 5.1 is that scarcely any significant differences exist between teaching-oriented and research-oriented faculty. According to this analysis of the Carnegie data, teaching orientation does not appear to have a significant impact in how faculty approach their classroom instruction activities. There are a few regional variations observed in the data. For example, Japanese faculty whose interest lie more in teaching than in research were significantly (r=.12) less likely to rely on the lecture method in their classrooms. However, no relationship was found among Japanese faculty between teaching orientation and time spent on classroom discussion or laboratory work. Further, no other Asian country's faculty data reflect a significant relationship between teaching orientation and classroom instructional method.

The use of lectures in the classroom is quite strong among all faculty surveyed in Asia. According to Lee (1996), "the majority of Korean academics rely on the lecture method, a reflection of Confucianism's powerful hold on education in Asia" (p.121). Here, "a majority of faculty devote three quarters of class time to lecturing, and the other one-quarter to discussion, laboratory work, and other instructional activities" (Lee, 1996: 122). "A majority of all Japanese faculty members surveyed report that more than 60 percent of their classroom time is spent in lectures . . . this is the case in all disciplines, at both types of universities, research and nonresearch, except in physical education and arts, where other methods are dominant" (Arimoto, 1996: 168). In Hong Kong, "faculty surveyed report that on average, 56 percent of course time is devoted to lectures" (Postiglione, 1996: 207).

Thus, with such a strong reliance on lectures among all faculty surveyed in Asia, it is unusual to find this relationship among the responses from teaching-oriented Japanese faculty. Perhaps one explanation for this trend appearing in the data for Japan but not for other Asian countries is that

TABLE 5.1

Are teaching-oriented faculty **more or less likely** than their research-oriented colleagues to spend classroom time on the following activities? (Q35a,b,c)

MORE Likely	LESS Likely	No Significant Relationships Found	
Lectures			
	Israel r= -.10	Australia	Korea
	Japan r= -.12	Brazil	Mexico
	United States r= -.13	Chile	the Netherlands
		England	Russia
		Germany	Sweden
		Hong Kong	
Class Discussions*			
Israel r= .17		Australia	Japan
United States r= .04		Brazil	Korea
		Chile	Mexico
		England	Russia
		Germany	Sweden
		Hong Kong	

* This item was omitted from the survey administered in the Netherlands.

MORE Likely	LESS Likely	No Significant Relationships Found	
Laboratory Work			
Israel r= .08	Germany r= -.21	Australia	Japan
United States r= .08		Brazil	Korea
		Chile	Mexico
		England	Russia
		Hong Kong	Sweden
		the Netherlands	

NOTE: All correlations presented were significant at the .05 level.

Japanese faculty are considerably less teaching-oriented than faculty in Hong Kong or Korea. This would tend to emphasize the importance of teaching orientation, as it is a rarity. Also, as Arimoto (1996) observed, "the reliance on the lecture as the predominant method of instruction is so wide-spread that the Japanese Ministry of Education has been compelled to rec-ommend that each university undertake teaching method innovations by introducing devices such as small classes, seminars, and discussions in the classrooms" (p. 163). It can be expected that these reforms will be first adopted by faculty whose interests lie more in teaching than in research. Thus, teaching-oriented faculty in Japan would be less likely to rely on the lecture method in their classrooms.

In his analysis of the survey responses from faculty in the United States, Haas (1996) observed that "research-oriented faculty lean more heavily toward lecturing than do teaching-oriented academics—64 percent and 59 percent respectively" (p. 355). His finding is corroborated by this analysis of the data—indeed, as shown in Table 5.1, this analysis found that in both the United States and Israel, teaching-oriented faculty were significantly less likely to spend their classroom hours lecturing, and more likely to spend time on class discussions or laboratory work. This pattern seems intuitive, as described in the above explanation of how this question was asked on the Carnegie survey—if a higher percentage of class time is spent on one activity, then one can expect lower percentages of time spent on the other available activities. However, there does not appear to be a reasonable explanation for why this pattern was found among the responses from only Israel and the United States.

Considerably more faculty are oriented toward teaching in the United States (63%) than in Israel (38%). In Israel, faculty do not appear to spend considerably more or less time lecturing than faculty in any other country surveyed. "On average, Israeli faculty spend 68 percent of their undergraduate classroom time in lectures, and 26 percent on class discussions" (Chen, Gottlieb & Yakir, 1996: 646). In the United States, "about 60 percent of class time is devoted to lectures, with class discussions and laboratory work accounting for roughly equal proportions of the remaining class time" (Haas, 1996: 355). These percentages are comparable to data reported from all the countries participating in the Carnegie survey, and thus do not explain the trend indicated in Table 5.1. Perhaps one reason why teaching orientation plays an important role in these countries—in terms of instructional method—lies in the academic culture of these countries. New and innovative approaches to teaching in higher education have been pioneered in these countries, such as student portfolios (e.g., Crouch & Fontaine, 1994; Smith, 1998), collaborative learning (e.g., Bruffee, 1991: Panitz & Panitz, 1998), and institutional teaching and learning centers (e.g., Hargreaves, 1993). However, more research is needed on the role of teaching orientation in these countries before any conclusive explanation can be reached.

No significant correlations between method and teaching orientation were found in the data from Latin American faculty. Among the European faculty, only the data from Germany indicate that teaching orientation has some relationship with classroom activity. In this case, although no correlation was found between teaching orientation and time spent on lectures or classroom discussions, German faculty whose preferences lie in teaching are considerably (r=.21) less likely than their colleagues to spend their classroom time on laboratory work. This trend, the only one of its kind throughout the countries surveyed, is better understood within the unique context of how teaching duties are distributed among all faculty in Germany. "Both university professors and *Fachhochschule* (vocational/professional college) professors state that they spend about two-thirds of their time on lecturing—higher than the average in Europe—while junior staff spend more time on supervising laboratory work" (Enders & Teichler, 1996: 476). However, "only a small number of junior staff at universities are expected to focus solely on teaching; they generally teach smaller classes on average and are responsible for fewer examinations" (Ibid.: 455). There are more positions established exclusively or primarily for research purposes. Thus, junior staff in Germany are considerably more focused on research—only 28% of university junior staff in Germany indicated that their preferences lie in the direction of teaching (Ibid.: 460). Also, junior staff spend only six hours of teaching, clearly less than the nine hours reported by university professors. An explanation of the trend indicated in Table 5.1 thus begins to emerge—in Germany, the faculty who are most likely to engage in laboratory work are the least likely to be oriented towards teaching. In other words, because of this distribution of professional activity, teaching-oriented faculty are considerably less likely to engage in laboratory work.

In summary, one might reasonably expect that teaching-oriented faculty would tend to approach classroom instruction in different ways than their research-oriented colleagues. However, no international or regional patterns emerged in the data—in other words, no clear consensus was found among teaching-oriented faculty on the use of lectures, classroom discussion or laboratory work. Only data from Israel and the United States indicate a clear relationship between faculty preferences and their choice of instructional method, favoring class discussions and laboratory work rather than lecturing. Unique trends were found in Japan and Germany, which can be partly explained by the respective contexts of the academic profession in these countries. Thus, one cannot conclude that greater orientation towards teaching necessarily leads to different approaches to methods of classroom instruction. This is a fairly surprising finding, and suggests that orientation toward teaching or research may have less impact on an academic's professional actions than believed. At the same time, perhaps classroom instruction is not an appropriate arena in which to determine the effect of teaching orientation. Indeed, perhaps it is how a professor approaches his or her duties outside the classroom where teaching orientation matters more.

SHOULD FACULTY SPEND MORE TIME WITH STUDENTS OUTSIDE THE CLASSROOM?

Another important element of teaching in higher education concerns whether faculty are intellectually engaged with their students outside the classroom. A large amount of research exists on the importance of interaction between teachers and students beyond the traditional classroom setting (Astin, 1993; Pascarella & Terenzini, 1991). Scholars have observed that student academic success is considerably enhanced through faculty mentoring and support (cf. Howe, 1993; Olson & Ashton-Jones, 1992). Oxford University's historic tutorial approach, which involves a large amount of one-to-one discussion between teacher and student, is widely considered one of the best pedagogical approaches in existence, although not feasible for institutions with large student enrollments. As one might expect teaching-oriented professors to have a relatively strong interest in the academic success of their students, this study looked at how these faculty responded to the statement, "Faculty should spend more time with students outside the classroom." In over half of the countries in which this question was asked (6 out of 11), teaching-oriented faculty are significantly more likely than their colleagues to indicate that faculty should spend more time with students outside the classroom (see Table 5.2).

TABLE 5.2

Are teaching-oriented faculty **more or less likely** than their colleagues to indicate that faculty should spend more time with students outside the classroom? (Q39f)*

MORE Likely		LESS Likely		No Significant Relationship
Australia	r= .18	Mexico	r= -.06	Chile
Brazil	r= .01			Hong Kong
Israel	r= .25			Russia
Japan	r= .19			Sweden
Korea	r= .11			
United States	r= .13			

* This item was omitted from the survey administered in England, Germany, and the Netherlands.

As observed in the earlier discussion on instructional methods, teaching-oriented faculty in Israel and the United States appear to be significantly different from their research-oriented colleagues in their approach to teaching. They are joined here by faculty from Australia, Brazil, Japan and Korea. A variety of explanations may be possible for the relationship found in these countries between teaching orientation and agreement with this statement.

To begin with, the correlation between teaching orientation and views toward faculty spending more time with students outside the classroom is considerably strongest among the Israeli academics surveyed (r=.25). A significant correlation (r=.13) was also found among responses from the United States. As observed earlier, teaching-oriented faculty in both the United States and Israel were significantly less likely to spend their classroom hours lecturing, and more likely to spend time on class discussions or laboratory work. However, this analysis found few other trends in common from both the Israeli and United States data samples that would account for the relationship between teaching orientation and support for faculty spending time with students outside the classroom. Considerably more faculty in the United States are teaching-oriented than in Israel. Although the academic systems of both countries have similar historical influences and roots, these are also shared by other countries surveyed by the Carnegie Foundation in which the correlation was not found. More research in this area beyond the scope of the Carnegie data may prove useful for determining meaningful similarities between these countries in how their faculty approach their teaching responsibilities both within and beyond the classroom.

Strong correlations between teaching orientation and support for faculty spending time with students outside the classroom were also found in the data from faculty in Asia. There is considerably stronger agreement with the need for faculty to spend time with students outside the classroom among teaching-oriented faculty in Japan (r=.19) and Korea (r=.11). The similarities between Japan and Korea are more apparent than between Israel and the United States. The faculty in both countries are relatively research-oriented, although Japanese faculty are much stronger in this preference. Of all the countries surveyed, Japan and Korea have the highest percentages of female faculty, and as observed earlier in this study, female faculty are considerably more likely to be teaching-oriented. However, Japanese and Korean faculty also registered lower opinions of their students than faculty elsewhere, with less than a quarter of faculty in these countries rating their students as "excellent" or "good." Researchers on teaching in Asia (e.g., Watkins, 1998) have observed that the ability of teachers to foster responsibility and good moral conduct in their students is widely viewed as a sign of a good teacher. This conception of good teaching may also play a role in this correlation between teaching orientation and support for faculty spending time with students outside the classroom.

Japan and Korea also have considerably more full-time faculty than in any other country surveyed, which may have some influence on the correlations found here. As described in the previous chapter of this volume, part-time faculty often have full-time jobs off campus, often in a profession such as law, management, or accounting, and are only available on campus during the time the class meets. Additionally, few part-time faculty are provided with office space with which to meet with students outside the classroom. In general, there appear to be few incentives for part-time faculty to want to spend time with students outside the classroom.

Thus, in Latin America, where part-time faculty dominate the academic profession, one would expect that responses to this statement—"Faculty should spend more time with students outside the classroom"—would be considerably negative. However, among teaching-oriented faculty, only the data collected from faculty in Mexico support this expectation. Moreover, this correlation observed here is not particularly strong (r= -.06). This finding reflects a unique trend among the responses from faculty in Mexico.

Other studies of the Mexican faculty data (cf. Anton, 1996) indicate no significant differences comparatively on this topic—that is, faculty in Mexico do not appear to be any more or less likely than their colleagues in other countries to agree with the need for faculty to spend more time with students outside the classroom. Thus, there is no clear explanation why the teaching-oriented faculty in Mexico—and not other Latin American countries—are less supportive of spending time with students outside the classroom.

On the other hand, the data from faculty in Brazil indicate that teaching-oriented faculty are surprisingly *more likely* to agree with the need for faculty to spend time with students outside the classroom. As discussed in the previous chapter, Brazil is also the only Latin American country where a significant correlation was found between faculty data on working time and on teaching orientation. This correlation was positive in nature—that is, part-time faculty were significantly more likely than their colleagues to indicate that their preferences lie more in teaching than in research. This would seem to indicate that, at least in Brazil, part-time faculty remain committed to the importance of facilitating student academic achievement both within and outside their classrooms. This is an important distinction to make when discussing the pros and cons of hiring "taxicab professors" (Altbach, 1995). Certainly, more research on the relationship between teaching orientation and the nature of part-time academic work would be useful for furthering this discussion.

In summary, there appears to be very little relationship internationally, or even regionally, between teaching orientation and faculty approaches to teaching. Although it might seem intuitive that faculty whose interests lie more in teaching than in research would have significantly different views toward teaching than their research-oriented colleagues, the Carnegie survey data do not support this assertion. However, another relationship seems equally intuitive—one would expect faculty whose interests lie more in teaching than in research to have significantly different views toward the assessment of teaching than their research-oriented colleagues. After all, when a faculty member indicates that a particular activity which they engage in is very important to them (in this case, teaching), it is reasonable to assume that they would also take a strong interest in how that activity is evaluated. In other words, faculty whose interests lie more in teaching than in research are likely to have considerably stronger views than their colleagues toward the assessment of their teaching. Thus, it is useful to explore the Carnegie survey data to determine whether there exists a significant relationship between teaching orientation and faculty views toward the assessment of teaching.

IMPROVING THE EVALUATION OF TEACHING

Boyer's (1990) *Scholarship Reconsidered* summed up the situation nicely. "Today, at most four-year institutions, the requirements of tenure and promotion continue to focus heavily on research and on articles published in journals, especially those that are refereed. Good teaching is expected, but it is often inadequately assessed" (p.28). Boyer calls for redefining the term *scholarship* to incorporate the importance of effective teaching and college classroom interaction. However, the term *effective teaching* has yet to find a common definition in many academic circles. Indeed, anyone who carries out research on teaching effectiveness quickly runs into the problem of evaluating the outcomes of teaching (McKeachie, 1990). How do classroom processes affect learning outcomes? Students react differently to the same teacher, and yet the majority of current teaching assessment methods throughout the world rely on student evaluations. There is worldwide concern over the inadequacies of current methods for evaluating teaching, a concern which has fostered a growing body of research and suggestions. One idea for improving the assessment of teaching is provided in Murray's (1995) discussion of teaching portfolios. Also, Wright (1998) and others have continually advocated the use of instructional development workshops and institutes to bring faculty together around this issue, and for this "community" to decide how best to evaluate their teaching.

The notion of a unified "academic community" is particularly important when revisiting Gouldner's (1957) distinction between "local" and "cosmopolitan" academics. As earlier chapters of this volume have described, the Carnegie data appear to indicate that teaching-oriented faculty lean more toward "local" affiliations—particularly, their institution—while research-oriented faculty are more concerned with "cosmopolitan" affiliations—mostly, their academic discipline. Some researchers in academic management theory have adopted Gouldner's distinction in exploring differences between professional and administrative concerns. As Hughes (1979) observed, the standards by which professionals judge their work are likely to be closely related to the intellectual discipline of their specialist field and less directly to the instrumental expediences of their employing organization. Loyalty to the organization is thus liable to take a second place to the concept of solidarity with professional colleagues outside the boundaries of the organization itself.

The Carnegie survey data provides an international dimension to the discussion of faculty views toward the assessment of their work. "Respondents in all countries note that teaching is evaluated most often, with research coming second; service activities are seldom assessed" (Altbach & Lewis, 1996: 33). According to the data collected by the Carnegie international survey, a majority of faculty in all countries surveyed indicated that their teaching is regularly evaluated, but that better ways to evaluate teaching performance were needed. The strongest agreement with the need for better ways of evaluating teaching performance was found among Latin American faculty—Mexico (80%), Chile (75%) and Brazil (75%). The weakest (yet still quite significant) agreement with the need for better ways of evaluating teaching performance was found among the European countries—Sweden (59%), Russia (59%), England (61%) and the Netherlands (63%). As stated earlier, it seems intuitive that faculty who prefer teaching over research would be more likely to harbor strong views toward the evaluation of their teaching. Indeed, the data reflect a correlation of this kind in 8 of the countries surveyed (see Table 5.3).

TABLE 5.3

Are teaching-oriented faculty **more or less likely** than their colleagues to indicate that better ways are needed for evaluating teaching effectiveness? (Q38c)

MORE Likely		LESS Likely		No Significant Relationship
England	r= .14	Mexico	r= -.07	Australia
Germany	r= .06			Brazil
Israel	r= .04			Chile
Japan	r= .16			Hong Kong
The Netherlands	r= .15			Korea
Sweden	r= .18			Russia
United States	r= .07			

As observed earlier, teaching-oriented faculty in Israel and the United States have markedly different views toward teaching than their colleagues. In these countries, it was found that they also have different views toward the assessment of teaching. However, the reasons for this common trend in the data may not be the same. Faculty in the United States are considerably more likely than their Israeli colleagues to have their teaching assessed, and the assessment policies and reward structures are notably different between the two countries. In Israel, "there are few established criteria for evaluating teaching, and standards of excellence are fraught with ambiguity" (Chen, Gottlieb & Yakir, 1996: 646), while in the United States, assessment of teaching is virtually universal, although the standards upon which teaching is assessed are not often the same between institutions. Faculty in the United States are considerably more likely than faculty in Israel to have their teaching assessed by students, department heads, peers, or senior administrative staff. However, these many differences notwithstanding, teaching orientation in both countries has a significant relationship with faculty support for new ways of evaluating teaching.

This correlation was also found among the faculty responses from all the European countries surveyed, as well as Japan. One possible explanation for this trend emerging in the data from these particular countries is that, with the exception of the United States, all of the countries where this data relationship was found comprise a professoriate more oriented towards research than teaching. That is, when asked where their preferences lie, a majority faculty in these countries chose research over teaching: England (55%), Germany (66%), Israel (62%), Japan (72%), the Netherlands (76%), and Sweden (67%). Perhaps it can thus be said that the impact of teaching orientation on views toward the assessment of teaching is stronger in countries where research orientation is more predominant than teaching orientation.

However, there are also important differences between these countries. For example, regular evaluation of teaching is quite common among faculty in England (94%) and Israel (87%), while relatively uncommon among faculty in Japan (45%) and Germany (42%). External reviewers play an important role in evaluating teaching in England and the Netherlands, but is virtually non-existent in Japan and Germany. Thus, while a significant relationship was found in all of these countries between teaching orientation and support for new ways of evaluating teaching, there are few international similarities that would lend themselves to an explanation for this trend.

Perhaps the most curious trend overall was found in the data from faculty in Latin America. No significant relationship was found in Brazil or Chile, but in Mexico, teaching-oriented faculty were less likely to agree with the need for better ways of evaluating teaching performance. Faculty in Latin America indicated the highest levels of teaching orientation of all countries surveyed, as well as the highest levels of dissatisfaction with current ways of evaluating teaching performance. Faculty were also highly likely to indicate that their teaching is evaluated regularly in Brazil (93%), Chile (88%) and Mexico (92%). However, in Brazil and Chile, no relationship was found between teaching orientation and agreement with the need for better ways of evaluating teaching performance. Perhaps agreement with the need for better ways of evaluation teaching performance is so commonly shared by faculty in these countries that the importance of personal preferences becomes diminished.

An even more surprising trend was found in the responses from Mexico, where more faculty (80%) than in any other country surveyed indicated a need for better ways of evaluating teaching performance. Here, a negative correlation was found—that is, teaching-oriented faculty were actually *less* likely to agree with the need for better ways of evaluating teaching performance ($r = -.07$; significance $=.009$). In Mexico, significantly more faculty (55%) than in either Brazil (28%) or Chile (23%) indicated that their teaching is regularly evaluated by senior administrative staff at their institution. External review of teaching is also twice as common in Mexico as it is in either Brazil or Chile (Altbach & Lewis, 1996). Perhaps these differences in who evaluates their teaching influences the relationship observed in the data from teaching-oriented faculty. Surely, a closer look at what teaching evaluation activities currently exist in Mexico would yield a better understanding of this trend, and particularly why teaching orientation plays a different role in Mexico than in Brazil or Chile in terms of views toward the need for better assessment of teaching.

In summary, a majority of faculty in every country surveyed indicated that better ways are needed for the evaluation of teaching performance. This view is strongest among faculty in Asia, Israel, Latin America and the United States. In the European countries surveyed, this view is considerably stronger among faculty whose interests lie more in teaching than in research. This is also the case among faculty in Israel, Japan and the United States, while teaching-oriented faculty in Mexico were considerably *less* likely to indicate that better ways are needed for evaluating their teaching. Interestingly, faculty in Mexico—as well as the other Latin American countries surveyed—are less likely than most other parts of the world to have students involved in the evaluation of their teaching. On the other hand, they are considerably more likely to have members of other departments evaluating their teaching than most of the countries surveyed. Thus, perhaps faculty satisfaction with the evaluation of their teaching has some relationship with who is involved in the evaluation activities. Certainly, it would be useful to take a closer look at who faculty feel *should* be involved in the evaluation of their teaching. The Carnegie survey provided some input on this topic, by asking faculty about their views toward the involvement of students in the evaluation of their teaching.

THE ROLE OF STUDENTS IN EVALUATING TEACHING EFFECTIVENESS

The power exercised by students in higher education varies from country to country and institution to institution. "Few systems accord them the pre-eminence they once enjoyed in the earlier medieval European universities; and even in countries with a sizable private sector, their potential as paying clients is rarely exploited" (Beecher, 1985: 2247). Indeed, the primary influence students enjoy in modern times is in the evaluation of teaching effectiveness. Many scholars have argued that student opinions can and should inform efforts to improve one's teaching (e.g., Cross & Angelo, 1988). McKeachie (1990) observed that "despite faculty doubts about the ability of students to appreciate good teaching, the research evidence indicates that students are generally good judges–surprisingly so, in view of the fact that most research on student evaluation has been carried out in introductory classes, in which one would expect the students to be less able to evaluate them than in more advanced classes" (p.191). However, evaluation instruments tend to favor teachers adept in observable or measurable teaching behaviors, while teachers who stress abstract or divergent thinking often do not fare well on such evaluations (Wright, 1998).

According to the Carnegie Foundation's initial report, a majority of faculty in all countries surveyed indicate some level of student involvement in the evaluation of their teaching, with the exception of Japan (37%) and Korea (12%) (Boyer, Altbach & Whitelaw, 1994: Table 27). Further, a majority of faculty in every country surveyed felt that student opinions *should* be used in evaluating teaching effectiveness. In fact, over 70% of faculty in 10 of the countries surveyed felt this way, with slightly lower majorities in Germany (67%), Russia (65%), Korea (64%) and Japan (50%). Fewer than one-fourth of all faculty surveyed (and in most countries, fewer than 15%) were opposed to student involvement in evaluations of faculty teaching effectiveness. As discussed earlier, it could be expected that considerably stronger support of student involvement in teaching evaluation would be found among teaching-oriented faculty throughout the survey. However, this was not the case—in only half the countries surveyed, teaching orientation provided some predictive value in whether faculty agreed with the statement, "student opinions should be used in evaluating teaching effectiveness" (see Table 5.4).

TABLE 5.4

Are teaching-oriented faculty **more or less likely** than their colleagues to agree that student opinions should be used in evaluating teaching effectiveness? (Q38a)

MORE Likely		LESS likely		No Significant Relationship
Australia	r= .14	Mexico	r= -.05	Brazil
England	r= .12			Chile
Germany	r= .03			Hong Kong
Japan	r= .11			Israel
The Netherlands	r= .13			Korea
Sweden	r= .13			Russia
United States	r= .07			

There are several interesting comparisons to be drawn from these findings. To begin with, there is considerable agreement with this statement among teaching-oriented faculty in countries where a high percentage of faculty indicated that students currently evaluate their teaching, including Sweden (96%) and the United States (91%). Here, student involvement in teaching evaluation is high, but if does not appear to have created a significant problem for faculty. However, there is also considerable support for student involvement in evaluating teaching among faculty where this is not so common. For example, only 37% of Japanese faculty indicated that students evaluate their teaching. Also, faculty in Japan were considerably more likely (23%) than in any other country to indicate that students *should not* be involved in evaluating teaching. However, there is significantly stronger support for student involvement in teacher evaluation among teaching-oriented faculty in Japan (r= .11). Thus, it does not appear that existing levels of student involvement in the evaluation of teaching has a direct correlation with faculty support for it.

Another interesting trend is that, with the exception of the United States, all countries where this correlation was found are predominantly research-oriented countries, including Australia and all the European countries surveyed. This mirrors the findings presented earlier which showed that teaching orientation appears to play a more significant role in countries where a minority of faculty are teaching-oriented.

Curiously, although support for student involvement in teaching evaluation is quite strong among all faculty surveyed in Latin America, different trends emerge when looking at teaching-oriented faculty. Fairly similar percentages of all faculty surveyed in the three Latin American countries indicated that students currently evaluate their teaching, and comparable percentages in all three indicated that student opinions should be used for evaluating teaching effectiveness. However, the data do not show significantly stronger or weaker agreement with this statement among teaching-oriented faculty in Brazil or Chile. Further, teaching-oriented faculty in Mexico were actually slightly *less* likely to agree that student opinions should be used for evaluating the effectiveness of teachers. This trend mirrors an earlier finding of this analysis, where faculty in Mexico were less likely than their Latin American colleagues—indeed, less likely than all faculty surveyed—to indicate that better ways are needed for the evaluation of teaching.

As indicated earlier, faculty in Mexico were significantly more likely than in either Brazil or Chile to indicate that their teaching is regularly evaluated by senior administrative staff at their institution. External review of teaching is also twice as common in Mexico as it is in either Brazil or Chile (Altbach & Lewis, 1996). Perhaps these differences in who evaluates their teaching influences faculty perspectives toward the use of student opinions in evaluating teaching effectiveness, which in turn would help explain why Mexican faculty stand out among all the other countries surveyed along these lines. However, other studies of the Mexican faculty data (cf. Anton, 1996) show that students are neither more nor less involved in evaluating teaching in Mexico than in most other countries surveyed. Further, Mexican respondents were not significantly different from their colleagues in other countries in reporting regular evaluation of teaching. Surely, a closer look at what teaching evaluation activities currently exist in Mexico would yield a better understanding of this trend. While the Carnegie survey collected information on who evaluates teaching, no comparative data is currently available on the *types* of instruments or procedures used in these activities. This is one area of further research which would certainly enhance our understanding of these and other issues related to faculty support for new ways of evaluating their work. However, the Carnegie survey data address a related topic of importance by collecting information from faculty on whether teaching effectiveness—assuming it is properly assessed—should be the primary criterion for the hiring and promotion of faculty.

TEACHING EFFECTIVENESS AS CRITERION FOR FACULTY HIRING AND PROMOTION

In a recent study, Wright (1998) found that faculty and deans in Canada, Australia, the United Kingdom and the United States felt that the "recognition of teaching in tenure and promotion decisions" is the most important element for improving the evaluation of teaching. This finding held true for faculty in research universities and liberal arts colleges alike, as did a common feeling among faculty that "teaching performance only seems to make a difference in cases when it is done poorly" (p.7). That is, when teaching effectiveness *is* used as a criterion for faculty hiring and promotion, it is only in situations where dramatically poor teaching leads to denial of job or promotion opportunities, while good teaching performance is scarcely rewarded (Wright, 1998).

In a recent analysis of teaching in the United States, Lewis (1996) noted that "for many academics, teaching is an intrinsically motivated activity . . . it is a task that motivates, not because of the promise of some external reward, but because it is something they simply enjoy doing" (p.147). This perspective may indeed be shared by faculty worldwide. According to the data collected by the Carnegie survey, there is considerable support among faculty worldwide for a stronger recognition of the importance of teaching effectiveness—a majority of faculty surveyed in all countries indicated that teaching should be the primary criterion for the promotion of faculty.

The wording of this item on the Carnegie survey warrants special attention. The survey asked respondents to indicate their agreement with the statement, "Teaching effectiveness should be the primary criterion for faculty hiring and promotion." Note that this statement proposes that teaching performance should be "**the**" primary criterion, not simply "**a**" criterion, for faculty hiring and promotion decisions. According to the data collected by the Carnegie survey, more faculty worldwide agree than disagree with this statement. With the exception of Russia—where, as indicated earlier in this volume, the data collected are particularly suspect—teaching-oriented faculty in all countries surveyed are significantly more likely to indicate that teaching effectiveness should be the primary criterion for faculty hiring and promotion (see Table 5.5).

The strength of the data relationships in many of these countries is impressive. Correlations in the United States (r=.59), Israel (r=.56), Australia (r=.52) and England (r=.51) indicate that teaching orientation has a very strong relationship with how faculty responded to this survey item. Further, this analysis found a correlation in the Carnegie survey data that holds true in virtually every country surveyed—an unusual rarity, given the

TABLE 5.5		
Are teaching-oriented faculty **more or less likely** than their colleagues to indicate that teaching effectiveness should be the primary criterion for faculty hiring and promotion? (Q38d)*		
MORE Likely	**LESS Likely**	**No Significant Relationship**
Australia r= .52 Brazil r= .26 England r= .51 Chile r= .43 Germany r= .32 Hong Kong r= .48 Israel r= .56 Japan r= .35 Korea r= .13 Mexico r= .22 Sweden r= .47 United States r= .59		Russia

* This item was omitted from the survey administered in the Netherlands.

multiple dimensions of variety between each country's academic culture, system, and data sample. Could this international trend be related to the cosmopolitan/local distinction (Gouldner, 1957) described in previous chapters of this book? Certainly, one might expect that faculty whose interests are more oriented towards their institution and towards "campus-related activities" (Altbach & Lewis, 1996) would have stronger views toward issues related to teaching and learning. This analysis adds a compelling international dimension to this issue. In Asia, Latin America, Europe and the United States, in research institutions and liberal arts colleges, teaching-oriented faculty seem to be indicating that they have had enough of the emphasis on research publication in their hiring and promotion activities.

This call for recognizing and rewarding good teaching in higher education is certainly not a new one. Indeed, decades ago, Caplow and McGee's (1958) study of U.S. institutions found that faculty in research universities were primarily evaluated on the basis of their research. Indeed, according to Caplow and McGee, not only was teaching not rewarded at these institutions, but "academic success is likely to come to the man [sic] who has learned to neglect his assigned [teaching] duties in order to have more time and energy to pursue his private professional interests" (p.221). According to recent studies of the academic profession (Lewis, 1996; Murray, 1995; Tierney & Bensimon, 1996), this perspective towards faculty hiring and promotion is as common today as it was in the late 1950s.

In a related study, which found that a majority of academics in the U.S. believed that teaching effectiveness should be a primary criterion for promotion, Boyer (1990) sought to introduce the idea of viewing teaching as a form of scholarship, one which should be rewarded equally with other forms. In the U.S., his notion of the "scholarship of teaching" is most commonly found among liberal arts colleges, but has still not found much support among research universities. Boyer argues that, rather than rewarding research activities to the exclusion of teaching, these institutions must "set a demanding standard—To bring teaching and research into better balance, we urge the nation's ranking universities to extend special status and salary incentives to those professors who devote most of their time to teaching and are particularly effective in the classroom. Such recognition will signify that the campus regards teaching excellence as a hallmark of professional success" (p. 58).

According to the data collected by the Carnegie international survey, faculty—and particularly those faculty whose primary area of interest and activity is more in teaching than in research—want a change. The relatively widespread agreement worldwide with the notion of teaching performance being the primary criterion for faculty hiring and promotion may indicate movement in a new direction of faculty evaluation policies. Further, the data show that teaching orientation is strongly correlated with agreement with this statement, perhaps indicating that institutions should make special efforts to include teaching-oriented professors on hiring and promotion review committees. Regardless of how institutions address this issue of rewarding teaching performance, the Carnegie international survey data clearly show that this issue cannot be ignored.

CONCLUSION

This analysis of the Carnegie survey data sought to determine whether teaching-oriented faculty were significantly different from their colleagues in responding to survey questions related to classroom instruction and the assessment of teaching. For any that were found, this study also sought to determine whether these differences existed internationally or for only faculty in a few of the countries surveyed. The research presented in this chapter tested the validity of a hypothesis which stated that teaching-oriented faculty view classroom instruction and the assessment of teaching differently than do research-oriented faculty. The opposite of this, the null hypothesis, states that there are no significant differences between how teaching-oriented faculty and research-oriented faculty view classroom instruction and the assessment of teaching. According to this analysis of the Carnegie data, we can reject the null hypothesis—there are significant differences between teaching-oriented faculty and research-oriented faculty in their views toward teaching and the assessment of teaching.

However, this analysis did not always find internationally-shared similarities in the relationships between teaching orientation and faculty responses to the Carnegie survey. Rather, this study of the Carnegie data uncovered several kinds of trends, which can be meaningfully organized into one of four categories:

I. Internationally significant - trends in the data that were shared throughout a majority of the countries surveyed;
II. Internationally modest - relationships that were found in the data from fewer than half (but more than two) of the countries surveyed;
III. Mixed results - the data indicate a relationship in one direction in some countries, and a relationship in the opposite direction in others; and
IV. Unique findings - data relationships that were found only among the responses from one country or specific region.

The following discussion reviews the findings of this analysis in relation to these four sub-topics, and explores implications of the more significant trends. Also, in presenting the findings of this analysis, the view is taken that where teaching orientation had no significant relationship whatsoever with faculty responses to a particular item on the survey, this itself is an international trend of sorts.

(I) Significant International Trends

In several cases, the regression analyses showed correlations that were either always positive or always negative for all or most countries surveyed. These findings provide an international insight into what it means to prefer teaching over research.

1. In virtually every country surveyed, faculty with stronger preference for teaching than for research were more likely than their colleagues to indicate that "teaching effectiveness should be the primary criterion for the hiring and promotion of faculty." Further, the correlations observed in this analysis are strong, with r=.5 or higher for several countries.

2. In a majority of countries surveyed, teaching-oriented faculty were more likely than their colleagues to indicate that "faculty should spend more time with students outside the classroom." This trend was strongest among faculty responses from Australia, Israel and the United States.

3. In general, faculty with stronger preference for teaching than for research are not significantly different from research-oriented faculty in their approaches to teaching—that is, teaching orientation does not appear to play a major role regarding the amount of the time they spend in their undergraduate classrooms on lectures, classroom discussions, or laboratory work.

(II) Internationally Modest Findings

Several of the relationships found in this analysis of the Carnegie data are shared by more than a few countries, but not enough to consider them internationally significant.

> 1. In a considerable minority of countries surveyed, teaching-oriented faculty were more likely than their colleagues to indicate that "better ways are needed for evaluating teaching effectiveness." This trend was observed most often among faculty responses from Australia, Europe, Israel and the United States.

> 2. When asked whether "student opinions should be used in evaluating teaching effectiveness," teaching-oriented faculty in Europe, Australia, Japan and the United States are more supportive than their research-oriented colleagues. However, this is not true among teaching-oriented faculty in Latin America, Israel, Russia, Hong Kong and Korea.

> 3. When looking at responses to the survey items addressed in this chapter, teaching orientation plays a significant role more often in faculty responses from Australia, Europe, Israel and the United States, and less often in responses from Asian and Latin American faculty.

(III) Mixed Results

There are also several cases in which teaching orientation had a positive correlation in some countries, and a negative one in others.

> 1. Teaching-oriented faculty in Israel and the United States are more likely to spend classroom time engaged in laboratory work while in Germany they are less likely to do so.

(IV) Unique Findings

In several cases, this analysis of the Carnegie data found a relationship between teaching orientation and faculty response to a particular survey item that was not shared with any other country surveyed.

> 1. Teaching-oriented faculty in Mexico are different than in any other country surveyed, in that they are less likely than their research-oriented colleagues to indicate that "better ways are needed for evaluating teaching effectiveness," that "student opinions should be used in evaluating the effectiveness of teaching," or that "faculty should spend more time with students outside the classroom." These findings reflect a unique

trend in the Carnegie data, for which there is no explanation provided by either the country's case study (see Anton, 1996) or other trends in the survey responses from Mexican faculty.

2. Teaching orientation plays a more prominent role in faculty responses from Israel and the United States than from any other country surveyed. Throughout this chapter, teaching-oriented faculty were consistently found to have responded differently to the Carnegie survey than their research-oriented colleagues. Further, faculty responses from these two countries were the only ones to indicate a significant relationship between teaching orientation and faculty approaches to classroom instructional activities. Teaching-oriented faculty in Israel and the United States were less likely to spend their classroom time in lectures, and more likely to spend their time in class discussions and laboratory work.

3. Japanese faculty whose interest lie more in teaching than in research were significantly (r=.12) less likely to rely on the lecture method in their classrooms. However, no relationship was found among Japanese faculty between teaching orientation and time spent on classroom discussion or laboratory work. Further, no other Asian country's faculty data reflect a significant relationship between teaching orientation and classroom instructional method.

4. Teaching orientation does not appear to play any significant role in how Russian faculty responded to the Carnegie survey. However, as described in Chapter 3, there are problems with the Russian faculty data which must be accounted for in any analysis of the Carnegie data.

Summary and Implications

While the mixed and unique findings are compelling reasons for further research, this study adopts the research philosophy that cross-national similarities inform more of our understanding of the academic profession than do cross-national differences. Additionally, "cross-national similarities lend themselves readily to sociological interpretation, while cross-national differences are much more difficult to interpret" (Kohn, 1987: 31). Looking at cross-national consistencies in the data helps to reduce complex levels to meaningful comparisons—such as culture, language and geography—and gain a collective understanding of issues shared by faculty across the major regions of the world. Thus, national differences can be largely set aside in this study, in looking for a shared phenomenon.

The international findings presented in this chapter generally do not provide support for research on the relationship between faculty personality traits and teaching activities (cf. Murray, 1987; Sherman and Blackburn, 1975), as teaching-oriented faculty in most countries surveyed do not appear to approach classroom instructional activities differently than their research-oriented colleagues. However, teaching-oriented faculty in many countries are stronger than their research-oriented colleagues in support of spending time with students outside the classroom. Also, this study found significant international support among teaching-oriented faculty for better ways to evaluate teaching performance, as well as for student involvement in the evaluation of their teaching. The most significant international finding of the study was that teaching-oriented faculty throughout the survey strongly support the call by Boyer (1990) and others to recognize the importance of teaching in our faculty hiring and promotion activities.

The international dimension of this study brings an important element to our understanding of how faculty feel their teaching should be assessed. The Carnegie survey collected data from a diverse population of faculty, and yet there appears to be a great deal of similarity among their responses to questions on the assessment of teaching. These findings support existing research on the common values embedded in teaching throughout much of academe worldwide. As Watkins (1998) observed, "Western conceptions of what constitutes good teaching seem to have a high degree of cross-cultural validity" (p. 21). These similarities in perspectives are significantly strengthened when this population is divided into teaching-oriented and research-oriented academics. Thus, it can be concluded that orientation toward teaching plays a considerable international role in how faculty feel about the assessment of teaching.

One implication of this is that higher education worldwide must engage teaching-oriented faculty in efforts to improve the evaluation of teaching, as they show the strongest concern for this issue among all faculty. Additionally, as teaching-oriented faculty appear to significantly concerned about how teaching is rewarded in terms of faculty hiring and promotion, higher education administrators would do well to make new efforts at involving teaching-oriented faculty in hiring and promotion review committees and other related decision-making bodies. The amount of time faculty have available for spending with students outside the classroom also needs a closer look, and is certainly related to the overall need to more adequately recognize and reward the importance of teaching in the academy. Perhaps we should have different forms of assessment for different kinds of faculty, related to whether their primary areas of interest and activity are more in teaching or research. All of these topics warrant consideration for future research on the academic profession.

Before we can adequately assess and compare cross-nationally the need for better ways of evaluating teaching, we must first develop a more comprehensive understanding of the methods that are currently used in each of the countries surveyed. This research would necessarily involve in-depth analysis of evaluation instruments, procedures, organizational and political support within each department, and how the outcomes of these evaluation activities are communicated and used within the institution and, where applicable, in the larger national environment. There are several good studies available for the United States, England, Australia, and other countries, but the methodology of these studies, and often their scope, do not render them easily comparable. However, more important is the relative absence of accessible studies of this kind in most of the other countries surveyed. Thus, more research on this topic is needed in order to more completely gauge where things are in terms of the assessment of teaching in higher education on an international scale.

This analysis of the Carnegie data revealed that teaching-oriented faculty are significantly in favor of using teaching effectiveness as the primary criterion for faculty hiring and promotion. This would seem to indicate a significant dissatisfaction, at least among teaching-oriented faculty, with current hiring and promotion criteria, which in many places emphasizes research productivity rather than teaching effectiveness. This dissatisfaction may carry forward into their views toward other dimensions of their academic work. For example, their satisfaction with the conditions under which they labor could very well have negative implications for how faculty approach the teaching function of their profession. Thus, it seems useful next to explore whether teaching-oriented faculty are different from their colleagues in how they view their institutional working conditions.

CHAPTER 6

Institutional Working Conditions

INTRODUCTION

This chapter continues an exploration of whether teaching orientation is related to how faculty responded to the Carnegie international survey. While the previous chapter focused on issues of classroom instruction and the assessment of teaching, this chapter expands the area of focus to include issues related to institutional working conditions. "The working conditions of faculty, inevitably, influence both productivity and morale" (Boyer, Altbach & Whitelaw, 1994: 13). A significant portion of this study thus explores whether the Carnegie data indicate that teaching-oriented faculty have different views toward morale or job satisfaction than research-oriented faculty. Given the widespread disparity in rewards for teaching and research activities, which have been described in previous chapters of this volume, it is likely that teaching-oriented faculty feel less positively about their daily working lives than their research-oriented colleagues. The research presented in this chapter sought to identify internationally significant trends in the Carnegie survey data that would indicate a relationship between teaching orientation and faculty perspectives toward their institutional working conditions.

"There is ample evidence that professorial working conditions are deteriorating in most of the countries included in this survey" (Altbach & Lewis, 1996: 16). Indeed, there is a concern worldwide that being a professor is becoming a less enviable career choice. The Carnegie survey collected data on faculty perspectives toward a wide range of issues regarding their place of work. A majority of survey items related to this topic asked for the respondent's agreement with a particular statement or satisfaction with a particular element of their institutional daily lives, such as their collegial relationships or the quality of institutional resources. The responses to these survey items indicate that faculty worldwide are not an entirely happy lot, particularly regarding their salaries, institutional resources, and institutional administration. However, faculty worldwide are also mostly satisfied with the courses they teach and with their collegial relationships.

As discussed earlier in this study, there are bound to be some differences in opinion between faculty in relation to whether they are more oriented towards teaching or research. The nature of academic work has certainly become more research-oriented in many parts of the world, raising questions about the commitment to—and quality of—teaching in higher education. This in turn has led to a decrease in public support for professorial autonomy and has made life difficult for those who defend traditional definitions of academic work. Faculty who prefer to teach are rarely mentioned by institutions or professional disciplines as "stars" or "experts"—rather, these labels are awarded most often to the productive researcher (Gumport, 1991). As Lewis (1996) and other scholars have shown, academic reward structures tend to favor research productivity, and not teaching effectiveness. Thus, one might expect teaching-oriented faculty to feel the brunt of these "deteriorating" working conditions in the academic professions. The Carnegie survey provides a unique opportunity to examine whether teaching-oriented faculty, being somewhat less positive in their views toward current methods of assessing their work, are also less likely to indicate positive views toward academic life in general.

Are teaching-oriented faculty more or less upbeat than their research-oriented colleagues in their survey responses about working conditions at their institution? This chapter tests the validity of the following hypothesis:

> Teaching-oriented faculty have different perspectives than their research-oriented colleagues towards their institutional working conditions.

Specifically, this analysis of the Carnegie survey data sought to determine the relationship of teaching orientation with faculty views on working conditions at their institution, including issues such as the influence of bureaucracy, the quality of institutional resources, and satisfaction with collegial relationships. The chapter is organized around these themes for reasons of data comparability—almost no country omitted any of these items from their survey—and personal research interests. In analyzing and presenting the data relationships found in this study, it is assumed that the more countries in which a trend in the Carnegie data exists, the more international that trend is. The following internationally significant relationships were found in this analysis of the Carnegie survey data:

> • In a majority of the countries surveyed, teaching-oriented faculty are considerably more likely than their colleagues to indicate satisfaction with the undergraduate courses they teach.

• Teaching orientation has a significant relationship in virtually every country surveyed with how faculty responded to the statement, "the pressure to publish reduces the quality of teaching at this institution."
• Teaching orientation has a significant correlation in most countries surveyed with how faculty rate their institution's resources for teaching.

Overall, teaching-oriented faculty appear to be significantly less satisfied than their colleagues with several dimensions of their jobs, including the pressure to publish and their prospects for promotion. However, they are more satisfied than their colleagues with the courses they teach, and with some of their institution's resources for teaching.

As described in Chapter 2, research has shown that a faculty member's preferences can often drive their behavior (cf. Clark, 1987; Clark, 1992; Sherman and Blackburn, 1975). Thus, one can assume that teachers who are unhappy with their working conditions are likely to approach their work differently than their colleagues who are more satisfied with their surroundings. Indeed, few would argue that a faculty member's teaching is not influenced to some degree by their working conditions. The effectiveness of a teacher is most likely affected by the quality of resources which are available to them, as well as their relationships with co-workers and their overall happiness in their job. As observed in the initial Carnegie report, "the working conditions of faculty, inevitably, influence both productivity and morale" (Boyer, Altbach & Whitelaw, 1994: 13).

Clearly, there is an assumption beneath all these observations that an unhappy faculty member most likely makes for a less effective teacher. Thus, this chapter addresses an important question: Are teaching-oriented faculty any more or less happy than their research-oriented colleagues with their institutional working conditions? For the purposes of this discussion, it may be useful to look at this issue through the eyes of the survey respondent, the typical faculty member whose desk the Carnegie international survey came across earlier this decade. In responding to this survey, the faculty member would likely ask himself or herself questions related to their institutional working conditions, such as:

• Am I satisfied with my work environment?
• What kinds of pressures are there from within my institution?
• Am I likely to stay here or am I considering leaving this institution?

The analysis presented in this chapter sought to determine whether a teaching-oriented faculty member responded differently to these questions than their research-oriented colleagues. The chapter is organized around these themes for reasons of data comparability—almost no country omitted any of these items from their survey—and personal research interests. It is possible that teaching-oriented faculty may have a different set of grievances than their research-oriented colleagues toward their institution. If teaching-oriented faculty overall appear to be more satisfied (or less satisfied) in their jobs than their research-oriented colleagues, then this provides a unique dimension to discussions of improving higher education, and in particular points to the need for tying professional roles with appropriate institutional support and professional rewards in the academic profession.

AM I SATISFIED WITH MY WORK ENVIRONMENT?

A driving force behind a good deal of research on the academic profession is the goal of enhancing or improving the daily work lives of faculty members, and perhaps help them become more effective in their roles and responsibilities. The Carnegie survey collected data on several important dimensions of faculty working conditions, including satisfaction with institutional resources for teaching, courses taught, and collegial relationships. Each of these issues provides an opportunity to explore whether teaching-oriented faculty feel differently than their research-oriented colleagues about the places in which they work.

Satisfaction with Institutional Resources

How an institution maintains its resources for teaching has become an increasingly worrisome topic of debate worldwide. Recent decades have witnessed a trend of declining financial support for higher education worldwide, and institutions are increasingly forced to make hard decisions as to the distribution of its resources. One observed trend in these resource distribution decisions is that the most "revenue-generating" departments receive a favorable share of the available resource pool, often at the expense of liberal arts departments, maintenance needs, or support for teaching. The well-publicized critically poor condition of classrooms at Yale University is an excellent example of this trend.

The Carnegie survey data on how faculty view their institutional resources is thus useful here—looking at how faculty view their institution's resources, particularly those that directly relate to the teaching component of their jobs, provides an important insight into the learning environment that institutional resource distribution decisions have produced. In most countries surveyed, less than half the faculty indicated positive views of their institutional resources in support of teaching. Respondents in Hong Kong, the Netherlands, Sweden, Germany and the United States were consistently the most positive in their evaluation of these resources, with faculty in the remaining countries registering markedly lower opinions, particularly in Japan, Russia and Korea (Boyer, Altbach & Whitelaw, 1994: Tables 33-36).

However, along another dimension, one may argue that the relationship between teaching orientation and satisfaction with institutional resources for teaching is a more important one to consider. As teaching-oriented faculty tend to have more daily interaction with their institution's resources for teaching and learning, their views are considerably important, and might tend to be more critical of these resources than their research-oriented colleagues. Indeed, as Altbach and Lewis (1996) observed, faculty most involved in research have fewer complaints about facilities than do those most involved in teaching. This analysis of the Carnegie data confirm their observation, in finding that teaching orientation appears to have a significant relationship with how faculty evaluated their institution's classrooms, technology for teaching, laboratories, computer facilities, or libraries in most of the countries surveyed. When looking at responses from those faculty who indicated a stronger preference for teaching than their colleagues, we find significantly more satisfaction with classrooms and with technology for teaching, but significantly less satisfaction with laboratories and computers facilities (see Table 6.1).

This table represents several curious trends within the Carnegie data. First, teaching-oriented faculty in many countries were both more satisfied with technology for teaching and less satisfied with computer facilities. In fact, in no country were teaching-oriented faculty less satisfied with their institution's technology for teaching nor more satisfied with their computer facilities. A close look at what these terms may represent provides a possible explanation for this. "Technology for teaching" may include equipment like overhead projectors, screens, film projectors, microphones and other audio equipment, while "computer facilities" may include word processor laboratories, personal computers for faculty offices, database number crunching, access to the Internet, printers, and so forth. Teaching-oriented faculty have decidedly more interaction with the former than the latter, while research-oriented faculty likely use their institution's computer facilities more. Thus, perhaps this increased interaction has an effect on faculty satisfaction with these resources.

Institutional library holdings are considerably important to teaching-oriented faculty—poorly-equipped libraries make it difficult for students to do quality research for their term papers. Throughout the Carnegie survey, a majority of faculty in only Germany, Sweden and the Netherlands rated their library holdings as "excellent" or "good", while most faculty in all other countries responded "fair" or even "poor" on this survey item. However, teaching-oriented faculty in Israel, Japan and Mexico are significantly more satisfied than their colleagues with their institution's library holdings. Teaching-oriented faculty in Israel and Mexico were also significantly more satisfied with their institution's laboratories. The reverse trend was found in England, the Netherlands and the United States, where teaching-oriented faculty were significantly less satisfied with both laboratories and library holdings.

TABLE 6.1

Are teaching-oriented faculty **more or less likely** to indicate high satisfaction with their institution's resources?

MORE Likely	LESS Likely	No Significant Relationship
CLASSROOMS (Q24A)*		
Australia r= .01	England r= -.01	Chile
Japan r= .08	Germany r= -.06	Hong Kong
Mexico r= .14	Sweden r= -.01	Israel
the Netherlands r= .10		Korea
United States r= .08		Russia
		*Not asked in Brazil
TECHNOLOGY FOR TEACHING (Q24B)		
Australia r= .01		Brazil
Chile r= .01		Hong Kong
England r= .10		Korea
Germany r= .11		Russia
Israel r= .18		
Japan r= .10		
Mexico r= .15		
the Netherlands r= .13		
Sweden r= .02		
United States r= .03		
LABORATORIES (Q24C)		
Chile r= .01	England r= -.09	Australia Russia
Israel r= .14	Germany r= -.12	Brazil Sweden
Mexico r= .11	Japan r= -.01	Hong Kong
	the Netherlands r= -.13	Korea
	United States r= -.05	
COMPUTER FACILITIES (Q24E)		
	Brazil r= -.09	Australia
	Chile r= -.15	Hong Kong
	England r= -.09	Korea
	Germany r= -.05	Mexico
	Israel r= -.01	Russia
	Japan r= -.01	Sweden
	the Netherlands r= -.03	
	United States r= -.12	

Several regional variations in these correlations were found. In Japan, where all faculty had more complaints than in most other countries about their institutional resources for teaching, teaching-oriented faculty were more likely to give positive reviews of the classrooms and libraries, but less likely to be satisfied with their technology for teaching, computer facilities, and laboratories. However, while Korean faculty also had more complaints than in most other countries about their institutional resources for teaching, no significant correlations were found to indicate that teaching-oriented faculty have stronger opinions in this area. This was also the case for faculty responses from Hong Kong and Russia

In Latin America, teaching-oriented faculty in Chile were more satisfied with their institution's technology for teaching and laboratories, but less satisfied with their computer facilities. Teaching-oriented faculty in Mexico were more likely to indicate satisfaction with their institution's classrooms, technology for teaching, laboratories, and libraries, but were not significantly more or less satisfied then their colleagues with their computer facilities. In Brazil, a significant correlation was found only between teaching orientation and greater dissatisfaction with computer facilities. Regional variations were found among the countries surveyed in Europe as well. Teaching-oriented faculty in England and the Netherlands were more likely to indicate dissatisfaction with their institution's laboratories, computer facilities, and libraries, but were also more likely to give a positive evaluation of technology for teaching. Overall, the Carnegie data indicate that teaching orientation plays a more prominent role in Europe and the United States than in any other part of the world when looking at faculty satisfaction with institutional resources for teaching.

In summary, teaching orientation in most countries surveyed appears to play some role in how faculty rated their institutional resources for teaching. However, the relationship between teaching orientation and faculty satisfaction with resources does not lend itself readily to a globally comparative interpretation, as the data correlations observed are mixed. No clear international—or even regional—correlations were found between orientation towards teaching or research and greater or less faculty satisfaction overall with their institutional resources for teaching and learning. As teaching-oriented faculty spend considerably more time in the classroom than their research-oriented colleagues, their satisfaction in this area is an important area for further research.

Satisfaction with Courses

As Lewis (1996) points out, "for many academics, teaching is an intrinsically motivated activity . . . it is a task that motivates, not because of the promise of some external reward, but because it is something they simply enjoy doing" (p.147). Assuming that faculty who are more satisfied with their courses may tend to have more intrinsic motivation to do well in their classrooms, it is useful to look at faculty responses to this item on the Carnegie survey. A majority of faculty in all countries surveyed indicated satisfaction with the undergraduate courses they teach, ranging from 54% in Japan to 86% in the United States (Boyer, Altbach & Whitelaw, 1994: Table 38). However, this analysis found significantly stronger satisfaction among teaching-oriented faculty in a majority of the countries surveyed (see Table 6.2).

TABLE 6.2

Are teaching-oriented faculty **more or less likely** than their colleagues to indicate high satisfaction with the undergraduate courses they teach? (Q27a)*

MORE Likely		LESS Likely	No Significant Relationship
Australia	r= .23		Brazil
Chile	r= .13		Hong Kong
England	r= .25		Russia
Germany	r= .33		
Israel	r= .09		
Japan	r= .18		
Korea	r= .07		
Mexico	r= .10		
Sweden	r= .29		
United States	r= .18		

* this item was omitted from the survey administered in the Netherlands

One might expect teaching-oriented faculty to have stronger views than most faculty toward the courses they teach. Thus, it is considerably important that this analysis found teaching-oriented faculty to be significantly more satisfied in this area in all but three of the countries surveyed. For teaching orientation to be positively correlated with faculty satisfaction with courses taught, the reverse must be true for research orientation. That is, according to this analysis, research-oriented faculty are significantly less satisfied than their colleagues with the courses they teach. This trend has broad implications for discussions on the relationship between faculty work preferences and the work they are assigned to do by their departments. Perhaps there is a need to further explore efforts in some countries—notably, the Netherlands—to divide up the academic professional workload based on whether a faculty member's work preferences lie in teaching or research. However, as observed earlier in this discussion, such a division poses an entirely new set of problems and issues to address.

The international similarities found in this trend in the Carnegie data are compelling. This trend was found in most of the Latin American, European and Asian countries. The strength of the data relationship in several countries is also important, particularly in Germany (r=.33), Sweden (r=.29) and England (r=.25). Further, there are few similarities among the countries where this relationship was not found. None of them—Brazil, Hong Kong, or Russia—are among the predominantly English-speaking countries, and they are each from separate geographic regions. Curiously, there were no significant correlations found in any of these three countries between teaching orientation and satisfaction with institutional resources for teaching. Generally speaking, there are no apparent explanations for why this relationship between teaching orientation and satisfaction with undergraduate courses taught was found in the data from so many of these countries, and not in these few others.

There are many possible dimensions to this relationship that warrant more extensive research. As indicated in Chapter 3, the nature of the survey data is such that strong teaching orientation can be easily interpreted as weak research orientation, and vice versa. Thus, an interesting question this analysis raises is why are research-oriented faculty worldwide less satisfied with the courses they teach? Faculty who are oriented towards teaching may tend to have more personal involvement than their research-oriented colleagues in the courses they teach. Or perhaps high satisfaction with the courses a faculty member teaches influences his or her preference for teaching. On yet another dimension, it could be that teaching orientation influences a greater likelihood for a faculty member to like virtually any course they teach. These issues bear particular relevance for discussions of faculty workload, assessment and rewards in academic organizations worldwide. Thus, future research is certainly warranted for answering these and other compelling questions raised by this analysis of the Carnegie data. One related question concerns collegial relationships within a faculty member's department, a particularly important issue given that course loads and curriculum changes are often the result of department-level negotiations.

Collegial Relationships

The academic world is a particularly competitive one, often involving debate, acceptance (or rejection) by colleagues in one's discipline, and comparisons with others in the field. Another dimension of this competitive environment involves comparisons between academic departments and institutions, although often based on the research productivity of particular faculty members within these departments. These comparisons often lead to national rankings of institutions within a particular field, both formal and informal—in virtually any academic discipline, one can discover who is the "best" in their field. Prestige and reputation drive these academic competitions to a significant degree. Those at the top of the prestige hierarchy are easily identified—look at who is invited to be a keynote speaker at an academic conference, or who is cited the most frequently in the publications within that discipline.

In recent decades, a growing number of scholars have pointed to the more negative aspects of this competitive environment within the academic profession and higher education generally (cf. Gumport, 1993; Lewis, 1996; Tierney & Bensimon, 1996). Some individuals have become disillusioned with the academic profession altogether, finding it less egalitarian—and far more political—than at first imagined. Particularly at the departmental level, collegiality has suffered from increased competitiveness for new positions, promotional opportunities, curriculum changes, and other internal negotiations. Indeed, for many reasons, there have been considerable changes in the way faculty relate to each other. One example of collegial relationships can be observed through changes in faculty decision-making activities. In a study of U.S. faculty, Zemsky (1996) observed that the nature of discussion about departmental curriculum reform has shifted from theoretical to procedural:

> [faculty] understood that the preservation of what community remained was dependent on making discussions within the department more narrow, more concerned with nuts and bolts—with procedures—and less given to wide-ranging discourse on either the nature of the canon or the components of a comprehensive undergraduate education (p. 83).

However, the Carnegie international survey results do not indicate widespread dissatisfaction in terms of collegial relationship—with the exception of Russia, a majority of faculty in all countries responded that their relationships with colleagues are at least satisfactory. Thus, it seems that this competitive environment has not led to a high level of animosity among faculty worldwide

Certainly, life in the academic profession is decidedly different for faculty who are not primarily engaged in these competitive worlds of academic research. Thus, it stands to reason that teaching-oriented faculty would be more likely to have stronger bonds with their colleagues, in that they are not competing against each other for higher prestige rankings. Indeed, it might be expected that faculty with strong teaching preference would be concerned more with the students and colleagues in their institution, while research-oriented faculty might focus more on academic relationships outside their institution. As described earlier in this discussion, Gouldner (1957) and other scholars of higher education have suggested a distinction between "local" and "cosmopolitan" professors along these lines.

However, the Carnegie data support this expectation for faculty responses from only three of the countries surveyed—Mexico, Sweden and the United States. The correlation between teaching orientation and satisfaction with collegial relationships is strongest in Mexico ($r = .12$), and significant in both Sweden and the United States. In each of these countries, teaching-oriented faculty are more satisfied than their research-oriented colleagues in their collegial relationships. Although this trend is only modest in its significance internationally, it nonetheless provides an important dimension to our understanding of how faculty feel about their working conditions.

However, a unique trend was found among the responses from faculty in Germany, where 66% of faculty surveyed indicated a preference for research over teaching, and 71% of faculty reported satisfaction with their collegial relationships. Here, teaching orientation is related to a *lower* likelihood of being satisfied with one's relationships with colleagues. Does this indicate lower academic collegiality among teachers than among researchers in this country? Other analyses of the Carnegie data do not seem to indicate this to be true. "Overall, satisfaction in the German professoriate is clearly influenced by the satisfaction of the German respondents with the position they have obtained" (Enders & Teichler, 1996: 469). "University Junior Staff are considerably more satisfied with their collegial relationships than their colleagues in other positions. However, a regression analysis provides evidence that relationships with colleagues plays a very minor role in how German faculty indicated satisfaction with their job overall" (Ibid: 471). Clearly, a comprehensive study of the negative correlation observed in this study between teaching orientation and satisfaction with collegial relationships would generate some interesting contributions to our understanding of the academic profession in Germany.

Overall, however, this analysis of the Carnegie data found that there are scarcely any significant differences between teaching-oriented and research-oriented faculty in how they feel about their relationships with their colleagues. Thus, despite considerable differences in work preferences and roles, faculty worldwide seem to be getting along quite well with each other. Perhaps there are some cultural elements embedded within the academic profession that contribute to this trend. The academic profession is an excellent example of a "one life, one career" profession (Furniss, 1981). For those going into the professoriate, there is a vague but nonetheless real understanding that an academic career is a calling as well as a job (Shils, 1983). Like other professions such as law, medicine, or the clergy, faculty are conditioned to believe they are committing themselves for a lifetime to a discipline (Simpson, 1990).

The international trend found in this analysis of the Carnegie data contributes to current discussions in higher education circles regarding the need for intellectual collaboration among academics. Recently, scholars such as Damrosch (1995) and others have raised a number of questions about the nature of academic work, much of which is conducted in isolation. With the exception of some fields in science, where collaboration is an important rule, certain aspects of academic culture seem to prohibit faculty members from working together, which arguably can produce research of higher quality and broader scope. Decisions of tenure and promotion review committees reflect this aspect by their emphasis on singly-authored publications as having more "weight" than co-authored works. Supporters of collaboration in classroom instruction (cf. Panitz & Panitz, 1998) can also take heart in the international academic camaraderie reflected in the Carnegie survey data.

While this study has found considerable differences between teaching-oriented and research-oriented faculty, there are no significant international differences in how they view their relationships with each other. However, this analysis of the Carnegie data has revealed some relationship between teaching orientation and faculty views toward their institutional resources and the courses they teach. There are other issues of satisfaction with the academic work environment which the Carnegie survey collected faculty responses on, including administrative bureaucracies and the pressure to publish. These pressures are also worth exploring, for they can enhance our understanding of how teaching-oriented faculty and research-oriented faculty feel differently about their working conditions.

WHAT KINDS OF PRESSURES ARE THERE FROM WITHIN MY INSTITUTION?

The issue of work pressures is arguably important for the study of any profession. Particularly, it is important to come to terms with the perceptions of the work environment held by the participants themselves—the ways in which they construct their own reality (Greenfield, 1975). Certainly, academic work is complex. Thus, any analysis of academic organization must involve multiple dimensions and issues. While classrooms and colleagues are two dimensions, others which seem salient for this discussion include how faculty feel about bureaucracies, the pressure to publish, and the struggle for promotion through the academic ranks.

The Pressures of Increasingly Bureaucratic Institutions

Studies of academic organizations have indicated that, owing the relatively autonomous nature of academic work, faculty are generally resistant to administrative control (Abrahamson, 1967; Kornhauser, 1962; Hughes, 1979). Thus, one might expect to find a tension globally between academics and administrators. Indeed, "throughout the world, faculty dissatisfaction with their institutional governance and administrators is high" (Altbach & Lewis, 1997: 27). For example, in the United States, the largest data sample collected, "almost nine out of ten faculty agree that the effectiveness of higher education is being threatened by growing bureaucracies" (Haas, 1996: 347). One possible explanation for this is mentioned in the initial Carnegie survey report:

> As higher education dramatically expanded to accommodate increasing numbers of students, colleges and universities developed a hierarchical "industrial model" of governance. Layers of administrators were created to handle everything from personnel policies to facilities for financial aid . . . creating within the institution a climate of confusion and sometime mistrust. (Boyer, Altbach & Whitelaw, 1994: 15)

For centuries, higher education institutions were run largely by their faculty. Today, the bureaucratic model is the norm throughout much of higher education. Bureaucracies are epitomized by goals of efficiency, often by introducing standard procedures for daily operations, as well as by which human and material resources get committed. The common flaw in these bureaucratic environments is that when presented with a situation that is not standard—in other words, is not accounted for in the "procedures manual"—personnel often do not know how to respond, and any resulting organizational action can be quite slow. This can cause the most frustration for faculty who wish to try new or innovative approaches in their work.

Overall, faculty throughout the Carnegie survey reported widespread dissatisfaction with the governance and administration of their institutions. Faculty in Russia expressed "considerable frustration with the obstacles to obtaining their goals both for themselves and their students" (Levin-Stankevich & Savelyev, 1996: 569). In every country surveyed, faculty tended to indicate little or no influence in their institution's decision-making process, and were quite negative in their views on relationships between the faculty and administration. However, in looking at the Carnegie survey results, Altbach and Lewis (1996) found that "those who prefer teaching over research spend somewhat more time on local or campus-related activities (teaching, service, and administration) than do those who prefer research over teaching" (p.21). Thus, a regression analysis was performed on the Carnegie survey data to determine whether research-oriented faculty are more or less resistant to bureaucracy than their teaching-oriented colleagues.

Somewhat surprisingly, teaching-oriented professors do not appear to be significantly different than their colleagues in their views about the impact of bureaucracies in higher education. Indeed, no significantly positive relationships were found in a majority of countries between teaching orientation and agreement with the statement, "The effectiveness of higher education is being threatened by growing bureaucracies." Further, teaching-oriented faculty in four countries—Japan ($r= -.10$), Mexico ($r= -.17$), Russia ($r= -.10$) and Sweden ($r= -.12$)—are considerably *less* likely to agree with this statement. This raises an obvious question of why, in these countries, do teaching-oriented faculty seem to feel relatively more positive towards bureaucracies than their research-oriented colleagues. Perhaps the reverse angle of this relationship—that research-oriented faculty are significantly less satisfied than their teaching-oriented colleagues—provides a more useful way of exploring the trend. It cannot be said that bureaucracies are relatively more or less significant in these countries than in the other countries surveyed, although faculty in Japan, Russia and Sweden (but not Mexico) were considerably less likely than in most other countries to indicate that a lack of faculty involvement in institutional decision-making was a significant problem. According to Levin-Stankevich & Savelyev (1996), "Russian universities have always had a system of shared governance, although the operations and autonomy of institutions of higher education were highly proscribed by legislation, ministerial orders, and constant vigilance on the part of the state and political organizations" (p. 597).

"Japanese faculty enjoy a substantial involvement in the decision-making process through the chair system and departmental representation" (Arimoto, 1996: 175), and "a majority of Japanese faculty surveyed agree that top administrators are providing competent leadership" (Altbach & Lewis, 1997: 29). However, faculty in Japan—as well as in Mexico, Russia and Sweden—tend to view the decision-making process as centralized. In Mexico, "only 12 percent of faculty consider themselves very influential at the departmental level in helping to shape key academic policies, and 59 percent consider bureaucracy a real threat to higher education" (Anton, 1997: 337), with similar perspectives shared by their Swedish colleagues. However, these trends do not distinguish these countries in any meaningful way from the other surveyed. Indeed, "faculty dissatisfaction with current administrative and governance arrangements is high" (Altbach & Lewis, 1997: 27), and "a majority of faculty in every country surveyed indicated that they have little or no influence in shaping key academic policies at their institution" (Ibid: 28).

Overall, while correlations were found in four countries which indicate a relationship between teaching orientation and faculty views toward bureaucracy, there are no clear structural or systemic explanations for this trend. Further, there are no obvious explanations for why there is less of a negative view toward bureaucracies among these teaching-oriented professors than among their colleagues elsewhere. Overall, the most significant finding of this analysis of the Carnegie data on this issue is that there are no internationally significant differences between teaching-oriented and research-oriented faculty in how faculty view the impact of bureaucracies in higher education. As this study is concerned mostly with internationally significant trends in the data, this trend—although certainly interesting—will require further research at some other time. Rather, it is important here to explore how teaching orientation may relate to other pressures faculty may encounter in their workplace. In addition to the pressures of bureaucracies, most faculty also face mounting pressures to publish, particularly those faculty employed by research universities.

The Pressure to Publish

A significant theme of discussion throughout higher education concerns the relationship between publishing one's research with the effectiveness of one's classroom instruction. To date, no definitive proof has been found that publishing adds to or takes away from a teacher's effectiveness in the classroom. There are two ideological camps in academe that bear different views toward the relationship between teaching and research in the academic profession. On the one hand, there are academics who feel that teaching and research are necessarily complimentary—good teaching informs good research, and vice versa—and, therefore, faculty should be hired and promoted on the basis of excellence in both areas. On the other hand, there are academics who argue that a faculty member's skills, interest, and available time permit excellence in only one or the other. Their argument is that, given naturally limited resources, one can excel only in teaching or in research, but not in both. Certainly, they argue, a professor's time is not infinite—more time spent on one activity must certainly leave less time to engage in another.

However, as observed throughout this analysis, institutions of higher education do not reward both teaching and research equally. Gumport (1991) observed that as higher education institutions have increasingly adopted a "research imperative," faculty who are not considered productive researchers are frequently labeled "deadwood." Decisions are made daily at academic institutions which clearly indicate to faculty members what is valued, and what will be rewarded, at that institution. Sabbatical leaves, adjustments in teaching loads, support for attendance at conferences, and grants to support research all give clear indications of institutional priorities. And yet, while research is considered the 'coin of the realm' in academe, there are many faculty worldwide who prefer teaching over other academic activities. Certainly, one could expect to find difference of opinion towards institutional pressures for publishing among faculty who are plainly not interested in research.

The Carnegie survey collected data from faculty on this important topic by asking faculty to respond to the statement, "The pressure to publish reduces the quality of teaching at this institution." With the exception of Hong Kong, faculty throughout the survey were more likely to disagree than agree with this statement. In other words, "faculty worldwide do not endorse the view that teaching and research necessarily work at cross-purposes" (Altbach & Lewis, 1996: 25). Indeed, a majority of faculty appear convinced that their research has a positive influence on their teaching.

This study of the Carnegie data sought to determine whether this "pressure to publish" is interpreted differently by teaching-oriented faculty than by their research-oriented colleagues. Certainly, as described earlier in this discussion, the Carnegie data indicate that teaching-oriented faculty publish less than their research-oriented colleagues. Indeed, faculty interested in teaching spend more time on teaching activities than faculty interested in research, while those interested in research spend more hours on research than teaching faculty (Gottlieb & Keith, 1996; Altbach & Lewis, 1996). However, just because a faculty member's primary interests lie in teaching does not necessarily free them from feeling a pressure to publish. In fact, one might expect that orientation towards teaching influences a stronger negative view toward the pressure to publish, particularly regarding its impact on their teaching. According to this analysis, the Carnegie data support this expectation for a majority of faculty surveyed. In fact, significant relationships were found between teaching orientation and faculty views toward the pressure to publish in virtually every country surveyed (see Table 6.3).

TABLE 6.3

Are teaching-oriented faculty **more or less likely** to agree with the statement, "The pressure to publish reduces the quality of teaching at this institution"? (Q38b)

MORE Likely		LESS likely		No Significant Relationship
Australia	r= .22	Brazil	r= -.06	Mexico
England	r= .06	Chile	r= -.01	
Hong Kong	r= .26	Germany	r= -.01	
Japan	r= .17	Israel	r= -.12	
Korea	r= .15	Sweden	r= -.08	
the Netherlands	r= .04			
Russia	r= .23			
United States	r= .02			

The strongest correlations were found among faculty responses from Hong Kong (r= .26), Russia (r= .23) and Australia (r= .22), all of which indicated higher agreement with this statement among teaching-oriented faculty. However, several interesting regional variations in this trend were found. Teaching-oriented faculty in all the Asian countries surveyed were significantly *more likely* to agree with this statement. Does this mean that the pressure to publish is stronger in Asia than in other regions of the world? Certainly, "faculty in Asia were significantly more likely than in other countries surveyed to agree with the statement, 'I frequently feel under pressure to do more research than I actually would like to'" (Altbach & Lewis, 1996: 26).

On the other hand, faculty in both Chile and Brazil were *less likely* to agree, with no significant relationship found among the responses from Mexican faculty. Does this mean that the pressure to publish is weaker in Latin America than in other regions of the world? As indicated earlier in this analysis, faculty in Brazil, Chile and Mexico are considerably more interested in teaching than in research. The Carnegie data also show that faculty in these three countries indicated that their institution is "very important" to them, while a large majority of faculty in every country surveyed say this about their academic discipline. Altbach and Lewis (1996) observed that "the professoriate in all three countries stand out as having the lowest commitment to research of any country surveyed, defined by faculty indications of interest in research overall, time spent in research activities, books and articles published, and the level of funding received for research" (p. 24). Thus, perhaps there is significantly less pressure to publish in Latin America than in the other countries surveyed by the Carnegie foundation, a trend which offers some explanation to why teaching-oriented faculty here are in considerable disagreement with the impact this pressure has on their teaching.

In Europe, the results are split—teaching-oriented faculty in England and the Netherlands are *more likely* to agree with the statement, while their colleagues in Germany and Sweden are *less likely* to agree. Certainly, "there is a considerably higher commitment to research in European countries than in most others surveyed, as defined by faculty indications of interest in research overall, time spent in research activities, books and articles published, and the level of funding received for research" (Altbach & Lewis, 1996: 24). It is thus unclear why such an intra-regional difference exists among responses from teaching-oriented colleagues.

Taken together, the findings of this analysis appear mixed. However, among teaching-oriented faculty worldwide there is considerably more agreement than disagreement with the statement, "the pressure to publish reduces the quality of teaching at this institution." While this relationship may seem intuitive, this is the first international collection of faculty perspectives to provide evidence for it. As indicated earlier, teaching-oriented faculty publish less, and academic reward systems are frequently geared to recognize productivity in publishing and not in teaching. Thus, the relationship with teaching orientation found here might also be found among responses to a Carnegie survey item concerning the respondent's prospects for promotion.

The Pressures of the Struggle for Promotion

Virtually all faculty feel at some point in their careers a certain amount of pressure over whether or not they stand a chance to be promoted through the ranks of their department. Granted, once tenure is achieved, some faculty are happy to remain associate professors for life. However, the Carnegie study found that faculty worldwide are relatively dissatisfied with their prospects for promotion—in most countries surveyed, less than half are satisfied in this area. This institutional pressure, faced by a majority of faculty, is another compelling point of concern. As other research studies have observed, these pressures can often drive their behavior (cf. Clark, 1987; Clark, 1992; Sherman and Blackburn, 1975). As this chapter has already observed several distinctions between teaching-oriented and research-oriented faculty in how they feel about their institutional working conditions, it is thus also useful to determine whether faculty preference for teaching or research plays a considerable role in their satisfaction in this area.

In the previous chapter, it was found that teaching-oriented faculty are significantly more likely than their colleagues to indicate that teaching effectiveness should be the primary criterion for the hiring and promotion of faculty. Obviously, this is currently not the case. As discussed earlier in this book, publishing has become the "coin of the realm" in academe—faculty hiring and promotion committees reward those who publish. Teaching-oriented faculty publish less than their research-oriented colleagues, and thus one could expect them to feel more negatively than their colleagues about their prospects for promotion. However, this was the case in slightly less than half the countries surveyed (see Table 6.4).

TABLE 6.4

Are teaching-oriented faculty **more or less likely** to indicate high satisfaction with their prospects for promotion? (Q27d)*

MORE Likely	LESS Likely		No Significant Relationship
	Brazil	r= -.10	Australia
	England	r= -.06	Chile
	Germany	r= -.05	Hong Kong
	Israel	r= -.08	Japan
	Sweden	r= -.05	Korea
	United States	r= -.13	Mexico
			Russia

* This item was omitted from the survey administered in the Netherlands.

In every country where a significant relationship was found, this relationship was in the form of a negative correlation. That is, in no country surveyed were teaching-oriented faculty *more likely* than their research-oriented colleagues to indicate satisfaction with their prospects for promotion. Negative correlations were most noticeable among European faculty responses, where faculty tended to indicate that "it is difficult for a person to achieve tenure if he or she does not publish" and that "a strong record of successful research activity is important in faculty evaluation." (Boyer, Altbach & Whitelaw, 1994: Tables 22-23) Further, as observed earlier in this discussion, faculty in these countries are more research-oriented than in many others surveyed, and loyalty to academic disciplines tends to run higher than loyalty to one's institution. Taken together, these trends appear to indicate a working environment in Europe that is significantly more oriented towards research than the teaching-oriented professoriate in these countries would like. This discussion raises a number of compelling questions. Are there real or perceived barriers to promotion for teaching-oriented faculty in these countries? Are prospects for promotion overall different here than in other countries surveyed? Further research beyond the scope of the Carnegie survey data is needed for addressing these and other issues regarding the prospects for promotion for teaching-oriented faculty.

The strongest correlation (r= -.13) observed in this data analysis came from the responses of faculty in the United States, where there are more teaching-oriented faculty (63%) than research-oriented faculty (37%). There are several important trends among the Carnegie survey responses from U.S. faculty which may help explain the relationship between faculty teaching orientation and dissatisfaction with prospects for promotion. For example, 75% of all respondents indicated that "it is difficult for a person to achieve tenure if he or she does not publish" (Altbach & Lewis, 1996: 25), a level of response that is considerably higher than nearly all other countries surveyed. Indeed, the future of the tenure system has seen considerable debate in the United States over several decades, perhaps more so than in any other country. The tenor of the debate has risen and fallen over the decades, but the current resurgence of attention towards academic tenure may in fact be leading us towards the development of something entirely new. Certainly, there is an increasing amount of agreement among faculty that "the promotion and tenure system as it exists in the late twentieth century is in need of dramatic overhaul" (Tierney & Bensimon, 1996, p. 125). While some scholars have proposed alternatives to the tenure system (cf. Chait & Ford, 1982), others have been less than diplomatic in their assessment of the tenure system, such as Sykes' (1988) *Profscam*, or Bloom's (1987) *The Closing of the American Mind*. One of the more pressing concerns of these debates is whether faculty with tenure are less likely to be concerned with their teaching activities than their colleagues. As described earlier in this volume, many observers of higher education have argued that the reward structure associated with the tenure system compels faculty to focus on research projects—preferably those which bring external funding to the department—while teaching gets a second class ticket.

In a recent analysis of teaching and the academic labor market, Lewis (1996) suggested that the motivation to teach is often intrinsic, and not related to extrinsic rewards such as tenure or promotion. The analysis of the Carnegie data presented earlier in this volume (see Chapter 4) appears to support Lewis' observation. Here, tenure status was not found to be a predictor of teaching orientation internationally. However, a modest correlation was found among responses from faculty in the United States, where faculty with tenure were slightly more likely than others to indicate that their primary interests were more toward teaching than research. Taken together, these trends in the Carnegie data may help explain the relationship in the U.S. between teaching orientation and dissatisfaction with prospects for promotion as indicated in Table 6.4.

These same trends were also found among responses from faculty in Brazil, where again there are more teaching-oriented faculty (62%) than research-oriented faculty (38%). As indicated in Chapter 4, tenure was found to be a modestly significant predictor of teaching orientation in this country. Further, more faculty (76%) in Brazil than in any other country indicated that their institution was "very important" to them (Boyer, Altbach & Whitelaw, 1994: Table 16). However, Brazilian faculty were also more significantly likely to disagree with the statement, "in my department, it is difficult for a person to achieve tenure if he or she does not publish" than in any other country surveyed. Thus, there are both similarities and differences among faculty in the United States and Brazil which may have mixed effects regarding the relative dissatisfaction with prospects for promotion observed among the teaching-oriented professoriate.

Overall, these findings may indicate a trend that in these six countries, orientation towards teaching has a stronger effect than elsewhere on one's prospects for promotion. However, it may instead be more a matter of perception in these countries, where teaching-oriented faculty view themselves, for whatever reasons, as having less potential for promotion than their colleagues, regardless of whether or not this is really the case.

Certainly, this analysis raises the question of why teaching orientation is correlated with responses from these countries and not others in terms of satisfaction with prospects for promotion. Further research and analysis of faculty views on this topic would surely provide an important dimension to our understanding of related issues, such as mobility in the academic profession. Taking issues of satisfaction with working conditions and pressures into account, are teaching-oriented faculty any more or less likely than their colleagues to consider leaving their institution?

AM I LIKELY TO STAY HERE OR LEAVE?

In designing the questionnaire, the Carnegie survey administrators sought to identify reasons why faculty leave or stay. Faculty were asked to indicate on a five-point scale the extent to which each of five working conditions was viewed as a reason to leave versus a reason to stay: income, resources for research, academic reputation of the institution or department, academic cooperation among colleagues, and region in which the institution is located. "For U.S. academics as a whole, financial considerations—income and resources for research—are the most powerful factors pushing the potentially mobile away from their current institutions" (Haas, 1996: 374).

As observed earlier in this discussion, research is a discipline-based activity, whereas teaching is an institution-based activity. This analysis of the Carnegie data found that teaching-oriented faculty indicated stronger affiliation with their institution higher than with their academic discipline, while the reverse trend was found among research-oriented faculty (see Chapter 1). The rewards for high research productivity may include offers from various institutions to move, saying "come here, bring us your prestige, and we will pay you more than your current institution." Teaching-oriented faculty are considerably less likely to receive these kinds of offers—and thus less likely to be lured away—than their research-oriented colleagues, because is it through research that academic departments gain visibility. Thus, one might assume that mobility is more often found among research-oriented faculty than among their teaching-oriented colleagues.

Indeed, the Carnegie data indicate that teaching orientation does play a significant role in how faculty responded to the survey question, "how likely is it you will leave this institution within the next five years?" Faculty in a majority of countries surveyed were *less likely* to indicate that they planned to leave within the next five years (see Table 6.5).

TABLE 6.5

Are teaching-oriented faculty **more or less likely** than their colleagues to indicate that they planned to leave their institution within the next five years? (Q29)*

MORE Likely	LESS likely	No Significant Relationship
Mexico r= .03	Australia r= -.01	Chile
United States r= .05	England r= -.08	Hong Kong
	Germany r= -.14	Israel
	Japan r= -.05	Russia
	Korea r= -.02	
	the Netherlands r= -.09	
	Sweden r= -.06	

* this item was omitted from the survey administered in Brazil.

Teaching-oriented faculty in Australia, Japan, Korea and all the European countries surveyed were significantly less likely to indicate plans to leave their institution within the next five years. In order to understand more fully the reasons for this trend, one must look at the important flip-side of the relationships indicated in Table 6.5. Wherever there is a significant trend in how teaching-oriented faculty responded to a particular survey item, there is also a significant relationship with how research-oriented faculty responded. Thus, the table above also indicates that research-oriented faculty are *more likely* than their teaching-oriented colleagues to leave their institution within the next five years.

As discussed in Chapter 1 of this study, research-oriented faculty are predominantly more "cosmopolitan" than "local", when looking at the issue through Gouldner's (1957) paradigm. Indeed, the Carnegie data clearly indicate that teaching-oriented faculty are significantly more likely than research-oriented faculty to indicate loyalty to their institution. Further, as described earlier in this section of the chapter, opportunities for "institution-hopping" are usually more available to research-oriented faculty—and more of them are likely to pursue these opportunities—than their teaching-oriented colleagues. Thus, when considering the many dimensions of differences between research-oriented and teaching-oriented faculty, it becomes clearer why teaching-oriented faculty in a majority of countries surveyed were significantly less likely to indicate that they were considering leaving their institution within the next five years.

However, what is more surprising among the findings presented in Table 6.5 is that in the United States and Mexico, the reverse relationship was found—teaching-oriented faculty were actually *more likely* to indicate plans to leave their institution within the next five years. Is this an indication of a particularly strong dissatisfaction among teaching-oriented faculty with their institutions? Alternatively, are there more opportunities for teaching-oriented faculty to be mobile in these countries? Overall, the Carnegie data do not indicate significantly higher dissatisfaction generally in these countries than elsewhere, nor are there significant comparative similarities between Mexico and the United States regarding the impact of teaching orientation on other questions asked on the Carnegie survey. Clearly, further research beyond the scope of the Carnegie survey data is necessary for addressing these questions, and would provide an important dimension to our understanding of satisfaction in the academic profession.

CONCLUSION

This chapter has addressed only some of the many issues related to faculty satisfaction with institutional working conditions. Given the widespread disparity in rewards for teaching and research activities, as described in previous chapters of this volume, it was originally suggested in this chapter that teaching-oriented faculty could be expected to feel less positively about their institutional working conditions than their research-oriented colleagues. The research presented in this chapter tested the validity of a hypothesis which stated that teaching-oriented faculty view their institutional working conditions differently than do research-oriented faculty. The opposite of this, the null hypothesis, states that there are no significant differences between teaching-oriented faculty and research-oriented faculty internationally in terms of how they view these issues. Overall, according to this analysis of the Carnegie data, we can reject the null hypothesis—differences related to teaching orientation were observed on international, regional, and national levels.

However, this analysis did not always find internationally-shared similarities in the relationships between teaching orientation and faculty responses to the Carnegie survey. Rather, this study of the Carnegie data uncovered several kinds of trends, which can be meaningfully organized into one of four categories:

I. Internationally significant - trends in the data that were shared throughout a majority of the countries surveyed;

II. Internationally modest - relationships that were found in the data from fewer than half (but more than two) of the countries surveyed;

III. Mixed results - the data indicate a relationship in one direction in some countries, and a relationship in the opposite direction in others; and

IV. Unique findings - data relationships that were found only among the responses from one country or specific region.

The following discussion reviews the findings of this analysis in relation to these four sub-topics, and explores implications of the more significant trends. When a trend is both internationally significant and yet somewhat mixed, this is indicated within each category of findings. Also, in presenting the findings of this analysis, the view is taken that where teaching orientation had no significant relationship whatsoever with faculty responses to a particular item on the survey, this itself is an international trend of sorts.

(I) Significant International Trends

In several cases, the regression analyses showed correlations that were either always positive or always negative for all or most countries surveyed. These findings provide an international insight into what it means to prefer teaching over research.

1. Teaching-oriented faculty are significantly more satisfied with the undergraduate courses they teach.

2. Teaching-oriented faculty are significantly more satisfied than their research-oriented colleagues with their institution's technology for teaching.

3. Teaching-oriented faculty are significantly less satisfied than their colleagues with their institution's computer facilities.

4. Teaching-oriented faculty in a majority of countries surveyed were significantly more likely than their colleagues to agree with the statement, "The pressure to publish reduces the quality of teaching at this institution." However, in Brazil, Chile, Germany, Israel and Sweden, teaching-oriented faculty were less likely to agree with this statement.

(II) Internationally Modest Findings

Several of the relationships found in this analysis of the Carnegie data are shared by more than a few countries, but not enough to consider them internationally significant.

1. Teaching-oriented faculty in Brazil, England, Germany, Israel, Sweden and the United States were significantly less likely to indicate satisfaction with their prospects for promotion.

2. Teaching-oriented faculty in Japan, Mexico, Russia and Sweden are considerably less likely than their colleagues to agree with the statement, "the effectiveness of higher education is being threatened by growing bureaucracies."

(III) Mixed Results

There are also several cases in which teaching orientation had a positive correlation in some countries, and a negative one in others.

1. In several countries teaching-oriented faculty are *more satisfied* than their colleagues with their classrooms, laboratories, and libraries, yet in several other countries teaching-oriented faculty are *less satisfied* with the quality of these resources.

2. Teaching-oriented faculty in Australia, Japan, Mexico, the Netherlands, and the United States are *more likely* to indicate satisfaction with their classrooms, while their teaching-oriented colleagues in England, Germany and Sweden are *less likely* to do so.

3. Teaching-oriented faculty in Chile, Israel and Mexico are significantly *more likely* to indicate satisfaction with their laboratories, while their teaching-oriented colleagues in England, Germany, Japan, the Netherlands and the United States are *less likely* to do so.

4. Teaching-oriented faculty in Israel, Japan and Mexico are significantly *more likely* to indicate satisfaction with their institution's' library holdings, while their teaching-oriented colleagues in England, the Netherlands and the United States are *less likely* to do so.

5. Teaching-oriented faculty in Mexico, Sweden and the United States are *more satisfied* than their research-oriented colleagues in their collegial relationships, while teaching-oriented faculty in Germany are *less satisfied* with their relationship with their colleagues.

6. Teaching-oriented faculty in Mexico and the United States were *more likely* to indicate plans to leave their institution within the next five years, which teaching-oriented faculty in Australia, England, Germany, Japan, Korea, the Netherlands and Sweden were *less likely* to do so.

7. Teaching-oriented faculty in a majority of countries surveyed were significantly *more likely* than their colleagues to agree with the statement, "The pressure to publish reduces the quality of teaching at this institution." However, in Brazil, Chile, Germany, Israel and Sweden, teaching-oriented faculty were *less likely* to agree with this statement.

(IV) Unique Findings

In several cases, this analysis of the Carnegie data found a relationship between teaching orientation and faculty response to a particular survey item that was not shared with any other country surveyed.

1. Among the Mexican professoriate, teaching-oriented faculty were more likely than their colleagues to indicate high satisfaction with the courses they teach, with their institutional resources for teaching, and with their relationships with colleagues.

2. Teaching-oriented faculty in the United States were *more likely* than their colleagues to indicate high satisfaction with the courses they teach, with their institutional resources for teaching, with their relationships with colleagues.

3. Teaching-oriented faculty in the United States were *less likely* than their colleagues to indicate satisfaction with their prospects for promotion and were more likely than their colleagues to indicate that they planned to leave their institution within the next five years.

4. Teaching orientation plays a more prominent role in Europe and the United States than elsewhere when looking at faculty views toward institutional resources.

Summary and Implications

While the mixed and unique findings are compelling reasons for further research, this study adopts the research philosophy that cross-national similarities inform more of our understanding of the academic profession than do cross-national differences. Additionally, "cross-national similarities lend themselves readily to sociological interpretation, while cross-national differences are much more difficult to interpret" (Kohn, 1987: 31). Looking at cross-national consistencies in the data helps to reduce complex levels to meaningful comparisons—such as culture, language and geography—and gain a collective understanding of issues shared by faculty across the major regions of the world. Thus, national differences can be largely set aside in this study, in looking for a shared phenomenon.

In looking at the responses from faculty in the United States, Haas (1996) observed that in general, faculty in the United States reflect a distinct contradiction in terms of job satisfaction:

> How can these professionals, specifically 78 percent of the respondents, be satisfied with their job situation as a whole while at the same time expressing dissatisfaction with so many elements of the setting in which they practice their profession? (p. 349)

This contradiction was observed throughout the responses to the Carnegie survey. The international dimension of this trend provides an important opportunity to explore how orientation towards teaching or research is related with faculty satisfaction with institutional working conditions, particularly those which may influence a decision to leave their institution. While teaching orientation does not have an internationally-similar relationship with faculty perspectives toward institutional working conditions altogether, the data relationships found here do lead to some suggestions for future research. Certainly, as "the working conditions of faculty, inevitably, influence both productivity and morale" (Boyer, Altbach and Whitelaw, 1994: 13), understanding how different kinds of faculty feel about these conditions informs our understanding of the academic profession and higher education organizations.

Certainly, one might expect that teaching-oriented faculty have stronger views than their research-oriented colleagues toward the quality of resources they have to work with in their teaching. After all, teaching-oriented faculty spend more time in the classroom than their research-oriented colleagues. This analysis found that indeed, teaching orientation is significantly correlated with faculty satisfaction with their classrooms, their laboratories, their technology for teaching, their computer facilities, and their library holdings. While the nature of the relationships in the survey data on these items vary between country, it is nonetheless an important distinction to make for our understanding of how teaching orientation is related worldwide with how faculty view academic work.

It is also important to note that the teaching-oriented professoriate worldwide are significantly more satisfied than their research-oriented colleagues with the courses they teach. In other words, faculty who prefer to teach spend more time teaching and are significantly more satisfied with the courses they teach than is the case for their research-oriented colleagues. Thus, one important area for further research is why, do research-oriented faculty worldwide indicate stronger *dissatisfaction* with the courses they teach? Is it because they would simply rather be researching than in the classroom, or is this an indication that they are not teaching the kinds of specialized courses that could be more closely associated with their research agenda? Are there significant differences worldwide between courses that teaching-oriented faculty teach, and courses that research-oriented faculty teach? Clearly, further research beyond the Carnegie survey data is necessary for addressing these compelling questions.

An important dimension of this issue concerns the relationship between research and effective teaching. There are two ideological camps in academe that bear different views toward the relationship between teaching and research in the academic profession. On one hand, there are academics who feel that teaching and research are necessarily complimentary—good teaching informs good research, and vice versa—and, therefore, faculty should be hired and promoted on the basis of excellence in both areas. On the other hand, there are academics who argue that a faculty member's skills, interest, and available time permit excellence in only one or the other. Their argument is that, given naturally limited resources, one can excel only in teaching or in research, but not in both. Certainly, they argue, a professor's time is not infinite—more time spent on one activity must certainly leave less time to engage in another.

This analysis of the Carnegie data found that teaching orientation is internationally correlated with faculty views toward pressure to publish. Although the nature of the relationships in the survey data vary between countries, a majority of teaching-oriented faculty surveyed were significantly more likely than their research-oriented colleagues to agree with the statement, "the pressure to publish reduces the quality of teaching at this institution. At first glance, this relationship in the data seems intuitive— faculty whose interests lie more strongly in teaching can largely be expected to feel that research negatively impacts their teaching, while their research-oriented colleagues can be expected to feel that this is not that case. The Carnegie data provide a new, international dimension to this issue, and suggests that teaching-oriented faculty may not only have a weak interest in research, but also a somewhat negative view towards the impact of research on that which they hold dear—classroom instruction. This has considerable implications for current discussions of faculty reward structures.

A recent study by the National Center on Postsecondary Teaching, Learning and Assessment (NCPTLA, 1995) found that "faculty with the least amount of student contact hours earn the highest salaries," and that "the more refereed publications a faculty member publishes, the higher their salary" (p.17). If teaching-oriented faculty are more likely to emphasize the importance of teaching effectiveness in faculty hiring and promotion decisions (as observed in Chapter 5), one may wonder whether they are not less disillusioned with current academic reward systems, which typically emphasize research productivity. Further analysis and interpretation of the Carnegie survey data—as well as future studies on the influence of faculty reward systems on professional satisfaction—would be useful in addressing this and other related questions. Overall, these trends indicate a mixed relationship between teaching orientation and how faculty view their institutional working conditions, but there is considerable international dissatisfaction among teaching-oriented faculty with their prospects for promotion. It is likely that this dissatisfaction carries forward to other views they may have about life in the academic profession. The institutional context is but one of several—including the contexts of nation and discipline—that are important to faculty (Clark, 1987). Thus, we now widen the scope of this discussion to include issues beyond the institution, specifically concerning the academic discipline and the academic profession.

CHAPTER 7

The Academic Profession

INTRODUCTION

This chapter continues an exploration of whether teaching orientation is related with how faculty responded to the Carnegie international survey. While the previous chapter focused on issues of institutional working conditions, this chapter expands the area of focus to include issues related to academic disciplines and the academic profession. A prominent but underlying theme of the previous two chapters—differences in professional rewards for teaching versus research—is carried forward here. Given the propensity for institutions to reward research productivity considerably more than teaching effectiveness—particularly in hiring and promotion decisions—it is reasonably likely that teaching-oriented faculty feel less positively about academic life than their research-oriented colleagues. The research presented in this chapter sought to identify internationally-significant trends in the Carnegie survey data that would indicate a relationship between teaching orientation and faculty perspectives toward their academic disciplines and their overall satisfaction with being a member of the academic profession.

As observed earlier, the Carnegie survey data provide ample evidence that "professorial working conditions are deteriorating in most of the countries included in this study" (Altbach & Lewis, 1996: 16). The institutional context is but one of several—including the contexts of nation and discipline—that are important to faculty (Clark, 1987). For a variety of reasons, including the reward structure inherent in the "research imperative" (Gumport, 1991) combined with decades of institutional retrenchment—one might expect to find a tendency among today's faculty to be less "local" and more "cosmopolitan" overall. Indeed, the organizational perspective of faculty reliance on their employing institution for many aspects of what defines their profession is certainly disconcerting, particularly when demographic portrait research shows that many colleges and universities do a relatively poor job in paying attention to the human needs of their instructional staff (Schuster and Bowen, 1985). However, as described earlier in this volume, there are significant proportions of "local" teaching-oriented faculty in every country surveyed by the Carnegie study. Certainly, one might expect that these faculty feel the same as their research-oriented colleagues about their disciplines or the academic profession.

Scholars of higher education have observed that the academic profession is for many a "one life, one career" profession (Furniss, 1981). For those going into the professoriate, there is a vague but nonetheless real understanding that an academic career is a calling as well as a job (Shils, 1983). However, this "understanding" may be significantly different between faculty whose interests lie primarily in teaching and those who are more interested in research. Do teaching-oriented faculty tend to indicate greater or less enthusiasm toward their academic discipline? Certainly, the answer to this question has implications for our understanding of faculty worldwide. As Tiernery and Bensimon (1996) observed, "the beliefs one holds about the academy inevitably frames how one acts in a postsecondary institution" (p. 5). This chapter explores whether the Carnegie data indicate that faculty views toward life in the academic profession are significantly different among faculty whose interests lie primarily in teaching, by testing the validity of the following hypothesis:

> Teaching-oriented faculty have different perspectives than their research-oriented colleagues towards the academic profession.

Specifically, this analysis of the Carnegie survey data sought to determine the relationship of teaching orientation with faculty views on life in the academic profession, including issues such as overall job satisfaction, whether or not this is a creative and productive time in the profession, if they would encourage young people to become academics, and whether or not respect for academics is declining. The chapter is organized around these themes for reasons of data comparability—almost no country omitted any of these items from their survey—and personal research interests. In analyzing and presenting the data relationships found in this study, it is assumed that the more countries in which a trend in the Carnegie data exists, the more international that trend is. The following internationally significant relationships were found in this analysis of the Carnegie survey data:

> • In virtually every country surveyed, teaching-oriented faculty were considerably less likely than their colleagues to indicate that this is a creative and productive time in their field.
> • Internationally, teaching orientation has only a modest relationship with how faculty responded to Carnegie survey items related to their views toward the academic profession.

• Teaching orientation is significantly correlated with faculty responses to the Carnegie survey items discussed in this chapter in Germany, Japan, and the United States more frequently than in other countries surveyed.

Overall, teaching-oriented faculty are significantly different from their research-oriented colleagues in their views toward their academic disciplines. However, only modest differences were found between teaching-oriented and research-oriented faculty in terms of their views toward the academic profession. Mixed trends were observed more commonly than international similarities. Trends were most noticeable among responses collected from faculty in Germany, Japan and the United States—the three largest survey samples collected. Here, teaching-oriented faculty are more likely to indicate that academics are among the most influential opinion leaders, and less likely to indicate that respect for academics is declining. In total, enough significant differences were found in this analysis of the Carnegie data to suggest that teaching-oriented faculty do feel somewhat differently than their research-oriented colleagues about life in the academic profession.

Perhaps the most striking evidence of this difference was presented earlier in this study, where it was found that research-oriented faculty were significantly more likely to indicate that their discipline is very important to them, while teaching-oriented faculty were significantly more likely to indicate that their department and institution is very important to them. As described in Chapter 1, this finding lends international support for Gouldner's (1957) distinction between "local" and "cosmopolitan" faculty based on indications of where their primary affiliations lie. This distinction is made all the more interesting when combined with the findings presented in the previous chapter, which indicate that teaching-oriented faculty overall are considerably dissatisfied with several dimensions of their institutional working conditions. If indeed faculty who are relatively more concerned than their colleagues with institutional issues are relatively more dissatisfied with their institution, this has broad implications for discussions on the current state of affairs in the academic profession.

This chapter provides a unique opportunity to examine whether teaching-oriented faculty are also less likely to indicate positive views toward academic life in general. As described in Chapter 4, a majority of teaching-oriented faculty are female. As female faculty are particularly unsatisfied with their overall situation in higher education (cf. Altbach & Lewis, 1996), one might reasonably expect that teaching orientation would have some correlation with lower levels of satisfaction with life in the academic profession. This analysis of teaching-oriented professors thus sought to determine whether this expectation held true.

The Carnegie survey collected data on faculty perspectives toward a wide range of issues concerning the academic profession in general. A majority of questions related to this topic were worded in terms of the respondents satisfaction with a particular statement or a particular element of their profession, such as creativity and productivity. Overall, faculty tended to indicate satisfaction with having chosen an academic career. A majority of faculty in every country surveyed agreed with the statement, "this is an especially creative and productive time in my field." Further, "despite widespread dissatisfaction about many aspects of their day-to-day life, most academics indicate that they would again choose the academic profession if they were starting their careers over" (Altbach & Lewis, 1996: 16). This study sought to determine whether teaching-oriented faculty responded to these survey items differently than their research-oriented colleagues.

For the purposes of this discussion, it is useful to look at these issues through the eyes of the respondent, pencil in hand, as they read through the Carnegie survey questions and ask themselves questions such as:

- *How do I feel about my academic discipline?*
- *How do I feel about the academic profession?*
- *How do I feel about my job overall?*

The analysis presented in this chapter sought to determine whether a teaching-oriented faculty member responded differently to these questions than their research-oriented colleagues. The chapter is organized around these themes for reasons of data comparability—almost no country omitted any of these items from their survey—and personal research interests. If teaching-oriented faculty internationally appear to be more satisfied (or less satisfied) with life in the profession, then this could certainly spark an interesting new line of research on faculty and provide a unique dimension to discussions of improving higher education.

HOW DO I FEEL ABOUT MY ACADEMIC DISCIPLINE?

As Ruscio (1987) observes, while "the role of academics—their tasks and attitudes and behaviors, their sense of professionalism and sense of being part of a larger academic community—are functions of the institutions to which they are attached, the discipline also exerts a powerful influence" (p.439). The content knowledge required for effectively filling the expectations which our society holds for professors requires specialization—immersion—in a particular subject area. Certainly, the field of specialization a faculty member chooses has some influence on their overall impression of the academic profession. As the work of Tony Becher (1989) and others on the cultures of individual disciplines have shown, bodies of knowledge variously determine the behavior of individuals and departments. Thus, when considering the issues of how faculty preference for teaching or research relates to their views toward other dimensions of academe, the discipline is an important arena of focus.

How do faculty worldwide feel about their academic disciplines? As indicated earlier in this discussion, research-oriented faculty are significantly more likely than teaching-oriented faculty to indicate that their discipline is "very important" to them (see Chapter 1). This issue was also addressed in the Carnegie survey by asking respondents to indicate the level of their agreement with the following statement: "This is an especially creative and productive time in my field." Across all countries surveyed, faculty tended to indicate considerable agreement with this statement (Boyer, Altbach & Whitelaw, 1994: Table 37). In terms of response patterns between countries, agreement on this matter ranged from 51% in Russia to 75% in Korea.

For the purposes of this discussion, it is important to focus on one of the concepts embedded in this statement. The term "productive" is somewhat vague, and could reasonably draw multiple interpretations depending on what a particular respondent considers "productive." Here's an example: take a look at the index in the recent book of case studies produced from the Carnegie international survey of the academic profession (Altbach, ed., 1996). Under the term "productivity", one finds the sole entry: "*See Publications*." This seemingly minor detail speaks volumes about the dominant paradigm in academe regarding what is considered "productive." Certainly, faculty who prefer to teach are rarely mentioned by institutions or professional disciplines as "stars" or "experts"—rather, these labels are awarded most often to the productive researcher (Gumport, 1991).

This said, it becomes more clear why this study of the Carnegie data sought to determine whether teaching-oriented faculty responded differently than their research-oriented colleagues to the statement, "This is an especially creative and productive time in my field." A regression analysis of the Carnegie data produced dramatic international similarities. In almost every country surveyed, teaching-oriented faculty were *less likely* to indicate that this is an especially creative and productive time in their field (see Table 7.1).

In looking at the survey data from the United States, Haas (1996) observed that "research faculty are more satisfied to pursue their own ideas and are more likely to see this as an especially creative and productive time in their field." This analysis of the Carnegie data supports this observation and expands it to an international dimension. Further, the strength of the correlations observed in this analysis—most notably in England ($r= -.23$) and Australia ($r= -.20$) —indicate significant levels of disagreement with this statement worldwide. Could this international trend be related to the cosmopolitan/local distinction (Gouldner, 1957) described in previous chapters of this volume? Is this a reflection that teaching-oriented faculty are more likely than their research-colleagues to feel "burned out" or at least less enthusiastic about their academic discipline?

TABLE 7.1		
Are teaching-oriented faculty **more or less likely** than their colleagues to agree with the statement, **"**this is an especially creative and productive time in my field**"**? (Q28a)		
MORE Likely	LESS Likely	No Significant Relationship
	Australia r= -.20	Hong Kong
	Brazil r= -.13	Russia
	Chile r= -.17	
	England r= -.23	
	Germany r= -.08	
	Israel r= -.17	
	Japan r= -.10	
	Korea r= -.17	
	Mexico r= -.11	
	the Netherlands r= -.15	
	Sweden r= -.11	
	United States r= -.14	

NOTE: All correlations presented were significant at the .05 level.

Perhaps there is some relation here to the issue of connections within academic disciplines. Certainly, a great deal of creativity and productivity is found among both teaching and research academics. Teaching-oriented faculty are less likely to publish, but this is not to say that they are any less creative or productive members of their discipline. Research-oriented faculty are more likely to create knowledge through their publications, while teaching-oriented faculty are more likely to create knowledge through their teaching. However, there is arguably more room for flexibility and creativity in research activities than in classroom instruction. Further, as described throughout this study, productivity in academe is far more closely associated with research activity than teaching, most significantly reflected in the common academic reward structures found throughout the higher education systems included in this survey.

Gumport (1991) observed that as higher education institutions have increasingly adopted a "research imperative," faculty who are not considered productive researchers are frequently labeled "deadwood." Decisions are made daily at academic institutions which clearly indicate to faculty members what is valued, and what will be rewarded, at that institution. Sabbatical leaves, adjustments in teaching loads, support for attendance at conferences, and grants to support research all give clear indications of institutional priorities. And yet, while research is considered the 'coin of the realm' in academe, there are many faculty worldwide who prefer teaching over other academic activities. Thus, one implication of this analysis of the Carnegie international survey data is that we need to explore new avenues for teaching-oriented faculty to feel more connected with the creative and productive dimensions of their respective disciplines.

In addition to the important context of academic disciplines, it is also useful in this study to examine whether there are distinct differences in faculty opinion toward the academic profession. One could reasonably expect that if teaching-oriented faculty are relatively dissatisfied with their academic discipline, they would also feel this way about the academic profession generally. Teaching is the essence of the academics' work, since it is the nearest thing to a common activity that nearly all professors do. If teaching-oriented are relatively dissatisfied with the academic profession, this is an important issue for us to address, for it could be the sign of a significant fissure within the academic profession. These issues are addressed in the next section of this chapter.

HOW DO I FEEL ABOUT THE ACADEMIC PROFESSION?

The views one holds toward the academic profession can certainly affect the attitude with which they approach their work. As indicated in Chapter 2, research has shown that a faculty member's preferences can often drive their behavior (cf. Clark, 1987; Clark, 1992; Sherman and Blackburn, 1975). This analysis subscribes to several of these researchers' assumptions that an unhappy faculty member most likely makes for a less effective teacher. As previous chapters have described various levels of satisfaction and dissatisfaction among teaching-oriented faculty toward their classrooms and their institution, it is next important to look at how faculty view life in the academic profession in general. This section of the chapter addresses the following important question: Are teaching-oriented faculty any more or less happy than their research-oriented colleagues with their life in the academic profession?

Across all countries surveyed, most faculty indicated optimistic views about beginning a career in the academic profession. However, in most countries surveyed, more than a quarter of respondents agreed with the statement, "this is a poor time for a young person to begin an academic career." Patterns of agreement with this statement by country ranged from 13% in Japan to 48% in Brazil. However, in Japan, where faculty overall were the least likely to agree with this statement, there is significantly more agreement among teaching-oriented faculty (r=.07), while in four of the countries surveyed, teaching-oriented faculty were *less* likely to agree with the statement (see Table 7.2).

Overall, Table 7.2 reflects scarcely any significant differences in opinion toward the academic profession—in most countries, teaching-oriented faculty were neither more likely nor less likely to indicate that this is a poor time for a young person to begin an academic career. However, in Germany, Hong Kong, Mexico and the United States, teaching-oriented faculty were significantly more likely than their colleagues to encourage a young person to begin an academic career. As described in Chapter 3, a significant relationship in the data with orientation towards teaching is also a relationship with orientation towards research. In other words, Table 7.2 also indicates that research-oriented faculty in Germany, Hong Kong, Mexico and the United States were significantly more likely to indicate that this is a poor time to begin an academic career. While this trend is only modest in an international sense—in that it is observed in a minority of countries surveyed—it is nonetheless a significant cause for further examination.

TABLE 7.2

Are teaching-oriented faculty **more or less likely** than their colleagues to indicate that this is a poor time to begin an academic career? (Q28b)

MORE Likely		**LESS Likely**		**No Significant Relationship**	
Japan	r= .07	Germany	r= -.05	Australia	Israel
		Hong Kong	r= -.05	Brazil	Korea
		Mexico	r= -.05	Chile	Russia
		United States	r= -.05	England	Sweden
				the Netherlands	

Are there common elements of the profession in these countries that might explain more positive feelings among teaching-oriented faculty than among research-oriented faculty? There are differences in orientation towards teaching among the four countries—commitment to teaching dominates in Mexico and the United States, while faculty interests lean toward research in Germany and Hong Kong. The professoriate in three of these countries—Hong Kong, Germany, and Mexico—are the youngest on average of any country surveyed, were more likely than faculty elsewhere to indicate that communication between the faculty and administration is poor, and were less likely than respondents from other countries to agree that "top-level administrators are providing competent leadership." While these similarities are interesting, they do not provide much in the way of explanation for why teaching-oriented faculty are more positive then research-oriented faculty regarding new entrants to the academic profession. Thus, more study beyond the scope of the Carnegie survey data is needed to adequately address this issue.

The reverse was found among Japanese faculty, where teaching-oriented faculty were significantly *more likely* to indicate that this is a poor time for a young person to begin an academic career. This relationship in the data is made all the more significant when considering that among all the countries surveyed, Japanese faculty overall were the least likely (only 13%) to indicate that this is a poor time for a young person to begin an academic career. If such a strong majority of faculty in Japan disagreed with this statement, the fact that teaching-oriented faculty in this country are more strongly in agreement is compelling. Are there some elements in Japanese academic work that lead to an explanation for this? Perhaps the relative lack of evaluation for teaching is one—in this country, "research is evaluated at

41 percent of the institutions surveyed, but at more than four-fifths of the institutions, teaching and service are not evaluated" (Arimoto, 1996: 187). At the time the Carnegie survey was conducted (1991-93), evaluation of faculty teaching performance was a new and somewhat controversial issue for most Japanese faculty. Certainly, faculty whose interests lie more in teaching than in research can be expected to have stronger opinions about the evaluation of teaching—mainly because they do more of it—than their research-oriented colleagues. Thus, there appear to be relatively easy explanations for why Japanese teaching-oriented faculty were the only ones out of the all those surveyed to indicate stronger agreement with the statement, "this is a poor time to begin an academic career."

Looking at the Carnegie data internationally, Altbach and Lewis (1996) observed, "Despite widespread dissatisfaction about many aspects of their day-to-day life, most academics indicate that they would again choose the academic profession if they were starting their careers over again" (p. 17). Does this indicate that there are some things about being a faculty member that are worth the problems faced throughout the academic profession? There may be considerable support in the Carnegie data for many scholars' observations that the academic profession is a unique line of work, a "calling" rather than a career (cf., Furniss, 1981; Shils, 1983). Preparation for the academy involves a great deal of work and commitment, and yet higher education has not seen a shortage of faculty (or prospective faculty) for several decades.

However, given the findings of the previous chapters related to satisfaction with working conditions, it is clear that faculty who prefer to teach may have significantly different views about life in the academy than their research-oriented colleagues. Some of these differences are likely driven by the fact that the rewards gained by research are considerably more common than those gained by teaching. Further, these differences may evolve over time, through experience in the academy. As teaching-oriented faculty observe more frequent examples of their research-oriented colleagues receiving rewards for research (while, it is assumed, their own teaching activities go largely unrewarded), they may become less enthusiastic over time about life in the academy. Thus, one might expect that teaching-oriented faculty would feel markedly different than their research-oriented colleagues about whether they would become an academic again if provided the opportunity.

However, the Carnegie data do not support this expectation in any country surveyed. Throughout the survey responses, teaching-oriented faculty were not significantly more likely to agree with the statement, "If I had to do it over again, I would not become an academic." Rather, this analysis of the Carnegie data found that teaching-oriented faculty in a small minority of countries were actually *less likely* to indicate that if they had to do it over again, they would not become an academic. Perhaps Lionel Lewis (1996) hit the nail on the head when observing that "for many academics, teaching is an intrinsically motivated activity . . . it is a task that motivates, not because of the promise of some external reward, but because it is something they simply enjoy doing" (p.147). Perhaps these same intrinsic rewards are what steer teaching-oriented faculty towards an academic career in the first place, and continue to drive them throughout their careers. This would explain in part why teaching-oriented faculty in several countries surveyed—particularly Germany and the United States—are more supportive of young people starting a career in the profession, and more likely to do so themselves if given the opportunity. Further, despite all the research and hand-wringing over the disparities in rewards between research and teaching activities, faculty who prefer to teach are in no way significantly more negative in their views toward the academic profession.

Together, these findings have implications for studies of job satisfaction within the academic profession. Despite expectations to the contrary, teaching-oriented faculty in every country surveyed were not significantly more likely to indicate disillusionment with an academic career. Further, teaching-oriented faculty in several countries—within which there are few social-structural commonalities— appear to be even more enamored of life in the profession than their research-oriented colleagues. Is there really a deeper satisfaction with the academic profession among teaching-oriented faculty in these countries? Certainly, further research beyond the scope of the Carnegie survey would be useful for addressing this and related questions. Overall, however, the most important finding in this analysis is this: among faculty worldwide, stronger preference for teaching is not significantly correlated with greater dissatisfaction with the academic profession, despite the emphasis on rewards for research productivity that teaching-oriented faculty do not enjoy.

Previous chapters of this volume have shown that teaching-oriented faculty are different from their research-oriented colleagues in a variety of dimensions—the analysis presented here add an additional dimension to our understanding of faculty, as well as academic culture. However, there as several other dimensions yet to be explored in terms of how different faculty construct their sense of self in the academic world. Among them, an important context is how faculty view the relationship between the academic profession and society. A faculty member who believes that the public supports the values of the academic profession is likely to have markedly different views toward academic life than one who does not feel this way. Further, a faculty member's assessment of how members of the academic profession are viewed by the public at large may have some impact on how they approach academic work.

Certainly, society provides a variety of good reasons to want to become an academic. "Professors are an extraordinarily important group in any society, frequently involved in politics and the intellectual life of the nation" (Altbach, 1996: 133). They are influential through their research, their writing, and their advice given to political and social leaders. "Most professors, even in relation to controversial matters of public policy, see themselves as experts, providing information and research-based analysis rather than direct participation in political disputations" (Ibid.: 136). However, according to the Carnegie survey, faculty worldwide appear to feel quite negative on whether they are well-respected and supported by society. With the exception of Korea, only a minority of faculty in each country agreed with the statement, "Academics are among the most influential opinion leaders in my country," ranging from 40 percent in Japan and Brazil to 15 percent or less in England, Germany, and Israel. Thus, overall it would appear that faculty do not feel they have much support in their society for the academic profession.

However, the reality is that in virtually every country surveyed, faculty are featured on news programs, talk shows, and in newspapers as "expert" resources on a particular topic. How does a faculty become an influential leader of public opinion? In a word, publish. When you see a professor being interviewed as an "expert" in a particular field, the chances are quite high that a primary reason for their exhalted position is that they have published something that received a fair amount of widespread attention. Given the findings presented in the discussion thus far, one might suspect that teaching-oriented faculty are likely to feel differently about this subject than their research-oriented colleagues. Indeed, whereas researchers may view the value of their contribution to society in terms of their scholarly productivity, teaching-oriented faculty might feel that an academic's most important influence in society is through classroom instruction, where they have a great deal of power in shaping the perceptions of future generations of leaders. Faculty who do not publish are rarely recognized by the public media as an authority figure in a particular field. Thus, as teaching-oriented faculty are significantly less likely to publish than their research-oriented colleagues (Gottlieb & Keith, 1996; Altbach & Lewis, 1996), one would expect that teaching-oriented faculty are less likely to consider themselves as influential leaders of public opinion. However, the Carnegie data do not support this expectation (see Table 7.3).

TABLE 7.3
Are teaching-oriented faculty **more or less likely** to indicate that academics are among the most influential opinion leaders? (Q72c)

MORE Likely		LESS likely	No Significant Relationship	
Germany	r= .02		Australia	Israel
Japan	r= .02		Brazil	Korea
United States	r= .10		Chile	Mexico
			England	Russia
			Hong Kong	Sweden

* this item was omitted from the survey administered in the Netherlands.

This analysis of the Carnegie data found that internationally, teaching-oriented faculty are not significantly less likely to feel that their opinions have an influence in society. Rather, in most countries surveyed, teaching orientation is not correlated at all with faculty response to the statement "Academics are among the most influential opinion leaders." However, in three countries—Germany, Japan, and the United States—teaching-oriented faculty were actually *more likely* to indicate agreement with this statement. This raises some obvious questions: Why, and why in only these countries? What commonalities among these three nations might explain such a trend among the teaching-oriented professoriate? A comparison of faculty in Germany, Japan and the U.S. is a complex and difficult task. However, before embarking on such a discussion, an important additional trend observed in this analysis of the Carnegie data must be noted.

A related item on the Carnegie survey collected responses to the following statement: "Respect for academics is declining." The responses to this statement are surprisingly similar to the one above—in most countries surveyed, teaching orientation is not correlated at all with faculty response to the statement. Thus, internationally, teaching-oriented faculty are not significantly more likely to feel that respect for academics is declining. Further, in three countries—Germany, Japan, and the United States—teaching-oriented faculty were actually *less likely* to indicate agreement with this statement (see Table 7.4).

TABLE 7.4

Are teaching-oriented faculty **more or less likely** than their colleagues to indicate that respect for academics is declining? (Q72d)

MORE Likely	LESS likely	No Significant Relationship	
	Germany r= -.03	Australia	Israel
	Japan r= -.11	Brazil	Korea
	United States r= -.03	Chile	Mexico
		England	Russia
		Hong Kong	Sweden
		The Netherlands	

There are significant differences in only a few countries between teaching-oriented and research-oriented faculty responses to this survey item. As this table reflects, teaching-oriented faculty in Germany, Japan and the United States are *less likely* than their colleagues to indicate that respect for academics is on the decline.

When looking at these tables together, a pattern emerges. In both cases, teaching-oriented faculty were not found to be more negative than their research-oriented colleagues toward their view of the profession. Further, unique trends were found in the same three countries—Germany, Japan, and the United States—where teaching-oriented faculty were significantly more positive in their responses to both statements. The similarities in how teaching-oriented faculty in Germany, Japan and the U.S. responded to both of these questions warrants a brief comparative discussion.

To begin with, these three countries represent the largest sample sizes throughout the Carnegie survey. Thus, perhaps sample size has some relationship with the impact of teaching orientation in these countries. Certainly, the academic systems found in each of these countries bear similarities with one another. However, a good deal of what these countries have in common—academic traditions, economic industrialization, high research productivity, and more—are also found in other countries surveyed where this trend was not found. Further, there are important differences which must be accounted for. "German academics take a more "cosmopolitan" position than their colleagues in other countries—they place a strong emphasis on the discipline, but place little importance on their affiliation to their department and institution" (Enders & Teichler, 1996: 483). Japanese academics are significantly more likely than their German or American colleagues to indicate that respect for academics is declining and less likely to indicate that academics are among the most influential opinion leaders. These and other differences raise further questions of why teaching-oriented faculty in these countries (and nowhere else) responded similarly to the Carnegie survey items on how members of the academic profession are viewed by society at large.

In order to adequately explain the common relationship observed in the data between teaching orientation and faculty views toward how academics are perceived, one must find among the German, Japanese, and American professoriate some commonalities that do not exist in the other countries surveyed. Unfortunately, due to comparability issues in the data collected by the Carnegie survey, such an analysis is not currently available. Thus, addressing the questions raised above will require future studies of the profession in these countries.

Overall, the most significant trend observed here is that there is no significant relationship between strong preference for teaching and how faculty responded to the Carnegie survey items related to how members of the academic profession are viewed by society at large. Certainly, one might reasonably expect teaching-oriented faculty to feel less positively about their public image than research-oriented faculty, who are frequently more likely to be called upon to present an authoritative view in the public eye. However, significant trends were not found in the Carnegie survey data to support this notion. As both tables 7.3. and 7.4 show, there are significant differences in only a few countries between teaching-oriented and research-oriented faculty regarding responses to these survey items. Further, teaching-oriented faculty in three countries—Germany, Japan and the United States—indicated more positive feelings than research-oriented faculty about their public image, although reasonable explanations for this common trend are not easily found. Certainly, this is one area where more research, particularly that of a comparative nature, would significantly benefit our understanding of the professoriate in these three countries.

Thus far, this chapter—as well as the previous two chapters—have primarily explored issues of faculty satisfaction and perspectives toward various dimensions of their work and life as an academic. The findings presented in these chapters have suggested that teaching orientation is related to faculty perspectives toward their courses, their institutional resources for teaching, the assessment of their teaching, the pressures to publish, and the current state of their academic disciplines. All things considered, one would expect that at the most basic level, there is some core difference between teaching-oriented and research-oriented faculty in terms of overall job satisfaction. This study thus sought to determine whether this expectation is supported by Carnegie data.

HOW DO I FEEL ABOUT MY JOB OVERALL?

As "the working conditions of faculty, inevitably, influence both productivity and morale" (Boyer, Altbach & Whitelaw, 1994: 13), the issue of job satisfaction is an important one. In most countries surveyed by the Carnegie study, a significant proportion of faculty tended to indicate that their job was a source of considerable strain. The strongest showing of job strain was found among faculty in Japan (56%) and Korea (50%), with responses from Hong Kong (39%) not far behind. On the other hand, only a small minority of faculty in Brazil (25%), Mexico (21%) and Israel (19%) indicated that their jobs were a source of considerable strain (Boyer, Altbach & Whitelaw, 1994: Table 32).

As described throughout this chapter—as well as the previous chapters of this volume—there is a great deal of concern over changes in the academic work environment throughout the world. Research funding has become increasingly hard to find, greater attention toward improving student performance in the classroom and in the workforce has led to increased pressures for faculty to explain their work, and declining public support of higher education—combined with rising costs—have forced many departments to increase faculty workload and demands for "productivity" (however loosely defined). Indeed, "there is ample evidence that professorial working conditions are deteriorating in most of the countries included in this survey" (Altbach & Lewis, 1996: 16). Within the context of these changes, some faculty have risen to the challenge and thrived, others have struggled—and not always silently—while still other faculty members have become victims of retrenchment or restructuring schemes. Overall one may expect to find a wide range of difference in opinions among faculty toward their job.

Of particular importance to this analysis, it was expected that teaching-oriented faculty would indicate somewhat different views toward their job than their research-oriented counterparts. As described throughout the volume, one reason for this expectation is the difference in reward for research productivity versus reward for teaching effectiveness. Teaching-oriented faculty teach more often than research-oriented faculty, and class sizes have grown considerably over the last few decades. Yet, it is the faculty member who teaches less and publishes more who reaps the rewards of recognition, higher salary, and other benefits. Faculty who prefer to teach are rarely mentioned by institutions or professional disciplines as "stars" or "experts"—rather, these labels are awarded most often to the productive researcher (Gumport, 1991).

Given the earlier discussions in this book about the apparent decline of support for faculty, particularly in their role as teachers, one might expect that teaching-oriented faculty are more inclined than their research-oriented colleagues to agree with the statement, "My job is a source of considerable strain." However, the Carnegie data do not support this expectation for faculty in any of the countries surveyed. Further, in four countries—Australia, Chile, Korea and the United States—teaching-oriented faculty were actually *less likely* to indicate this. Thus, despite their views toward the pressure to publish, their dissatisfaction with institutional resources and the way their teaching is assessed, and their relatively negative feelings toward their academic disciplines, teaching-oriented faculty are not more likely to indicate that their job is a source of considerable strain.

While an overwhelming majority of the data show no significant relationship, it is interesting to note the diversity of countries where teaching-oriented faculty were less likely than their colleagues to indicate that their job is a source of considerable strain. The professoriate in two of them—Chile and the United States—are predominantly teaching-oriented, while in the other two—Australia and Korea—faculty overall indicate a higher preference for research. Geographically speaking, the four countries are all over the map. There is not much in common among the four in terms of social structure, political climate, higher education history, language, or many other potentially important dimensions. With the exception of Korea, the evaluation activities in these countries are similar to those found elsewhere. The common trend found in these four countries is thus not easily explained, and requires further research beyond the scope of the Carnegie data. As this study is concerned with more significant international trends than found here, this will have to wait for analysis sometime in the future.

Earlier in this discussion, teaching-oriented faculty worldwide were found to be considerably dissatisfied with some elements of their institutional working conditions, such as the pressure to publish and the way their teaching is assessed, and the level of importance currently awarded to teaching effectiveness as reflected in hiring and promotion decisions. Yet, teaching-oriented faculty were also found to be quite satisfied with the courses they teach and were less likely to indicate intentions of leaving their institution. An additional question on the Carnegie survey cuts to the very heart of this issue—faculty were asked to indicate their overall satisfaction with their job. According to this analysis, teaching-oriented faculty are not significantly more likely to indicate dissatisfaction with their overall job situation. Indeed, in four of the countries surveyed—Germany, Japan, Korea, and Mexico—teaching-oriented faculty are significantly *more* likely to indicate high satisfaction with their job overall. Again, a majority of the data show no significant relationship with where faculty preferences lie. Further, the diversity of countries where this relationship was found does not lend itself to any conclusive suggestions about the overall impact of teaching orientation in responses to this survey item. Surprisingly, given the discussion in this and previous chapters about the lack of rewards for teaching, faculty whose preferences lie primarily in teaching are *not less satisfied* with their job overall.

In sum, teaching-oriented faculty in no country are less satisfied with their job than research-oriented faculty. In most countries surveyed, there is no relationship between job satisfaction and teaching orientation, and in a small minority of countries, teaching-oriented faculty are actually *more satisfied* with their jobs. Overall, these trends indicate a mixed relationship between strong preference for teaching and satisfaction with life in the academic profession. Thus, it is unclear whether teaching-oriented faculty are more or less satisfied with academe than their research-oriented colleagues. This finding mirrors other analyses of the Carnegie data which determined that, "In sum, one could not readily conclude that faculty morale is either good or bad. The picture that emerges is quite blurred. The professoriate around the world may express considerable discontent, but is has not lost sight of the positive aspects of academic life" (Altbach & Lewis, 1996: 16).

Gaining a deeper understanding of these issues is important, as faculty satisfaction with academic life certainly has an important relationship with how they approach academic work. Teaching-oriented faculty have higher courseloads and reap fewer extrinsic rewards than their research-oriented colleagues, and yet are not significantly dissatisfied with their job overall. Exploring why this is so in future studies of the profession can inform our understanding of the relationship between faculty work preferences and satisfaction with life in the academic profession.

CONCLUSION

Thus far, this study has focused primarily on issues of faculty satisfaction toward various dimensions of their work and life as an academic. The primary concern of this chapter has been to determine whether teaching orientation has an internationally common relationship with faculty perspectives toward being a member of the academic profession. According to the analyses presented in this chapter, there is a difference between teaching-oriented faculty and research-oriented faculty in their responses to Carnegie survey questions on this topic. However, in many cases this difference is a modest one in international terms. Given the widespread disparity in rewards for teaching and research activities, which have been described in previous chapters of this volume, it was originally suggested in this chapter that teaching-oriented faculty would feel less positively about academic work and life than their research-oriented colleagues. Overall, the results of the study are mixed—teaching-oriented faculty are not convinced that this is a creative and productive time in their academic discipline, but they are also not overtly dissatisfied with the current state of the academic profession, nor are they dissatisfied with their job overall.

For the most part, this analysis did not find internationally-shared similarities in the relationships between teaching orientation and faculty responses to the Carnegie survey. Rather, this study of the Carnegie data uncovered several kinds of trends, which can be meaningfully organized into one of four categories:

> I. Internationally significant - trends in the data that were shared throughout a majority of the countries surveyed;
> II. Internationally modest - relationships that were found in the data from fewer than half (but more than two) of the countries surveyed;
> III. Mixed results - the data indicate a relationship in one direction in some countries, and a relationship in the opposite direction in others; and
> IV. Unique findings - data relationships that were found only among the responses from one country or specific region.

The following discussion reviews the findings of this analysis in relation to these four sub-topics, and explores implications of the more internationally significant trends. Also, in presenting the findings of this analysis, the view is taken that where teaching orientation had no significant relationship whatsoever with faculty responses to a particular item on the survey, this itself is an international trend of sorts.

(I) Significant International Trends

In several cases, the regression analyses showed correlations that were either always positive or always negative for all or most countries surveyed. These findings provide an international insight into what it means to prefer teaching over research.

> 1. In almost every country surveyed, teaching-oriented faculty were less likely to indicate that this is an especially creative and productive time in their field.

(II) Internationally Modest Findings
Several of the relationships found in this analysis of the Carnegie data are shared by more than a few countries, but not enough to consider them internationally significant.

> 1. Teaching oriented faculty in Germany, Hong Kong, Mexico, and the United States were significantly less likely than their research-oriented colleagues to indicate that "This is poor time for a young person to begin a career in the academic profession."
>
> 2. Teaching oriented faculty in Germany, Russia, the Netherlands, and the United States were significantly less likely than their research-oriented colleagues to agree with the statement, "If I had it do it again, I would not become an academic."
>
> 3. Teaching-oriented faculty in Germany, Japan and the United States are more likely than their colleagues to indicate that academics are among the most influential opinion leaders.
>
> 4. Teaching-oriented faculty in Germany, Japan and the United States are less likely than their colleagues to indicate that respect for academics is on the decline.
>
> 5. In Australia, Chile, Korea and the United States, teaching-oriented faculty were actually less likely to agree with the statement, "My job is a source of considerable strain."
>
> 6. In Germany, Japan, Korea, and Mexico, teaching-oriented faculty are significantly more likely to indicate high satisfaction with their job overall.

(III) Mixed Results
There are also several cases in which teaching orientation had a positive correlation in some countries, and a negative one in others.

> 1. In Australia, teaching-oriented faculty were less likely to indicate that if they had to do it over again, they would not become an academic, yet they were less likely to indicate that this is an especially creative and productive time in their field. However, teaching orientation is not related to faculty responses on whether they would become an academic again.

(IV) Unique Findings
In several cases, this analysis of the Carnegie data found a relationship between teaching orientation and faculty responses to the Carnegie survey that was not shared with any other country surveyed.

1. In Germany, Japan and the United States, teaching orientation has a significant relationship with faculty perspectives toward the academic profession on virtually every dimension included in the analysis of the Carnegie data presented in this chapter.

2. Japan is the only country in which teaching-oriented faculty were significantly more likely than their research-oriented colleagues to indicate that this is a poor time to begin an academic career.

3. Teaching-oriented faculty in Germany and the United States appear to have generally more positive feelings about the academic profession than their teaching-oriented colleagues elsewhere.

4. Responses from Korean faculty indicate that teaching-oriented faculty were significantly less likely than their colleagues to indicate that their job is a source of considerable strain and were more likely to indicate greater satisfaction with their job overall.

Summary and Implications

Overall, these trends indicate a mixed relationship between teaching orientation and how faculty view their academic discipline and the academic profession in general. For the most part, significant international relationships between teaching orientation and faculty views toward the academic profession were not found. In other words, faculty appear to feel basically the same about the current status of their profession regardless of the strength of their preference for teaching or research. However, correlations were found in several countries between teaching orientation and attitudes toward a career in the academic profession, and toward how the public views academics. Further, an international relationship was found in the Carnegie data between teaching orientation and faculty perspectives toward this being a "creative and productive time" in their field. This supports the earlier findings in the Carnegie data which indicated that teaching-oriented faculty indicate stronger loyalty to their institution and research-oriented faculty are more focused on their disciplines, trends which lend international validity to Gouldner's (1957) cosmopolitan/local paradigm.

The research presented in this chapter tested the validity of a hypothesis which stated that teaching-oriented faculty view life in the academic profession differently than do research-oriented faculty. The opposite of this, the null hypothesis, states that there are no significant differences between teaching-oriented faculty and research-oriented faculty internationally in terms of their perspectives toward life in the academic profession. Based on the findings presented in this chapter, we can only partially reject the null hypothesis—differences related to teaching orientation were observed on regional and national levels, but rarely on an international level. However, while the differences overall are modest in international terms, there are some compelling questions which this study raises.

In almost every country surveyed, teaching-oriented faculty were *less likely* to indicate that this is an especially creative and productive time in their field. We need to explore more fully why this is so, and develop new ways to change the situation. Certainly, faculty who prefer to teach are rarely mentioned by institutions or professional disciplines as "stars" or "experts"— rather, these labels are awarded most often to the productive researcher (Gumport, 1991). Thus, one implication of this analysis of the Carnegie international survey data is that we need to explore new avenues for teaching-oriented faculty to feel more connected with the creative and productive dimensions of their respective disciplines.

One could reasonably expect that if teaching-oriented faculty are relatively dissatisfied with their academic discipline, they would also feel this way about the academic profession generally. However, while this study found that teaching-oriented faculty worldwide are considerably dissatisfied with the level of creativity and productivity in their academic discipline, in most countries they are neither more nor less likely than research-oriented faculty to indicate satisfaction with the academic profession overall. Further, previous chapters of this volume presented findings in the Carnegie data which indicated that teaching-oriented faculty appear to be significantly less satisfied than their colleagues with several dimensions of their jobs. However, they are not significantly less satisfied with their jobs overall, nor are they more likely to indicate that their "job is a source of considerable strain." Thus, there appears to be a contradiction in how faculty overall responded to the Carnegie survey. In looking at the responses from faculty in the United States, Haas (1996) observed that in general, faculty in the United States reflect a distinct contradiction in terms of job satisfaction:

> How can these professionals, specifically 78 percent of the respondents, be satisfied with their job situation as a whole while at the same time expressing dissatisfaction with so many elements of the setting in which they practice their profession? (p. 349)

This contradiction was observed throughout the responses to the Carnegie survey explored in this chapter. The international nature of this trend provides an important opportunity to explore how orientation toward teaching or research may not have much impact on how faculty view the academic profession overall.

The unique trends found in this study also warrant further attention. For example, teaching-oriented faculty in Germany and the United States appear to have relatively *more positive* feelings about the academic profession than their teaching-oriented colleagues elsewhere. In these two countries, teaching-oriented faculty were significantly less likely to indicate that this is a poor time to begin an academic career, and were less likely to indicate that if they had to do it over again, they would not become an academic. They were also less likely to indicate that respect for academics in their country is on the decline, and were more likely to indicate that faculty in their country are among the most influential opinion leaders. The uniqueness of these trends raises several questions. What do teaching-oriented faculty in Germany and the United States have in common that is not found elsewhere? "German academics take a more purely "cosmopolitan" position than their colleagues elsewhere—they place a strong emphasis on the discipline, but place little importance on their affiliation to their department and institution" (Enders & Teichler, 1996: 483). In the United States, faculty are generally more teaching-oriented, and clearly more institution-oriented, than their German colleagues. However, faculty in both countries were significantly more likely than most other countries surveyed to indicate considerable satisfaction with their institutional resources—such as research equipment, technology for teaching, computer facilities and library holdings—as well as with their academic salary. Perhaps these commonalities among the faculty of the two countries have some relationship with the trends observed in this chapter.

Overall, however, this study considers the most important trends as those with the most international significance. The analysis of the Carnegie data presented in this chapter found that internationally, strong preference for teaching is not significantly correlated with faculty views toward the academic profession. Faculty appear to feel basically the same about the current status of their profession regardless of the strength of their preference for teaching or research.

The findings presented in this chapter have particular implications for current discussions of faculty reward structures. A recent study by the National Center on Postsecondary Teaching, Learning and Assessment (NCPTLA, 1995) found that "faculty with the least amount of student contact hours earn the highest salaries," and that "the more refereed publications a faculty member publishes, the higher their salary" (p. 17). If teaching-oriented faculty are more likely to emphasize the importance of teaching effectiveness in faculty hiring and promotion decisions, one may wonder why they are not less disillusioned with current academic reward systems, which typically emphasize research productivity. Further analysis and interpretation of the Carnegie survey data—as well as future studies on the influence of faculty reward systems on professional satisfaction—would be useful in addressing this and other related questions.

Also, if teaching orientation has little or no relationship with how faculty feel about the academic profession, as this study indicates, then it is likely that there is also little difference between teaching-oriented and research-oriented faculty in how they view the academic profession's place in society. The following chapter addresses this issue, by examining the Carnegie survey responses for relationships between teaching orientation and faculty views toward the relationship between higher education and society.

CHAPTER 8

Higher Education's Role in Society

INTRODUCTION

This chapter continues the discussion of how teaching-oriented faculty view their working conditions differently than their research colleagues. While the previous chapter focused primarily on issues related to their academic discipline and the profession, this chapter broadens the scope of discussion to include how faculty view the relationship between higher education and society at large. There are many questions which this chapter addresses: Is teaching orientation related to how faculty view intellectual inquiry or the creation of knowledge? Are teaching-oriented faculty any less concerned than their research-oriented colleagues with applying their knowledge to solving problems in society? Is there a relationship between orientation towards teaching and faculty perspectives toward access to higher education? Faculty views toward higher education's role, and particularly how academics view their potential contribution to society at large, is thus the focus of this chapter.

In most countries, higher education has an impact on society in providing at least three important roles: the development of human resources, providing for (or preventing) changes in social stratification, and transferring culture from one generation to the next. Certainly, the most recognized impact of higher education on society is connected with the graduation of students—on various levels—and their subsequent employment in productive work. Indeed, work force requirements are usually important elements in any state or national higher education planning efforts. Granted, there is never a perfect fit between the courses a student takes, the skills he acquires, and the skills he finds himself needing in his immediate employment following graduation. However, workforce demands play an important role in the courses offered at many institutions of higher education. This is particularly true in many countries today, as the need for technically-proficient computer programmers, information technology managers, and senior technology administrators is dramatically under-met by current graduates of higher education.

Another important role higher education plays in society is in providing opportunities to change (or, in some countries, to further support) social stratification. In some countries, higher education is made available only to the elite, thus reinforcing their privileged status in society, while in other countries, access to higher education is more open, thus providing a mechanism for social advancement for members of various underclasses. Yet another significant effect of higher education is found in preserving and replicating the cultural heritage of society. Indeed, as the transfer of "book" knowledge is fundamental to higher education, so is the transfer of "cultural" knowledge—including society's values, customs, and beliefs.

There are other roles that higher education—through their faculty—can play in society. For example, society inevitably benefits from research undertaken by faculty to address social problems related to health, education, human welfare, and other important social issues. Academics often provide consulting and other important services to their communities, businesses and governments. For many, the academic profession is not simply an occupation, it is viewed as a calling to serve humankind, to search for ways to better the lives of all. Indeed, the initial report of the Carnegie survey observed this perception among faculty worldwide. "Overwhelmingly, [faculty] feel a professional obligation to apply their knowledge to the problems of society, building a bridge between theory and practice" (Boyer, Altbach & Whitelaw, 1994: 22).

Although only a minority of faculty in each country surveyed agreed with the statement, "Academics are among the most influential opinion leaders in my country" (as discussed in the previous chapter) they are nonetheless an extraordinarily important group in any society. Indeed, as Altbach (1997) and others observed, "faculty are frequently involved in politics and the intellectual life of the nation" (p. 133). Higher education has played a particularly important role in the political history of many countries. Over the years, campus protests from Korea to the United States have led to significant changes in national government policies. Through student and faculty political activism—as well as through faculty writing for newspapers and magazines, appearing on television, and advising key government officials—higher education plays an important role in focusing public attention on societal issues (Altbach, 1997).

Of course, the contribution to society of an individual professor is often related to their academic discipline—for example, faculty in applied economics, environmental science, or nuclear physics are likely to be called upon for expertise more often than faculty in Shakespearean literature or Greek philosophy. There are also a variety of differences in higher education's role in society between private and public institutions of higher education, and there are differences between countries based upon the level of governmental involvement in their nation's higher education systems. However, there are clearly many points at which higher education has some impact on society. How faculty worldwide view these points of impact was an important question which the Carnegie survey administrators sought to answer.

Based on the observations made earlier in this discussion, it is reasonable to suggest that teaching-oriented faculty might feel significantly different—and perhaps more strongly—than their research-oriented colleagues about these issues. As observed earlier, Altbach and Lewis (1996) found that throughout all countries surveyed by the Carnegie Foundation, "those who prefer teaching over research spend somewhat more time on local or campus-related activities (teaching, service, and administration) than do those who prefer research over teaching" (p.21). Further, as observed in Chapter 1, teaching-oriented faculty are significantly more likely than their research-oriented colleagues to indicate that their institution and department are more important to them, while research-oriented faculty are considerably more likely to indicate the importance of their academic discipline. Thus, given the significant differences in their views along these dimensions, one might reasonably expect teaching-oriented faculty to indicate different views about the role of higher education than their research-oriented colleagues.

The analysis of teaching-oriented professors presented in this chapter thus sought to determine whether this expectation held true. This chapter tests the validity of the following hypothesis:

Teaching-oriented faculty have different views than research-oriented faculty regarding the role of higher education in society.

Specifically, this analysis of the Carnegie survey data sought to determine the relationship of teaching orientation with faculty perspectives toward: (1) what the priorities of higher education should be; (2) higher education's role in addressing basic problems of society; and (3) access to higher education. The chapter is organized around these themes for reasons of data comparability—almost no country omitted any of these items from their survey—and personal research interests. In analyzing and presenting the data relationships found in this study, it is assumed that the more countries in which a trend in the Carnegie data exists, the more international that trend is. The following internationally significant relationships were found in this analysis of the Carnegie survey data:

- Internationally, teaching-oriented faculty were considerably less likely than their colleagues to indicate that higher education should place a high priority on promoting intellectual inquiry

• Internationally, teaching-oriented faculty were considerably less likely than their colleagues to indicate that higher education should give high priority on promoting research and scholarship.

• Teaching-oriented faculty internationally are significantly more likely than their colleagues to indicate that higher education should place a high priority on lifelong learning for adults.

• With the exception of the United States, teaching orientation appears has no significant relationship with how faculty responded to questions of access to higher education.

Overall, teaching-oriented faculty worldwide appear to share similar views toward higher education's role in society that distinguish them from their research-oriented colleagues. In an international perspective, these trends are related to a number of cultural and social influences, such as language, religion and history. For example, the orientation towards "universal" higher education (Trow, 1970) adopted in the United States has a great deal to do with faculty perspectives toward issues of access in this country. However, the international findings presented in this chapter transcend a number of nationally distinct social or structural dimensions of these issues, in showing that teaching-oriented faculty around the world are significantly different from their research-oriented colleagues in how they view the role of higher education in society.

These findings have implications for our understanding of how academics approach their work. For example, if a professor feels that higher education institutions should focus their resources on solving the problems of society, this view surely has some influence on the way he or she conducts their research or course discussions. Further, if teaching-oriented faculty are less supportive of the need to support intellectual inquiry and the creation of knowledge, this too may have some impact on how they approach their teaching activities. This chapter addresses these issues by examining the Carnegie data for relationships between teaching orientation and faculty perspectives toward several key issues, presented in the following order: (1) what the priorities of higher education should be; (2) higher education's role in addressing basic problems of society; and (3) access to higher education.

WHAT SHOULD BE THE PRIORITIES OF HIGHER EDUCATION?

There are several dimensions to the benefits higher education provides society, including research and scholarship, workforce development, lifelong learning, preserving cultural heritage, and educating future generations of leaders. Each of these dimensions have certain social and political implications, and thus how faculty feel about the priorities of higher education is an important issue to explore. As observed earlier, research studies have suggested that how faculty view their role in higher education may have some impact on how they approach academic work. For the purpose of this study, where the specific unit of analysis is teaching-oriented faculty, it is useful to ascertain whether teaching-oriented faculty were significantly different from their research-oriented colleagues in responding to these survey items.

Intellectual Inquiry and the Creation of Knowledge

As information and expertise become increasingly central to contemporary societies, those involved in the knowledge industries and especially in higher education will inevitably play a key societal role (Altbach, 1997: 144). The academic profession has always provided a significant benefit to society through focusing their considerable intellectual firepower on some of the more complex issues of the day. Scholarly research can influence change in society, illuminate overlooked problems and potentials, and generally inform a wide variety of social problems. In the United States—indeed, in democracies worldwide—intellectual inquiry is an important reflection of public freedom of thought and speech. Thus, it is useful to explore how faculty differ in their views toward whether higher education should focus on priorities related to intellectual inquiry and the creation of knowledge.

"Across all countries surveyed, faculty tended to indicate support for the idea that research and scholarship should continue to be a key part of the mission of the university and that intellectual inquiry should be protected" (Altbach & Lewis, p.43). "The strongest support for these dimensions of higher education was found among faculty surveyed in the industrial countries" (Enders & Teichler, 1996: 485). However, as observed in Chapter 1, teaching-oriented faculty in most countries were significantly less likely to indicate that their academic discipline—within which research and scholarship are rooted—is important to them, and were more likely to indicate that their institution and department were important. Thus, one might reasonably expect that teaching-oriented faculty would be less likely to indicate that intellectual inquiry, research and scholarship should be priorities of higher education Indeed, this analysis of the data supports this expectation. In a majority of the countries surveyed, teaching-oriented faculty were significantly less likely than other survey respondents to feel that protecting free intellectual inquiry should be a high priority for higher education (see Table 8.1).

TABLE 8.1

Are teaching-oriented faculty **more or less likely** than their colleagues to indicate that higher education in their country should give high priority to "protecting free intellectual inquiry"? (q69e)*

MORE Likely	LESS Likely		No Significant Relationship
Russia r= .17	Australia	r= -.08	Chile
	Brazil	r= -.10	Hong Kong
	England	r= -.11	Israel
	Germany	r= -.09	Korea
	Japan	r= -.06	
	Mexico	r= -.08	
	Sweden	r= -.08	
	United States	r= -.12	

NOTE: All correlations presented were significant at the .05 level. Also, please note that this item was omitted from the survey administered in the Netherlands.

Significant correlations were found throughout Europe, among Latin American and Asian countries, and in the former English colonies of Australia and the United States. The only exception was found among responses from faculty in Russia, where, as mentioned previously the data collected by the Carnegie survey are somewhat suspect. Here, teaching-oriented faculty are considerably more likely to indicate that higher education in their country should give high priority to protecting free intellectual inquiry. Certainly, there may be some political explanations for this trend—the government of this country has historically played a much more dominant role in higher education policy than in any other country surveyed. Four decades of Marxist-Leninist ideological domination in higher education—which certainly was not known for protecting free intellectual inquiry—may account for this anomaly in the Carnegie data.

Overall, it is significant that in most countries surveyed, teaching-oriented faculty responded differently than their research-oriented colleagues to the Carnegie survey item on protecting free intellectual inquiry. This finding has implications for our understanding of the differences between faculty in relation to the strength of their preference for teaching. A related item on the Carnegie survey also provides an important dimension to this discussion. Respondents were asked to indicate their agreement with the statement, "higher education in my country should give priority to promoting research and scholarship." As shown in Table 8.2, teaching-oriented faculty in a considerable majority of the countries surveyed were *less likely* to indicate that promoting research and scholarship should be a high priority of higher education in their country.

TABLE 8.2

Are teaching-oriented faculty **more or less likely** than their colleagues to indicate that higher education in their country should give high priority to "promoting research and scholarship" ? (q69f)

MORE Likely	LESS Likely		No Significant Relationship
	Australia	r= -.31	Chile
	Brazil	r= -.22	Israel
	England	r= -.31	Russia
	Germany	r= -.19	
	Hong Kong	r= -.33	
	Japan	r= -.15	
	Korea	r= -.06	
	Mexico	r= -.16	
	the Netherlands	r= -.06	
	Sweden	r= -.19	
	United States	r= -.32	

As one might expect, this analysis found that teaching-oriented faculty are not particularly interested in research or scholarship. Strong correlations were found in almost every country surveyed which indicate considerable disagreement with the need for higher education to place a high priority on promoting research and scholarship. Particularly strong correlations were found in Hong Kong (r=.33), the United States (r=.32), England (r=.31) and Australia (r=.31). As the higher education systems of these countries all stem from a common academic tradition, perhaps there is an element within their British roots that makes teaching-oriented faculty particularly unsupportive of research and scholarship, and more supportive of the teaching function of higher education.

Taken together, the findings presented in the two tables above represent an important difference in opinions toward higher education's priorities between teaching-oriented and research-oriented faculty. Earlier in this study, it was observed that teaching-oriented faculty overall are significantly less likely than their research-oriented colleagues to indicate that their academic discipline is important to them (see Chapter 1), which supports the distinction between "local" and "cosmopolitan" faculty made by Gouldner (1957) and other researchers. As research and scholarship are activities rooted within the academic discipline, the Carnegie data appear to indicate that the cosmopolitan/local paradigm is considerably prominent in most countries surveyed. Thus, the distinction between teaching-oriented faculty and research-oriented faculty does provide a useful dimension for analysis of the academic profession on a global scale, such as provided in this study.

Other items on the Carnegie survey concern the need for higher educa-tion to place a high priority on economic-related issues. This is an impor-tant area of concern given the current higher education environment of increased institutional accountability for student performance after gradua-tion. Indeed, frequent complaints are heard from business and political leaders that higher education is doing a relatively poor job in preparing stu-dents for the challenges of today's working environment. As teaching-ori-ented faculty spend considerably more time with students—in that they teach more—than their research-oriented colleagues, and thus have a rela-tively higher level of responsibility for the preparation of students, they tend to bear the lion's share of these criticisms. Thus, it is useful next to exam-ine how teaching-oriented faculty view the economic dimension of higher education's role in society.

Economic Priorities of Higher Education

Higher education in many countries worldwide have a relatively common mission of providing their respective country with its professional and busi-ness leadership. In the United States, higher education of the distant past prepared an elite for the clergy, medicine and the law, while higher educa-tion of more modern times also prepares students for vocational, agricul-tural, and a wide variety of other practical fields. In the decades following World War II, most countries of the Western world saw a dramatic increase in the supply of formally, highly-educated labor—sometimes more than the job market could absorb. Still, perhaps the single most commented-upon role higher education plays in virtually any society is the development of human resources to meet the demands of the national economy.

"Across all countries surveyed, faculty tended to indicate support for the idea that higher education should prepare students for the workforce" (Altbach & Lewis, 1996: 43). This should be expected, and faculty generally are concerned about the ability of their students to lead successful lives after they graduate. Certainly, one might expect teaching-oriented faculty—being more likely than their research-oriented colleagues to spend signifi-cant amounts of time with students—to indicate stronger support for this being a high priority of higher education. Indeed, this analysis supports this expectation. In half (7) of the countries surveyed, teaching-oriented faculty were significantly more likely than other survey respondents to feel that higher education should focus on preparing students for making productive contributions in the workplace (see Table 8.3).

Teaching-oriented faculty can be expected to have considerably high con-cern over the future success of their students. Thus, the trend indicated in Table 8.3 may simply indicate that this concern is stronger among teaching-oriented faculty in these countries than elsewhere. Or perhaps faculty in these countries are more supportive in general of a national economic agenda than elsewhere. In most of these countries, economic competitive-ness is a national priority—four of the G-7 countries are represented in the

"More Likely" column. However, one cannot conclude that teaching orientation plays a more prominent role in how faculty responded to this survey question in these countries because of the predominant overall public goal of economic development. In Hong Kong and the Netherlands, two countries in which there exists a strong focus on economic development, no significant differences were found between teaching-oriented and research-oriented faculty.

TABLE 8.3

Are teaching-oriented faculty **more or less likely** than their colleagues to indicate that higher education in their country should give high priority to "preparing students for making productive contributions in the workforce"? (q69b)

MORE Likely		LESS Likely	No Significant Relationship
Australia	r= .13		Chile
Brazil	r= .13		Hong Kong
England	r= .11		Israel
Germany	r= .10		Korea
Japan	r= .10		Mexico
Sweden	r= .10		the Netherlands
United States	r= .15		Russia

Overall, teaching orientation has some relationship with how faculty responded to this survey item. Particularly interesting is that in no country were teaching-oriented faculty *less likely* than their colleagues to indicate that higher education should focus on preparing students for making productive contributions in the workplace, and in many countries teaching-oriented faculty were *more likely* to express support for this agenda for higher education in their country. Thus, it may appear at first glance that teaching-oriented faculty are considerably different from their research-oriented colleagues in their views toward economic priorities of higher education. However, teaching orientation does not appear to have a significant relationship with how faculty answered a related question, concerning the importance of higher education in developing global economic competitiveness. Only in the Netherlands were teaching-oriented faculty different from their colleagues in their responses to this survey item. Here, teaching-oriented respondents were significantly less likely than research-oriented faculty to indicate that "strengthening the nation's capacity to compete internationally" should be a high priority of higher education (r= -.08). Thus, the international trend observed here is that there appears to be no relationship between teaching orientation and responses to this survey item.

Overall, when looking at faculty views toward the economic dimensions of higher education's role in society, the data suggests that orientation toward teaching can mean stronger support for preparing students for the workforce, but not for enhancing their nation's global competitiveness. Perhaps the difference between how these survey items are worded has some impact on the different relationships observed in the data. That is, survey item q69b is concerned primarily with how higher education should impact the lives of students vis-à-vis the workforce, while q69g is more concerned with higher education's overall impact in strengthening a nation's global economic position. As teaching-oriented faculty spend more time with students—in that they spend more time in the classroom—than their research-oriented colleagues, it may be the case that teaching orientation has some relationship with how faculty view higher education's responsibility to students and their success.

Indeed, as observed earlier in this discussion, teaching-oriented faculty in many countries are significantly more likely than their research-oriented colleagues to indicate that faculty should spend more time with students outside of classrooms. Perhaps there is a significant relationship in these countries between teaching orientation and heightened faculty concern over the success of their students. Another item on the Carnegie survey contributes to this discussion—respondents were asked to indicate their level of agreement with the statement, "Higher education should give high priority to educating students for leadership."

Educating Students for Leadership

"The most easily recognized impact of higher education on society is connected with the graduation of students—on various levels—and their subsequent employment in productive work" (Bergendal, 1979: 2220). For years, members of the business community have observed that graduates of our higher education institutions need to be equipped with the leadership skills necessary to meet the changing needs of the marketplace. However, according to the Carnegie survey data, faculty in all countries surveyed indicated only lukewarm support for this idea. In no country did more than a third of respondents indicate that higher education should place a high priority on the education of students for leadership. In several countries, faculty ranked this item as the lowest priority of all those possible on the Carnegie survey. Given that teaching-oriented faculty are more locally-focused—that is, on the institution, the classroom, and their students—while research-oriented faculty are more concerned with their disciplines, one might expect to find considerable differences between them in how they view higher education's role in educating students for leadership.

However, the data do not support this expectation on an international level. In only 5 of the countries surveyed—Australia, England, Germany, Korea, and the United States—were teaching-oriented faculty significantly more likely than other survey respondents to feel that higher education should focus on educating students for leadership. Of course, this trend also indicates that in these countries, faculty with stronger preference toward research are *less likely* than their colleagues to indicate that higher education in their country should give high priority to educating students for leadership. This modestly international trend raises a curious question: What do the faculty in these countries have in common that might explain this trend?

The previous section of this chapter observed relatively stronger support among teaching-oriented faculty in these countries—with the exception of Korea—for higher education's role in preparing students for making productive contributions to the workplace. There are also considerable similarities among the historical roots and traditions of the academic professions in these countries. Indeed, the Carnegie data suggest many similarities among the faculty in these countries, but these similarities are also found among faculty from countries in which no relationship was found between teaching orientation and views toward higher education's role in educating students for leadership. This analysis of the Carnegie data could thus determine no clear explanation for why this relationship appeared among responses from teaching-oriented faculty from some countries and not others.

The most internationally significant trends observed here are that (1) in no country were teaching-oriented faculty *less likely* than their colleagues to indicate that higher education should focus on educating students for leadership; and (2) in most countries surveyed, teaching orientation has no significant relationship with how faculty responded to this survey item. This is somewhat surprising, given the results described thus far in this analysis. Perhaps the term "educating students for leaders" has connotations for most faculty surveyed that differ from my own, which views this as a vitally important role for teaching in higher education. Future study of faculty in these countries would be useful for obtaining a more concrete understanding of how faculty view this dimension of higher education's role in society.

Another survey item on the Carnegie survey reflects a different kind of role for higher education in society, a considerably more "humanistic" than economic one. Respondents were asked to indicate the importance of higher education's role in providing life-learning for adults. Their responses to this survey item—and particularly, the differences between teaching-oriented and research-oriented faculty in responding to this—provides another interesting dimension to our understanding of how faculty view the relationship between higher education and society.

Providing Lifelong Learning for Adults

Continuing education is not entirely an American phenomenon, but higher education systems outside of the U.S. do comparatively little to provide lifelong learning for adults. It is thus not surprising to find that, according to the Carnegie survey data, faculty are not very supportive of this being a primary role of higher education in their country. In most countries surveyed, faculty ranked this item among the lowest priorities of all those possible on the Carnegie survey. There are few regional differences here. In

Asia, faculty in Hong Kong were considerably more supportive than in Korea or Japan. Russian faculty placed lifelong learning at the bottom of the priority list, while European faculty were slightly more supportive. Faculty in all the Latin America countries surveyed indicated low support for higher education's role in providing lifelong learning for adults.

However, this study found major differences internationally between responses to this item based on faculty preference for teaching. In other words, teaching orientation has a significant international relationship with how faculty responded to this survey item. In a considerable majority of the countries surveyed, teaching-oriented faculty were significantly *more likely* than other survey respondents to feel that lifelong learning for adults should be a high priority for higher education (see Table 8.4).

TABLE 8.4

Are teaching-oriented faculty **more or less likely** than their colleagues to indicate that higher education in their country should give high priority to "lifelong learning for adults"? (q69c)

MORE Likely		LESS Likely	No Significant Relationship
Australia	r= .10		Brazil
England	r= .15		Chile
Germany	r= .13		Israel
Hong Kong	r= .17		Korea
Japan	r= .12		Mexico
the Netherlands	r= .08		
Russia	r= .08		
Sweden	r= .07		
United States	r= .12		

Here, the correlation with teaching orientation is considerably international in scope, encompassing all the European countries, Japan, Hong Kong, Australia and the United States. Teaching orientation does not appear to play a role in how Latin American faculty responded to this survey item, perhaps because there is low support for this in general among all faculty surveyed in Latin America (cf. Schwarzman & Balbachevsky, 1996; Schiefelbein, 1996).

The international dimension of this finding has several broad implications for our understanding of the teaching-oriented professoriate, and raises even more questions about the academic profession generally. Why do research-oriented faculty consider lifelong learning for adults as a relatively unimportant agenda item for higher education? Earlier findings presented in this chapter indicated that teaching-oriented faculty may have a considerably stronger concern for the overall success and well-being of their students. Is this another dimension of this same concern? Do teaching-oriented faculty care more about learning in general than their research-oriented colleagues? If so, this certainly has implications for how we address the issue of courseloads for faculty who would much rather be engaged in research than being compelled by their institution to deal with students. These issues surely warrant further investigation beyond the initial findings of the Carnegie survey, particularly from studies that involve a mixture of qualitative and further quantitative analyses.

Other dimensions of faculty views toward the role of higher education in society can further inform our understanding of the differences between teaching-oriented and research-oriented academics. One important area of concern is whether faculty view higher education as a mechanism for passing cultural and social history—termed "cultural heritage" in the Carnegie survey—from one generation to the next. Given the findings presented thus far in this chapter, it is possible that faculty with stronger preference for teaching than for research would have considerably different views than their research-oriented colleagues toward this dimension of higher education's role in society.

Preserving the Cultural Heritage

"One of the basic impacts of higher education on society is concerned with the formation of people's concept of knowledge" (Bergendal, 1979: 2222). Clearly, teaching can be seen as a way of preserving the cultural heritage, by passing customs, traditions, history to the younger generations. Indeed, many scholars have pointed to the role education plays in maintaining both social stratification and cultural knowledge through successive generations. In this manner, teachers play a prominent role in transferring to their students not just knowledge, but cultural understanding and interpretation. Thus, one might reasonably expect teaching-oriented faculty to feel differently than research-oriented faculty about this important function of higher education. However, this was found to be the case in only 3 of the countries surveyed—Germany (r=.05), Japan (r=.03), and the United States (r=.07). Here, teaching-oriented faculty were significantly *more likely* than other survey respondents to feel that preserving the cultural heritage should be a high priority for higher education. Thus, internationally-speaking, there is only a modest difference between teaching-oriented and research-oriented faculty in their responses to this survey item.

As in many other cases discussed in this chapter, no significant correlations were found among responses from Latin American faculty and most of Asia. However, teaching-oriented faculty in Korea were found to be slightly *less likely* than their colleagues to indicate the importance of higher education's role in preserving the cultural heritage (r=-.02). In most all relationships discussed so far in this study, correlations with teaching orientation have been the same in each country—either positive in all cases, or negative. However, the results of this analysis of the Carnegie data indicate that in this case, teaching orientation plays a different role in Korea than in the other countries where correlations were found. While the difference is quite small in statistical terms, it is an unusual anomaly in the data that may reflect larger issues about the role of teaching orientation in this country. Perhaps the relatively high level of governmental involvement in Korean higher education has some relationship to the trend found here. More than one-third of Korean faculty indicated that there are political or ideological restrictions on what a scholar can publish. And yet, responses from this country also indicate that faculty in Korea believe they have a higher level of influence in their country than faculty in other countries. Thus, the particular social, political and cultural environment in Korea may explain this singular relationship in the data between teaching orientation and faculty views toward higher education's role in preserving the cultural heritage.

Summary

Overall, teaching orientation does have some relationship with how faculty view the kinds of priorities about which their country's higher education enterprise should focus. This is particularly true for faculty perspectives toward protecting intellectual inquiry, promoting research and scholarship, student contributions in the workplace, and lifelong learning for adults. Teaching-oriented faculty are less supportive than their research-oriented colleagues of higher education's focus on promoting intellectual inquiry and scholarship. Teaching-oriented faculty were significantly more likely than their colleagues to indicate that higher education should focus on preparing students for making productive contributions in the workplace. Teaching-oriented faculty around the world also show considerably more support than their colleagues for higher education providing lifelong learning for adults.

Significantly international trends were not found between teaching orientation and faculty responses to the other survey items addressed here. However, this study did find strong support among teaching-oriented faculty in several countries for higher education's role in preserving the cultural heritage and for educating students for leadership. These and other findings presented in this study help to form an increasingly comprehensive view of who teaching-oriented faculty are and how they view the world of academe in different ways than their research-oriented colleagues.

Further studies in this area beyond the scope of the Carnegie data are needed, particularly comparative studies which examine the relationship between academic discipline and faculty views toward the priorities of higher education. To be sure, analyses of this kind are available for some countries surveyed by the Carnegie study. For example, Enders and Teichler found that among the German faculty responses, "professors of economics and business studies support a strong emphasis on educating students for leadership, while professors of fine arts give a high priority to the aim of preserving the cultural heritage" (p.485). However, due to comparability issues in how each country's survey administrators collected their faculty data, an international study of this kind is not yet available.

Having looked at several dimensions of faculty views toward what higher education should give priority to, it is next useful to examine their views toward higher education's role in addressing the problems of society. Clearly, the Carnegie data in this area indicate "the faculty's confidence in the practical value of their knowledge and their concern about larger social issues" (Boyer, Altbach & Whitelaw, 1994: 18). This analysis of the Carnegie data sought to determine whether this confidence is different among teaching-oriented faculty than among research-oriented faculty.

HIGHER EDUCATION AND THE PROBLEMS OF SOCIETY

Across all countries surveyed, faculty tended to indicate that higher education should play an important role in addressing their country's social problems. A strong majority of faculty in every country surveyed agreed with the statement, "Faculty in my discipline have a professional obligation to apply their knowledge to problems in society," ranging from 61% of faculty in Russia to 93% in Germany. As observed in the initial Carnegie report, this represents "the faculty's confidence in the practical value of their knowledge and their concern about larger social issues" (Boyer, Altbach & Whitelaw, 1994: 18). Indeed, there has always been a strong sentiment throughout the academic profession that higher education has some responsibility for serving the needs of society, and this sentiment is reflected in the responses internationally to several Carnegie survey items.

This analysis of the Carnegie data set out to determine whether teaching-oriented faculty are significantly more likely than their research-oriented colleagues to indicate that they have an obligation to apply their knowledge to problems in society. As Table 8.5 shows, correlations were found among the data from several countries, but overall there appears to be only a modest difference between teaching-oriented and research-oriented faculty.

TABLE 8.5

Are teaching-oriented faculty **more or less likely** than their colleagues to agree with the statement, "faculty in my discipline have an obligation to apply their knowledge to problems in society?" (q54a)

MORE likely		LESS Likely		No Significant Relationship	
Brazil	r= .03	Chile	r= -.01	Australia	Korea
Japan	r= .06	Germany	r= -.01	England	Mexico
United States	r= .03	Israel	r= -.03	Hong Kong	Russia
		Sweden	r= -.03	the Netherlands	

While the correlations here are not particularly strong (r=.03 in Brazil and the United States, and r=.06 in Japan), they indicate that teaching-oriented faculty in these countries may be more supportive than their research-oriented colleagues of the ideal that higher education should provide service to society. Does this indicate that teaching-oriented faculty in these countries are more socially-conscious than their research-oriented colleagues? Why might research-oriented faculty in these countries be less likely than their teaching-oriented colleagues to feel that their academic disciplines—which they indicated are more important to them than their institutions—have an obligation to apply knowledge to social problems?

To make these matters even more complicated, teaching orientation has the reverse affect among responses from faculty in Chile, Germany, Israel, and Sweden. In these countries, teaching-oriented faculty were significantly less likely to indicate that faculty have an obligation to apply knowledge to social problems. However, again, the correlations found here are not particularly strong (r=-.01 in Chile and Germany, and r=-.03 in Israel and Sweden). Does this indicate that teaching-oriented faculty in these countries are less socially-conscious than their research-oriented colleagues? Or perhaps this is indicative of the trend (presented in Chapter 1) where teaching-oriented faculty are less concerned overall with their academic disciplines.

Overall, this analysis of the Carnegie data found that teaching orientation in half the countries surveyed does have some impact on whether a faculty member feels they have an obligation to apply their knowledge to problems of society, while correlations were not found in the other countries. Thus, the study indicates a mixed relationship between teaching orientation and views toward the obligation of faculty to apply their knowledge to problems in society. An important dimension for further analysis would be a comparative analysis of how faculty in different disciplines responded to this survey item, to determine whether teaching orientation has any more or less significance than found here. Unfortunately, such an analysis is not possible using the Carnegie data, due to a number of variances in the collection and coding procedures for each country's data collection, as described in Chapter 3. Perhaps future studies of this kind will enable a more comprehensive study such as suggested here.

However, a related question on the Carnegie survey adds an important dimension to this discussion. In addition to the above statement concerning "faculty in my discipline", respondents were also asked to indicate their agreement with the statement, "Higher education should give high priority to helping resolve basic problems." Here, the results of the regression analysis found no international differences between teaching-oriented and research-oriented faculty. In fact, only teaching-oriented faculty in the United States were significantly different from their colleagues in responding to this survey item. The question this raises is why teaching-oriented faculty in the United States—and nowhere else—are more likely than their research-oriented colleagues to feel that higher education should give high priority to helping resolve basic problems. Perhaps this means that teaching-oriented faculty are more engaged in social issues in the United States than in any other country surveyed. Or, perhaps this is reflective of the considerable history in the United States of faculty involvement in addressing societal problems. Or perhaps this is simply an anomaly in the data, and that the real story is that no significant differences are observed between teaching-oriented and research-oriented faculty views on this topic.

A further question is raised when looking at the two trends above side by side. While a significant—albeit mixed—relationship was found between teaching orientation and responses to the survey statement regarding the responsibilities of "faculty in my discipline," no relationships were found internationally between teaching orientation and higher education giving priority to helping resolve basic problems. Does this indicate that, when considering the role of higher education in society, faculty generally feel that academic disciplines have a stronger obligation to society than higher education generally? Further, why do research-oriented faculty in some countries feel that their academic disciplines have an obligation to solving society's problems, while research-oriented faculty in other countries do not feel this way?

Of course, the real story here is that the Carnegie data appear to reflect scarcely any significant differences between teaching-oriented and research-oriented faculty. Much has been made of the apparent over-emphasis on research in higher education, with many inferences made about the impact faculty reward structures may have on classroom instruction. As many scholars of higher education have observed, faculty are more likely to be rewarded when attracting external funding into their department than for any other activity (cf. Clark, 1995). Indeed, the initial Carnegie report noted a widespread problem with faculty engagement in addressing society's problems, with the observation that ". . . in many countries professional service is not regularly evaluated, which may mean that professors who spent too much time applying their knowledge to real life issues could compromise their careers" (Boyer, Altbach & Whitelaw, 1994: 22). However, this analysis shows that faculty who prefer teaching over research do not seem to be significantly different from their research-oriented colleagues in how they feel about higher education's role in society. Said differently, faculty whose primary interests lie in research are no less likely than their teaching-oriented counterparts to support the notion of higher education solving basic problems in society.

This has implications for our understanding of the differences between teaching-oriented and research-oriented faculty, between the "locals" and the "cosmopolitans." Regardless of their preference for research or for teaching, faculty appear to be alike in their concern for social problems, and higher education's role in addressing them. Thus, perhaps the differences lie more in faculty perspectives toward how higher education should address problems of society. Teaching-oriented faculty may view higher education's priority in this area as one involving the training of their students, equipping them with the skills and knowledge necessary to explore new and innovative solutions to problems. On the other hand, research-oriented faculty may be more likely to feel that it is through their research and scholarship—through the efforts of the faculty, and not necessarily the students—that higher education can most effectively address the problems of society. Certainly, research beyond the scope of the Carnegie data—particularly, comparative studies of both quantitative and qualitative angles—would help gain a more complete understanding of how faculty worldwide differ in their views toward higher education's role in society.

As described earlier in this study, the data show that teaching-oriented faculty are likely to spend considerably more time with students than their research-oriented colleagues, both in and outside the classroom. As higher education has expanded over the last few decades, and classrooms are swelling with increasing numbers of students, one might reasonably expect teaching orientation to play a significant role in how faculty responded to Carnegie survey items regarding access to higher education.

ACCESS TO HIGHER EDUCATION

Around the world, criteria and procedures for access to higher education vary. In many European countries, entry to higher education is determined chiefly by entry to—and successful completion of—secondary schools which provide some form of university preparatory studies. In some of these countries—notably Germany and France—certain highly competitive disciplines impose more strict admissions requirements, and even annual quotas in some cases. In other countries (for example, Japan) access to higher education is determined through highly competitive examinations. Still other systems rely on a mix of criteria for admission to higher education. For example, higher education in the United Kingdom and the United States look at secondary schools as but one of several factors, including national tests (such as the SAT) and personal attributes of the potential student.

All of the academic systems included in the Carnegie international survey are what Trow (1970) would refer to as either "mass" or "universal" systems of higher education systems, in that they accept considerably a large proportion of those young adults graduating from secondary school. Further, "all the systems included in the survey have dramatically increased enrollments in recent years, and, with the exception of the United States, enrollment growth continues" (Altbach & Lewis, 1996: 42). Faculty members in most countries surveyed expressed a strong commitment to expanding opportunity for attending higher education. "While cautiously concluding that not all young people in their countries are capable of completing secondary education, faculty strongly agree that access to higher education should be admitted to all who meet minimum entrance requirements"

(Boyer, Altbach & Whitelaw, 1994: 21). "Roughly a third of all faculty surveyed, with the exception of Germany, indicated some reservations about expanded educational opportunity, with all others responding in favor of the idea that any student who can meet minimum entrance requirements for postsecondary education should be permitted to pursue at least a bachelor's degree" (Altbach & Lewis, 1996: 43).

At the same time, "most faculty reject the idea of lowering academic standards to admit disadvantaged students. They also express frustration that college students are often inadequately prepared in the basic skills, indicating a continuing tension both here and abroad between access and excellence. Still, it's truly impressive that academics support the expansion of educational opportunities, which signals a continuing international movement from "elite" to "mass" higher education" (Boyer, Altbach & Whitelaw, 1994: 21).

As observed earlier in this discussion, teaching-oriented faculty are more likely to teach than research-oriented faculty, and are therefore more likely to have considerably higher levels of interaction with students. Thus, it seems useful to determine whether teaching-oriented faculty feel differently about these issues than their research-oriented colleagues. One might reasonably expect that teaching-oriented faculty, having to deal with crowded classrooms and increasingly high numbers of students to advise, would likely indicate that admission policies should be more stringent.

However, with the exception of the United States ($r=-.05$), teaching orientation appears to have no significant impact on how faculty feel about access to higher education in their country. The negative correlation found here indicates that the stronger the teaching orientation, the more likely the respondent indicated a higher percentage of high school graduates should be admitted to higher education. Further, teaching orientation has a relationship in only the United States ($r=.02$) with how faculty responded to a related survey item concerning access to higher education. In this case, teaching-oriented faculty were slightly more likely to agree with the statement, "Access to higher education should be made available to all who meet the minimum entrance requirements." Of course, this also indicates that research-oriented faculty in the United States are significantly less supportive of access to higher education than their teaching-oriented colleagues.

Thus, it is interesting to note that in virtually all countries surveyed, no significant relationship was found internationally between teaching orientation and faculty views toward access to higher education. This seems to fly in the face of at least two areas of academic concern. On the one hand, one would expect teaching-oriented faculty to feel strongly that access to higher education should be constricted, resulting in smaller classrooms, which in turn lead (in theory) to better instruction. On the other hand, one might expect teaching-oriented faculty to be significantly more interested in passing along existing knowledge to larger percentages of future generations. According to this analysis of the Carnegie data, neither of these possible scenarios hold true—in almost every country surveyed, faculty with a strong preference for teaching do not appear to feel any differently from their research-oriented colleagues toward the issue of access to higher education.

The findings presented here also have implications for our understanding of the differences between "local" and "cosmopolitan" faculty. Apparently, the differences between faculty—as related to where their preferences and professional loyalties lie—are relatively unimportant when it comes to questions of access to higher education. This discussion raises more questions than answers, and illustrates the need for more research on how faculty worldwide feel about higher education's role in their societies.

CONCLUSION

There are many unexplored dimensions to faculty views toward the priorities of higher education. There are likely to be significant differences among faculty by discipline, institutional type, training, political orientation, and a variety of other possible aspects to a faculty member's personal and professional identity. This study has adopted the view that the strength of a faculty member's preference is an intervening variable, an aspect of a faculty member's sense of self that can influence their views toward higher education and the academic profession. The Carnegie data findings presented in this chapter supports this view, as teaching-oriented faculty are significantly different from their research-oriented colleagues in responses to several survey items related to higher education's role in society.

The research presented in this chapter tested the validity of a hypothesis which stated that teaching-oriented faculty view the role of higher education in society differently than do research-oriented faculty. The opposite of this, the null hypothesis, states that there is no real difference between teaching-oriented faculty and research-oriented faculty in terms of their perspectives toward the role of higher education in society. According to this analysis of the Carnegie, data, we can reject the null hypothesis. Overall, this analysis of the Carnegie data found that teaching-oriented faculty indicated significantly different views than their research-oriented colleagues toward several dimensions of higher education's role in society. However, this analysis did not always find internationally-shared similarities in the relationships between teaching orientation and faculty responses to the Carnegie survey. Rather, this study of the Carnegie data uncovered several kinds of trends, which can be meaningfully organized into one of four categories:

  1. Internationally significant - trends in the data that were shared throughout a majority of the countries surveyed;

II. Internationally modest - relationships that were found in the data from fewer than half (but more than two) of the countries surveyed;

III. Mixed results - the data indicate a relationship in one direction in some countries, and a relationship in the opposite direction in others; and

IV. Unique findings - data relationships that were found only among the responses from one country or specific region.

The following discussion reviews the findings of this analysis in relation to these four sub-topics, and explores implications of the more internationally significant trends. Also, in presenting the findings of this analysis, the view is taken that where teaching orientation had no significant relationship whatsoever with faculty responses to a particular item on the survey, this itself is an international trend of sorts.

(I) Significant International Trends

In several cases, the regression analyses showed correlations that were either always positive or always negative for all or most countries surveyed. These findings provide an international insight into what it means to prefer teaching over research.

1. Internationally, teaching-oriented faculty were considerably less likely than their colleagues to indicate that higher education should place a high priority on promoting intellectual inquiry.

2. Internationally, teaching-oriented faculty were considerably less likely than their colleagues to indicate that higher education should give high priority on promoting research and scholarship.

3. Teaching-oriented faculty internationally are significantly more likely than their colleagues to indicate that higher education should place a high priority on lifelong learning for adults.

4. With the exception of the Netherlands, teaching orientation appears has no significant relationship with whether faculty feel that "strengthening the nation's capacity to compete internationally" should be a high priority of higher education.

5. With the exception of the United States, teaching orientation has no significant relationship with how faculty responded to questions of access to higher education.

(II) Internationally Modest Findings
Several of the relationships found in this analysis of the Carnegie data are shared by more than a few countries, but not enough to consider them internationally significant.

> 1. In half of the countries surveyed, teaching-oriented faculty are considerably more likely than their colleagues to indicate that higher education should place a high priority on preparing students for making productive contributions in the workplace.
>
> 2. Teaching orientation is correlated in several countries with how faculty responded to questions of higher education's role in addressing basic problems of society; however, in some countries this correlation was positive while in others it was negative, indicating no clear international trend.
>
> 3. Teaching orientation is modestly related internationally with how faculty responded to questions of higher education's role in educating students for leadership.
>
> 4. Teaching orientation is modestly related internationally with how faculty responded to questions of higher education's role in preserving the cultural heritage.

(III) Mixed Results
There are also several cases in which teaching orientation had a positive correlation in some countries, and a negative one in others.

> 1. Teaching orientation is related internationally with how faculty responded to the Carnegie survey question related to whether higher education should place a high priority on solving problems in society. However, in Brazil, Japan and the United States, teaching-oriented faculty were more likely than their colleagues to indicate that higher education should place a high priority on solving problems in society, while in Chile, Germany, Israel, and Sweden teaching-oriented faculty were less likely to indicate agreement with this statement.

(IV) Unique Findings
In several cases, this analysis of the Carnegie data found a relationship between teaching orientation and faculty response to a particular survey item that was not shared with any other country surveyed.

> 1. Teaching-oriented faculty in the United States were alone in showing significantly stronger support for higher education's role in solving basic social problems.

2. Teaching-oriented faculty in Russia were significantly more likely than their colleagues to indicate that higher education in their country should give high priority to protecting free intellectual inquiry, while teaching-oriented faculty in most other countries surveyed were less likely to indicate this than their colleagues.

3. Teaching-oriented faculty were alone in showing significantly stronger support than their colleagues for providing more access to higher education.

4. Only teaching-oriented faculty in the Netherlands were significantly more likely than their colleagues to indicate that higher education in their country should place a high priority on strengthening the nation's capacity to compete internationally.

Summary and Implications

Several unique and international trends were observed in the Carnegie survey data related to teaching orientation. Teaching-oriented faculty worldwide feel more strongly than their research-oriented counterparts that preparing students for making productive contributions in the workplace should be a high priority for higher education. Teaching-oriented faculty are more in favor than their colleagues of higher education providing life-learning for adults. Also, teaching-oriented faculty internationally are less inclined to feel that protecting free intellectual inquiry or promoting research and scholarship are important priorities of higher education's role in society.

What are the implications of these trends in the data? For one, these faculty responses support the distinction suggested by Gouldner (1957) and others between "local" and "cosmopolitan" faculty, based upon where a faculty member primary interests lie. Research-oriented faculty are relatively more supportive of higher education's role in promoting intellectual inquiry and scholarship—activities rooted in the academic disciplines, which is where their loyalties are the strongest. Teaching-oriented faculty appear more interested in ensuring that education helps students succeed in work and life, which reflects the concerns of institutions and departments, where students and teachers interact the most.

These trends raise questions and pose new challenges for the academic profession. How can the profession engage teaching-oriented faculty in a way that might strengthen their support for higher education's role in promoting intellectual inquiry and scholarship? Why do research-oriented faculty appear relatively less concerned with whether their students are adequately equipped to "make productive contributions to the workplace" or for leadership? Does being "cosmopolitan" mean relatively less concern for students overall, while "locally-oriented" faculty are more concerned with the impact of higher education on students? How the profession responds to these and other related questions will surely have implications for the future of higher education.

Another noticeable trend found in this analysis of the Carnegie data is that teaching-oriented faculty in England, Australia and the United States were similarly supportive of higher education's role in the preparation of students for the workforce and for leadership. This, combined with their support of faculty spending more time with students outside the classroom and their support for student involvement in the assessment of teaching (as evidenced in the previous chapter's findings) appears to indicate that teaching-oriented faculty in these three countries all seem to share a strong concern for the success of their students, in comparison to their teaching-oriented and research-oriented colleagues elsewhere. Why might this be so? Perhaps there is something embedded in the social or political structure of these three English-speaking democracies that would explain such a unique similarity. Certainly, the impact of British academic institutions in the United States and Australia—due at first to colonialism—provides for some common traditions and perspectives toward higher education among the faculty in these three countries. Certainly there is room for expansive quantitative and qualitative research in these areas in the future.

Another unique trend was observed among the data collected from the Russian professoriate. Here, teaching-oriented faculty are considerably *more likely* than their research-oriented colleagues to indicate that higher education in their country should give high priority to protecting free intellectual inquiry, while teaching-oriented faculty in almost every other country surveyed were significantly *less likely* to indicate this. Certainly, there may be some political explanations for this trend—the government of this country has historically played a much more dominant role in higher education policy than in any other country surveyed. Four decades of Marxist-Leninist ideological domination in higher education—which certainly was not known for protecting free intellectual inquiry—may account for this anomaly in the Carnegie data.

Still another trend found throughout these findings is in the direction of the correlations observed. In most cases, the regression analyses showed correlations that were either always positive or always negative. There is only one significant case in which teaching orientation had a positive correlation in some countries, and a negative one in others. Teaching orientation is related internationally with how faculty responded to the Carnegie survey question related to whether higher education should place a high priority on solving problems in society. However, in Brazil, Japan and the United States, teaching-oriented faculty were more likely than their colleagues to indicate that higher education should place a high priority on solving problems in society, while in Chile, Germany, Israel, and Sweden teaching-oriented faculty were less likely to indicate agreement with this statement. Overall the findings show that, teaching orientation is correlated in much the same way throughout all the countries surveyed. Thus, these findings provide an international insight into what it means to prefer teaching over research.

The international nature of the trends presented in this chapter (as well as previous chapters) lend support to many scholars' observations—many of which are provided in Chapter 2 of this volume—that the academic profession has become a truly international enterprise. However, while teaching-oriented faculty may have much in common internationally, they may be actually less internationally-minded than their research-oriented colleagues. Research is rooted in (and rewarded by) academic disciplines, which are very international, whereas teaching is located within the institution. Thus, it would be useful next to determine whether teaching-oriented faculty differ from their research-oriented colleagues in their perspectives toward the international dimensions of higher education.

International Dimensions of Higher Education

INTRODUCTION

This chapter continues the discussion of how teaching-oriented faculty view academic life and higher education differently than their research colleagues. While the previous chapter focused primarily on issues related to the relationship between higher education and society, this chapter expands the focus of the study to include international connections in the academic profession. "Academic institutions are linked across international boundaries by a common historical tradition, connected by an international knowledge network that communicates research worldwide through books, journals, and increasingly, databases" (Altbach, 1997: 207). An exploration of differences in faculty views toward the international dimensions of higher education is thus important and useful. There are many questions which this discussion addresses: Do teaching-oriented faculty consider international connections with their colleagues important? How does faculty orientation towards teaching or research relate to their views toward international study abroad programs for students or professors? Is there significant support among teaching-oriented faculty for a more international curriculum? This chapter seeks to address these important questions, the answers to which have implications for our understanding of the teaching-oriented professoriate as well as the academic profession overall.

"Events have fostered a more professionally connected, international community of scholars and scientists, and there is a deep conviction both that higher education is an international enterprise and that the academic profession is becoming a more global community" (Altbach & Lewis, 1996: 41). "As the world has become increasingly interdependent and national academic boundaries have been blurred, science and scholarship are becoming increasingly international" (Ibid: 36). Given the recent growth in international connections within the academy, the Carnegie survey admin-

istrators were particularly interested in discovering faculty opinions toward
how internationally-focused higher education should be. For the purposes
of this study, it is particularly useful to look at how orientation towards
research or teaching impacts faculty views in this area, as the Carnegie data
can provide an important international dimension to Gouldner's (1957) cos-
mopolitan/local dichotomy regarding the importance of faculty orientation
towards academic disciplines versus orientation towards their institutions.
Certainly, as international connections are fostered and nurtured within
academic disciplines, research has become a much more international
activity than teaching. Therefore, it can be reasonably expected that
research-oriented faculty and teaching-oriented faculty differ in their views
toward the international dimension of higher education.

This chapter explores thus how teaching orientation is related to faculty
perspectives toward the international dimension of higher education. This
chapter tests the validity of the following hypothesis:

> Teaching-oriented faculty have different views about the interna-
> tional dimension of higher education than their research-orient-
> ed colleagues do.

Specifically, this analysis of the Carnegie survey data sought to determine
the relationship of teaching orientation with: (1) indications of time spent
on international activities, such as collaborating with foreign colleagues, or
traveling abroad to study or do research; and (2) faculty views toward international dimensions of higher education, such as connections with colleagues in other countries, reading books and journals published abroad,
and the international focus on their institution's curriculum. The chapter is
organized around these themes for reasons of data comparability—almost
no country omitted any of these items from their survey—and personal
research interests. In analyzing and presenting the data relationships found
in this study, it is assumed that the more countries in which a trend in the
Carnegie data exists, the more international that trend is. The following
internationally significant relationships were found in this analysis of the
Carnegie survey data:

> • Teaching-oriented faculty worldwide are significantly less like-
> ly than their research-oriented colleagues to indicate that con-
> nections with faculty in other countries are important.
> • Internationally, teaching-oriented faculty are significantly less
> likely than their colleagues to agree that scholars should read
> books published abroad.
> • In a majority of countries surveyed, teaching-oriented faculty
> were significantly less likely than their research-oriented col-
> leagues to have collaborated with faculty from another country
> in the past 10 years.

- Teaching-oriented faculty in most countries surveyed were less likely than their colleagues to have traveled or worked abroad within the past 10 years.

Overall, teaching-oriented faculty appear to be significantly less internationally-minded than their colleagues. Thus, one implication of this study is that we must find new ways to engage teaching-oriented faculty so that they feel more strongly that they are a part of a vibrant and exciting international academic profession. Also, as teaching-oriented faculty are engaged more in campus-based activities than their research-oriented colleagues (Altbach & Lewis, 1996), they are considerably more likely to have a meaningful role in the adoption of a curriculum at any institution. However, according to the results of this analysis, there exists a significant challenge of convincing teaching-oriented faculty of the importance of an international curriculum. We must also determine why teaching-oriented faculty are less inclined to foster connections with their colleagues in other countries or to read books and articles published abroad, and we must find ways to change these attitudes in a direction more positive towards the international dimension of higher education. Our understanding of the academic responsibility of teaching needs to encompass an international dimension, in order for our university and college teachers–and their students–to adequately address the demands of this increasing global interdependence.

INTERNATIONAL ACTIVITIES OF TEACHING-ORIENTED FACULTY

International mobility of faculty is an important product of the international connectedness that has evolved in higher education over the last several decades. Regional cooperative efforts have been designed to promote academic staff exchanges, such as the European Union's European Community Action Scheme for the Mobility of University Students (ERASMUS), while institutional-based faculty exchange programs are common worldwide. "One of the main reasons for academic staff mobility has been the fostering of communication and cooperation among institutions and academia aimed at the advancement of knowledge" (Enders, 1998: 46). According to the Carnegie survey data, "over half the professoriate in ten countries made at least one trip abroad for study or research" (Altbach & Lewis, 1996, p. 38). However, "the range of international mobility varies widely, from Israel—where 90 percent of the respondents indicated experiences studying abroad—to Brazil, Russia and the United States, where only about one-third of respondents reported such activity" (Ibid.: 39).

International mobility in the academic profession is also significantly impacted by faculty orientation towards teaching or research. As Altbach and Lewis (1996) observed, "those more committed to research than teaching had a greater likelihood of international involvement. That is, professors oriented to research are, not surprisingly, the professors who more often write for an international audience, travel and work abroad, and have relationships with academics in other countries" (p. 38). This analysis of the Carnegie data confirms these scholars' observations, by revealing considerably significant correlations in a majority of countries surveyed between international mobility and orientation towards teaching. To begin with, teaching-oriented faculty in a majority of countries were significantly less likely than their research-oriented colleagues to have worked collaboratively with an academic from another country (see Table 9.1).

TABLE 9.1

Are teaching-oriented faculty **more or less likely** to indicate that they have worked collaboratively with an academic from another country within the past 10 years? (Q65a2)

MORE Likely	LESS likely		No Significant Relationship
	Australia	r= .26	Hong Kong
	Brazil	r= .25	Israel
	Chile	r= .24	Korea
	England	r= .24	Mexico
	Germany	r= .12	the Netherlands
	Japan	r= .13	Russia
	Sweden	r= .21	
	United States	r= .24	

NOTE: All correlations presented were significant at the .05 level. Also, please note that this item was omitted from the survey administered in the Netherlands.

It is important to note the strength of the correlations reflected in Table 9.1—as high as r=.26 (Australia), r=.25 (Brazil) and r=.24 (Chile, England and the United States). Thus, the data indicate that there is significantly less international collaboration among teaching-oriented faculty than among their research-oriented colleagues. This could be somewhat expected, given that opportunities for international collaboration are more available for research than for teaching. Indeed, no country's responses indicated that teaching-oriented faculty were *more likely* than their research-oriented colleagues to indicate that they had worked collaboratively with an academic from another country. However, although this analysis expected to find significant correlations in all the countries surveyed, this was not the case among the responses from six countries, among which there appear to be few similarities. Faculty in Mexico and Russia are considerably teaching-oriented, while the highest percentages of research-oriented faculty were found in Israel (72%) and the Netherlands (76%). Israel has by far the most internationally-active professoriate, indicated by numbers of faculty going abroad to study, teach or do research. Thus, a question emerges as to why teaching orientation does *not* appear to have a significant impact in these countries on whether faculty have collaborated with an academic from another country in the past ten years. More importantly, as shown in Table 9.2, teaching-oriented faculty appear significantly less internationally-active in only half or fewer of the countries surveyed.

TABLE 9.2		
Are teaching-oriented faculty **more or less likely** to indicate that they have engaged in any of the following international activities within the past 10 years? (Q65b2,c2,d2)		
Traveled abroad to study or do research (Q65b2)		
MORE Likely	**LESS likely**	**No Significant Relationship**
	Australia r= .22	Germany
	Brazil r= .24	Hong Kong
	Chile r= .19	Israel
	England r= .25	Korea
	Japan r= .16	Mexico
	Sweden r= .07	the Netherlands
	United States r= .20	Russia
Served as a faculty member at an institution in another country (Q65c2)		
MORE Likely	**LESS likely**	**No Significant Relationship**
	Brazil r= .16	Australia Japan
	Chile r= .20	Germany Korea
	England r= .14	Hong Kong Mexico
	United States r= .12	Israel Russia
		the Netherlands Sweden
Spent a sabbatical abroad (Q65d2)		
MORE Likely	**LESS likely**	**No Significant Relationship**
	Australia r= .15	Brazil Japan
	England r= .17	Chile Korea
	Israel r= .02	Germany Russia
	Mexico r= .10	Hong Kong Sweden
	United States r= .12	the Netherlands

This table reflects several important findings in the Carnegie data. To begin with, the most significant international trend observed in Table 9.2 is that in no country were teaching-oriented faculty *more likely* than their research-oriented colleagues to have traveled or worked abroad within the past 10 years. Thus, it is clear that faculty who prefer research over teaching also have had more international experiences than their teaching-oriented colleagues. Another significantly international trend observed in the data indicates that teaching-oriented faculty were considerably less likely to have studied or engaged in research abroad. The strength of these correlations were highest among the faculty responses from England (r=.25), Brazil (r=.24), Australia (r=.22), and the United States (r=.20). As observed earlier in this discussion, there are commonalities in the social and political structures of the three English-speaking democracies here that might help explain such a unique similarity. Certainly, the impact of British academic institutions in the United States and Australia—due at first to colonialism—provides for some common traditions and perspectives toward higher education among the faculty in these three countries.

This analysis of the Carnegie data also found that in several—but interestingly, not a majority—of the countries surveyed, teaching-oriented faculty were significantly less likely to have served as a faculty member at an institution in another country, or to have spent a sabbatical abroad. Since these trends are relatively modest internationally, perhaps there is little overall difference between teaching-oriented and research-oriented faculty in their responses to these Carnegie survey items. This also indicates that the most significant differences between teaching-oriented and research-oriented faculty—in terms of their international activities—lies in the area of research activities, and not in the others on which the Carnegie survey collected data.

Overall, the Carnegie survey responses indicate that teaching-oriented faculty in most countries surveyed were less likely than their colleagues to have traveled or worked abroad within the past 10 years. Further, as the findings presented in Tables 9.1 and 9.2 very clearly show, teaching-oriented faculty are certainly *not* more likely than their research-oriented colleagues to have traveled or worked abroad within the past 10 years, or to have collaborated with an academic from another country. However, when looking at faculty responses from each country individually, the findings may indicate that while teaching orientation does play an important role in the international dimension of faculty life in several countries—most noticeably in England and the United States—the Carnegie data reflect only modest support for the notion that teaching-oriented faculty are generally less internationally-active than their research-oriented colleagues.

One particularly useful area for further research would be in determining the level of *opportunities* to travel or work abroad found in each of these countries. It is most likely that opportunities to engage in international work are extremely limited if not tied in some way to a research agenda. Indeed, very few programs exist which encourage teachers to go abroad to teach. Faculty exchange programs, such as the world-renowned Fulbright program in the United States, typically pick recipients largely by scholarly reputation rather than anything related to their classroom instructional activities. To be sure, this is changing somewhat in parts of the world which have seen a rise of regionalism in economic and educational cooperation. Perhaps the most famous current examples are the SOCRATES and ERASMUS programs in Europe, which provide teaching fellowships "to stimulate the creation of new teaching materials" and "to support academics with exceptional abilities and teachers in developing a European dimension in their field" (deWitt, 1996: 2).

Certainly, more opportunities for teaching-oriented faculty to work abroad would have some impact on higher education internationally. However, if it could be proven that adequate opportunities are already available, then we might deduce that the primary reason teaching-oriented faculty do not go abroad is less a matter of resources or opportunity, and more a matter of personal choice. This would lead to a further understanding of the impact teaching orientation plays in the lives of faculty, particularly regarding the choices they make. Thus, it seems useful to look at what the Carnegie data show about whether teaching-oriented faculty feel there is indeed a need for opportunities to travel and do work abroad.

VIEWS TOWARD FACULTY AND STUDENT INTERNATIONAL MOBILITY

"Foreign students and scholars are a central part of academic life, reflecting a growing internationalism in higher education worldwide" (Altbach, 1997: 222). Indeed, concern for furthering international mobility of faculty and students has led to a blossoming of "sister-college" arrangements and international studies offices at many university and college campuses worldwide. International mobility is a primary focus of several organizations, such as the National Association for Foreign Student Affairs (NAFSA) and the Council on International Educational Studies (CIES), as well as government-sponsored efforts, such as the Fulbright and Rhodes scholarship programs, and the ERASMUS, SOCRATES and LEONARDO projects in Europe. "Japan, following a national study, established a goal of attracting 100,000 foreign scholars by the year 2000" (Altbach, 1997: 213). Clearly, there is a growing recognition worldwide of the importance of faculty and student international mobility.

As Altbach (1997) observes, "Foreign student and scholars are among the most visible aspects of the internationalism of higher education. They are concrete manifestations of the ways in which the knowledge network functions" (p. 207). However, according to the Carnegie data, "the range of international faculty mobility varies widely, from Israel—where 90 percent of the respondents indicated experiences studying abroad—to Brazil, Russia and the United States, where only about one-third of respondents reported such activity" (Altbach & Lewis, 1996: 39). The question then arises of whether faculty are not going abroad because they choose not to, or because they are not afforded the opportunity to do so by their institution. Thus, the Carnegie survey administrators sought to determine whether faculty believed that more opportunities are needed for studying and working abroad.

According to the Carnegie data, "faculty overall agree that colleges and universities should do more to promote student and faculty mobility from one country to another" (Altbach & Lewis, 1996: 40). In the United States, "the concept of learning by being there is extremely popular" (Haas, 1996: 378). The widespread agreement with this item on the survey may reflect worldwide dissatisfaction with current opportunities to study or teach abroad. Indeed, as one U.S. survey respondent indicated:

> I feel that much more should be done to promote international faculty exchanges. It was only with extensive personal networking that I was able to find a teaching position abroad. We have many international students, are teaching more international classes, but we don't have any methods or procedures for actively promoting faculty exchanges. (Haas, 1996: 377)

Clearly, most faculty worldwide feel that their institutions should provide more opportunities for international mobility. However, if teaching-oriented faculty are less likely to go abroad or to collaborate with the colleagues internationally (as indicated earlier in this chapter), one might expect to find that these faculty are also relatively less concerned with the need for more international student and faculty mobility. Indeed, teaching-oriented faculty in a majority of countries surveyed were significantly *less likely* to indicate agreement with the statement, "universities and colleges should do more to promote student and faculty mobility from one country to another." (see Table 9.3).

TABLE 9.3

Are teaching-oriented faculty **more or less likely** than their colleagues to agree with the statement, "Universities and colleges should do more to promote student and faculty mobility from one country to another"? (Q67c)*

MORE Likely	LESS likely		No Significant Relationship
	Australia	r= -.14	Brazil
	Chile	r= -.11	Hong Kong
	Germany	r= -.13	Japan
	Israel	r= -.35	Korea
	Mexico	r= -.09	Russia
	Sweden	r= -.06	
	United States	r= -.12	

* this item was omitted from the survey administered in England and the Netherlands.

With the exception of faculty in Asia, Brazil and Russia, teaching-oriented faculty were less likely than their research-oriented colleagues to indicate a need for more opportunities to study or work abroad. Interestingly, a much stronger correlation was observed in Israel (r= -.35) than in any other country. This indicates a pointedly strong negative reaction among teaching-oriented faculty to this survey item, which raises the question of "why." Is there too much opportunity already, or is there some reason why Israeli teaching-oriented faculty might rather stay home than travel? A qualitative analysis of Israeli faculty would surely prove useful for addressing these questions further.

As observed earlier, opportunities to engage in international work are much less common for teaching-oriented faculty than for their research-oriented colleagues. However, according to this analysis, teaching-oriented faculty in most countries surveyed do not seem to be particularly concerned about this. Further, teaching-oriented faculty worldwide are *not* more likely than their research-oriented colleagues to indicate that "universities and colleges should do more to promote student and faculty mobility from one country to another." In fact, in most countries surveyed, they are considerably less likely than their research-oriented colleagues to see a need for opportunities for going abroad.

Perhaps this finding is related to others presented in this study which reflect a relationship between orientation towards teaching and stronger loyalty to one's institution versus their academic discipline. As Altbach (1997) observes, "Foreign students and scholars are among the most critical parts of the international knowledge system . . . They are the "carriers" of knowledge across borders. They are the embodiment of the cosmopolitan scientific culture" (p. 211). The findings presented in this analysis of the Carnegie data indicate that the "cosmopolitan scientific culture" may not provide much in the way of international mobility for teaching-oriented faculty. Based on this distinction between "cosmopolitan" and "local" faculty (Gouldner, 1957), it is also likely that teaching-oriented faculty are generally less likely to see a need for developing connections with their colleagues in other countries.

CONNECTIONS WITH SCHOLARS IN OTHER COUNTRIES

"The relationships built up by foreign scholars are often quite productive not only for them and their research but also for developing institutional links and long-term collaboration" (Altbach, 1997: 211). It is widely agreed that the distribution of information and knowledge has reached new cross-national dimensions, and that this "international network" involves faculty and students worldwide. "Scholars are part of an "invisible college" that constitutes disciplines and specialties, directly involved in the international network" (Altbach, 1997: 207). Thus, the Carnegie survey administrators sought to determine how important international connections are to faculty. What they found is encouraging—"more than three quarters of faculty surveyed in most countries indicate that contacts with scholars in other countries are important for their professional work" (Altbach & Lewis, 1996, p.40). Notably, only the United States and England do not fall into this category, perhaps an indication of their dominance in professional conference markets and scholarly journal publishing.

In observing the development of an "international community of scholars," Altbach and Lewis (1996) noted that "as the world has become increasingly interdependent and national academic boundaries have been blurred, science and scholarship are becoming increasingly international" (p. 36). Perhaps it can even be said that science and scholarship are the prime arenas in which opportunities for international connections are most available. This has implications for our discussion regarding the teaching-oriented professoriate, for as they are less interested in research, they may also be less interested in international connections generally. Indeed, this analysis of the Carnegie data found that with the exception of Australia and Russia, teaching-oriented faculty worldwide were significantly *less likely* than research-oriented faculty to agree with the statement, "Connections with scholars in other countries are important." (see Table 9.4).

TABLE 9.4

Are teaching-oriented faculty **more or less likely** than their colleagues to agree with the statement, "Connections with scholars in other countries are very important to my professional work"? (Q67a)

MORE Likely	LESS likely		No Significant Relationship
	Brazil	r= -.17	Australia
	Chile	r= -.17	Russia
	England	r= -.31	
	Germany	r= -.19	
	Hong Kong	r= -.21	
	Israel	r= -.26	
	Japan	r= -.13	
	Korea	r= -.10	
	Mexico	r= -.20	
	the Netherlands	r= -.26	
	Sweden	r= -.22	
	United States	r= -.26	

The mirror to this trend is equally important—in no country were teaching-oriented faculty *more likely* than their research-oriented colleagues to indicate agreement with the importance of connections with scholars in other countries. Further, the strength of the correlations reflected in Table 9.4 are noteworthy, particularly in responses from faculty in England (r=-.31), Israel, the Netherlands and the United States (r=-.26 for each). Overall, according to the Carnegie data, faculty who are more focused in their work on teaching than research have significantly low concern for maintaining connections with their colleagues abroad. Also, the wording of the statement on the Carnegie survey perhaps contributed to the low response among teaching-oriented colleagues: "Connections with *scholars* in other countries are very important to my professional work." As teaching-oriented faculty may be less likely to consider themselves "scholars", this may have something to do with their response to this survey item.

To a degree, the findings presented here make considerable sense. There are few incentives for teaching-oriented faculty—who are more inclined to be concerned with their classrooms and institutions than their research-oriented colleagues—for maintaining connections with their colleagues abroad. On the other hand, research scholars, whose interests lie more in their discipline, have more incentive than their teaching-oriented colleagues to build international relationships, as disciplines themselves are international. This supports the argument earlier in this discussion that making a distinction between "cosmopolitan" and "local" faculty is both valid and useful.

Overall, as observed earlier in this study, there may be few reasons for teaching-oriented faculty to desire an international dimension to their work, unless it is entirely for reasons of personal curiosity. So far in this chapter, the findings have consistently indicated that teaching orientation is correlated with a significantly lower concern than other faculty over the international dimensions of academic work. Thus, one might also expect that teaching-oriented faculty are less likely to see a need to read books or journals published abroad.

READING BOOKS AND JOURNALS PUBLISHED ABROAD

In order to "stay connected" with one's discipline, it is important to attend professional conferences and keep abreast of relevant literature. As academic international connections foster and grow most usually within disciplinary contexts, faculty have an increasing need to read books and journals published beyond their nation's borders. To be sure, the need for this varies for faculty in different countries, particularly between those in "peripheral" nations. Faculty employed by universities in the developing world "find themselves at a disadvantage in the international network" (Altbach, 1997: 29). The Western world—and Western language—completely dominates the published world, which leads to a significant disadvantage for faculty elsewhere. Faculty in the United States have relatively less incentive than their (for example) Latin American colleagues to read books and journals published abroad, for the simple fact that there are far more books published in the U.S. than in all of Latin America.

The perceived value of reading books and journals published abroad can vary considerably depending on faculty location, interests, and discipline. However, "in all countries except the United States, more than 90 percent of faculty indicated that a scholar or scientist must read books and journals published abroad to keep up with his or her discipline" (Altbach & Lewis, 1996: 40). Such overwhelming support for this is certainly indicative of the growing international dimensions of higher education. However, it may also indicate that much of this growth in international connections is through the printed word—that is, there may be considerably stronger support among researchers than teachers for reading texts published abroad. A regression analysis of the Carnegie data confirmed this by finding that teaching-oriented faculty worldwide are significantly less likely than their research-oriented colleagues to indicate agreement with the statement, "A scholar must read books and journals published abroad" (see Table 9.5).

TABLE 9.5

Are teaching-oriented faculty **more or less likely** than their colleagues to agree with the statement, **"**A scholar must read books and journals published abroad**"**? (Q67b)*

MORE Likely	LESS likely		No Significant Relationship
	Australia	r= -.30	Hong Kong
	Brazil	r= -.19	Russia
	Chile	r= -.14	
	Germany	r= -.24	
	Israel	r= -.20	
	Japan	r= -.11	
	Korea	r= -.06	
	Mexico	r= -.15	
	the Netherlands	r= -.17	
	Sweden	r= -.24	
	United States	r= -.27	

* this item was omitted from the survey administered in England.

The mirror to this trend is equally important—in no country were teaching-oriented faculty *more likely* than their research-oriented colleagues to indicate agreement with the importance of reading books and journals published abroad. Further, it is important to note the strength of the correlations reflected in Table 9.5. The most significant correlation was found among faculty responses from Australia (r= -.30), where geographic insularity may have some impact on how "international" teaching-oriented faculty are likely to feel. In the United States (r= -.27), the relationship found here echoes concerns made by several other researchers. The Carnegie survey results also indicated that U.S. faculty were significantly less likely than their colleagues in any other country to agree with the statement, "Connections with scholars in other countries are very important to my professional work" and were less likely than elsewhere to have traveled abroad. "Is this because the United States is a worldwide center for academic publishing?" (Boyer, Altbach & Whitelaw, 1994: 20)

Indeed, "the American professoriate is at the center of an international knowledge network" (Altbach, 1997:114). However, "this has unfortunately fostered a unique American academic research system, in which scholars and scientists remain remarkably insular in their attitudes and their activities" (Altbach, 1997: 129). Overall, the Carnegie data indicate that faculty in the United States, regardless of whether their primary interests lie in teaching or research, are less internationally-minded than their colleagues in any other country surveyed. "American academics compare poorly with their colleagues in other countries when it comes to professional efforts to learn from and contribute to the international community of professionals in higher education" (Haas, 1996: 386). This parochial nature of U.S. faculty must change if we are to effectively rise to the challenge of an increasingly inter-connected world. One of the most important aspects of this challenge is how we communicate the values of globalism to future generations of leaders. Thus, our curriculum must reflect a more international focus.

INTERNATIONAL DIMENSIONS OF THE CURRICULUM

The primary teaching activities of many institutions worldwide are organized within a curriculum of some kind. However, the term curriculum does not garner the same definition cross-nationally. In countries with similar higher education systems as the U.S., discipline-based curricula are developed for particular stages of the higher education process, with basic review or "survey" courses provided in early undergraduate years, and more advanced research skills development courses and in-depth explorations of a particular topic are offered in graduate programs, or possibly the senior undergraduate years. In other countries, such as Germany, there is limited or no advanced study by coursework at all. These learning sequences and course patterns are regulated more closely in public education than in the private sector. In general, the past several decades have seen increasing diversification and specialization of higher education curricula. Also, there has been consistent pressure from the business community—as well as from members of the academic community—to make curricula more relevant to the skills needed in the job market. Clearly, there is a widespread belief that student success beyond graduation is influenced in some way by their institution's curriculum.

As Clark Kerr (1990) observed, "we live in a world where . . . the worldwide advancement of learning has become the single most influential factor affecting the human condition" (p. 12). This "internationalization of learning" is an important reason to develop the kinds of curricula that provide students with a reasonably useful sense of the world around them. As argued in earlier chapters of this volume, our understanding of the academic responsibility of teaching needs to encompass an international dimension in order for our students–and our colleagues–to adequately address the demands of this increasing global interdependence.

Few areas of academic work are more important for this to occur than in our curricular choices. It is thus a good sign that "faculty worldwide are convinced that the curriculum should be more international in scope" (Altbach and Lewis, 1996: 38). In Australia and the United States, less than half of the faculty were in agreement with this statement. However, teaching-oriented faculty, arguably those most concerned with their institution's curriculum, were significantly less likely to agree with this notion of internationalizing the curriculum (see Table 9.6)

TABLE 9.6		
Are teaching-oriented faculty **more or less likely** than their colleagues to agree with the statement, "The curriculum at this institution should be more international in focus"? (Q67d)*		
MORE Likely	**LESS likely**	**No Significant Relationship**
Israel r= .02 Mexico r= .08	Australia r= -.02 Brazil r= -.09 Chile r= -.10 Germany r= -.07 Korea r= -.04 United States r= -.05	Hong Kong Japan Russia Sweden

* this item was omitted from the survey administered in England and the Netherlands.

Responses from faculty in Israel and Mexico were the exception here— teaching-oriented faculty were significantly more likely to indicate a need for their institution's curriculum to be more international. The case of Israel is particularly unusual—less than a third of all Israeli faculty supported this idea, and as Altbach and Lewis (1996) observed, this may be a reflection of the fact that the curriculum in Israel is already international in scope. However, the situation is different in Mexico—even upon the heels of NAFTA, at the time the Carnegie survey was conducted, one could not reasonably describe the Mexican higher education curriculum at most institutions as being international in scope. Faculty in Mexico were more likely than in other countries to indicate that their students rarely or never have studied abroad, or that foreign students have been enrolled at their institutions. However, faculty in Mexico were stronger in their support for an international curriculum than in most of the countries in the survey, and teaching-oriented faculty here are considerably more in favor of an international curriculum than their colleagues.

This finding is particularly important for higher education policy in the United States and Canada. If teaching-oriented faculty in Mexico are considerably more supportive of an international dimension to their curriculum, there may be a considerable likelihood that they would also be willing to work with their international colleagues across the border in achieving that internationalism. This would seem an important window of opportunity to encourage Mexican higher education toward a direction which sheds favorable light on the goals of NAFTA and other North American regional policies. Certainly, this is worth exploring in some future research study.

Overall, the correlations presented in Table 9.6 indicate a mixed relationship between teaching orientation and faculty views toward internationalizing the curriculum. Among the teaching-oriented professoriate in many countries there is considerably less support for an international curriculum. This finding is somewhat problematic when considering that teaching-oriented faculty are those who are most likely to teach, and thus are more likely to have a more vocal involvement with curriculum policies at their institution. If we are to effectively rise to the challenges of our increasingly global environment, we must find ways to change teaching-oriented faculty views so that they are more supportive of an international focus in the curriculum. As British scholar W.H. Taylor (1993) observes, "the young need to be educated to realize how much of their lives will be determined by transnational forces" (p. 21).

CONCLUSION

"In a world where international relationships in commerce, science, and technology are seen as crucial to "competitiveness," the international role of academe is ever more important" (Altbach, 1997: 207). This study has adopted the view that the strength of a faculty member's preference is an important window through which to understand more fully how faculty view the international dimensions of higher education. The research presented in this chapter tested the validity of a hypothesis which stated that teaching-oriented faculty view the international dimension of higher education differently than do research-oriented faculty. The opposite of this, the null hypothesis, states that there is no real difference between teaching-oriented faculty and research-oriented faculty in terms of their perspectives toward the international dimension of higher education. According to this analysis of the Carnegie data, we can reject the null hypothesis.

However, this analysis did not always find internationally-shared similarities in the relationships between teaching orientation and faculty responses to the Carnegie survey. Rather, this study of the Carnegie data uncovered several kinds of trends, which can be meaningfully organized into one of four categories:

I. Internationally significant - trends in the data that were shared throughout a majority of the countries surveyed;

II. Internationally modest - relationships that were found in the data from fewer than half (but more than two) of the countries surveyed;

III. Mixed results - the data indicate a relationship in one direction in some countries, and a relationship in the opposite direction in others; and

IV. Unique findings - data relationships that were found only among the responses from one country or specific region.

The following discussion reviews the findings of this analysis in relation to these four sub-topics, and explores implications of the more significant trends. Also, in presenting the findings of this analysis, the view is taken that where teaching orientation had no significant relationship whatsoever with faculty responses to a particular item on the survey, this itself is an international trend of sorts.

(I) Significant International Trends

In several cases, the regression analyses showed correlations that were either always positive or always negative for all or most countries surveyed. These findings provide an international insight into what it means to prefer teaching over research.

1. Teaching-oriented faculty worldwide are significantly less likely than their research-oriented colleagues to indicate that connections with faculty in other countries are important.

2. Internationally, teaching-oriented faculty are significantly less likely than their colleagues to agree that scholars should read books published abroad.

3. In a majority of countries surveyed, teaching-oriented faculty were significantly less likely than their research-oriented colleagues to have collaborated with faculty from another country in the past 10 years.

4. Teaching-oriented faculty in most countries surveyed were less likely than their colleagues to have traveled or worked abroad within the past 10 years.

5. For the most part, teaching-oriented faculty worldwide are not *more* internationally minded than their research-oriented colleagues.

(II) Internationally Modest Findings

Several of the relationships found in this analysis of the Carnegie data are shared by more than a few countries, but not enough to consider them internationally significant.

1. In half the countries surveyed, teaching-oriented faculty were significantly less likely than their colleagues to indicate that their institution should do more to promote faculty and student mobility from one country to another.

2. In half the countries surveyed, teaching-oriented faculty were significantly less likely than their colleagues to indicate that the curriculum should be more international in focus.

(III) Mixed Results

There are also several cases in which teaching orientation had a positive correlation in some countries, and a negative one in others.

1. Teaching orientation has a relationship with how faculty view the need for an international focus in their institution's curriculum. In several countries surveyed, teaching-oriented faculty were significantly less likely than their colleagues to indicate that the curriculum should be more international in focus, while in others, teaching-oriented faculty were more supportive of an international dimension to their curriculum.

(IV) Unique Findings

In several cases, this analysis of the Carnegie data found a relationship between teaching orientation and faculty response to a particular survey item that was not shared with any other country surveyed.

1. Correlations between teaching orientation and views toward international dimensions of higher education are strongest and more frequent among faculty in Australia, England, and the United States.

2. Responses from Hong Kong indicate virtually no difference between teaching-oriented faculty and research-oriented faculty regarding their views toward the international dimensions of higher education. This is particularly interesting given the considerable international focus of higher education Hong Kong has had for years.

3. Responses from Russia indicate virtually no difference between teaching-oriented faculty and research-oriented faculty

regarding their views toward the international dimensions of higher education. However, the validity of the data here are considerably suspect.

Summary and Implications

One implication of these findings is that we must find new ways to engage teaching-oriented faculty so that they feel more strongly that they are a part of a vibrant and exciting international academic profession. "We live in a world where the worldwide advancement of learning has become the single most influential factor affecting the human condition" (Kerr, 1990: 12). Our understanding of the academic responsibility of teaching needs to encompass an international dimension, in order for our students—and our colleagues—to adequately address the demands of this increasing global interdependence. The findings of this study provide insight into how faculty who prefer to teach see the world and their place in it. Unfortunately, the picture we are presented with is not good in terms of international perspectives among the teaching-oriented professoriate. Throughout this analysis of the Carnegie survey, teaching-oriented faculty were considerably less supportive of the international dimensions of higher education. This has implications for both research and policy on institutional, national, regional and international levels.

To begin with, institutions of higher education must find ways to engage the teaching professoriate in a way that encourages a stronger international perspective. For the reasons described in this chapter, as well as previous chapters of this volume, teachers must recognize and convey to their students the importance of a global perspective. For the sake of a nation's current generation of students, governmental policies should also pay heed to fostering an international dimension in the classroom. The findings presented in this chapter inform these efforts. At any institution of higher education, teaching-oriented faculty will play a key role in the development and adoption of an international curriculum. As teaching-oriented faculty are engaged more in campus-based activities than their research-oriented colleagues (Altbach & Lewis, 1996), they are considerably more likely to have a meaningful role in the adoption of a curriculum at any institution. However, according to the results of this analysis, there exists a significant challenge of convincing teaching-oriented faculty that an international curriculum is important. Thus, the findings of this analysis of the Carnegie data suggest that we must develop new ways to change the way the teaching professoriate views the international dimensions of higher education, if we are to be successful in moving the curriculum toward a more international direction. We must find ways to encourage teaching-oriented faculty to recognize the important "internationalization of learning" (Kerr, 1990) in ways that will enable future generations to be successful in an increasingly global marketplace.

Regionally, issues of language, economic and political cooperation, and social understanding require an international perspective among faculty, students, and society at large. One of the most common and effective means for developing an international perspective is to travel and work in other countries. Indeed, at least among faculty in the United States, "the concept of learning by being there is extremely popular" (Haas, 1996: 378). However, if significant opportunities are not provided for teaching-oriented faculty to travel or work abroad, this can have negative implications for our efforts to internationalize our classrooms and our institutions—the arenas in which the loyalties of teaching-oriented faculty's are strongest. While opportunities are rare for teaching-oriented faculty to work abroad, they do not appear to feel that this is a significant problem. In fact, in most countries surveyed, they are considerably less likely than their research-oriented colleagues to see a need for opportunities for going abroad. Convincing the teaching-oriented professoriate otherwise is thus an important challenge to address in the coming years.

Overall, the findings presented in this study suggest that teaching-oriented faculty have much in common internationally, commonalities which provide an insight into what it means to prefer teaching over research worldwide. The importance of the international dimension of these findings cannot be overstated. Significant trends were found among faculty responses in virtually all of the countries surveyed by the Carnegie Foundation. Thus, despite significant structural or cultural differences, teaching-oriented faculty appear to feel the same around the world about the relative unimportance of the international dimension of higher education. These findings have particular significance for our growing understanding of academe as a truly international profession. While there is certainly an increasing amount of attention among research-oriented faculty towards the international dimension in higher education, this focus is not shared by teaching-oriented faculty. Indeed, how can this be any different? Teaching is basically an activity located within the institution, and is evaluated according to institutional guidelines of quality, whereas academic research is an activity generated primarily for the consumption of those outside the institution, and is thus compared with external measures of quality. The international dimension of this study provides an important addition the Gouldner's (1957) differentiation between "cosmopolitan" and "local" academics.

As international connections become increasingly common among academic disciplines, it may be expected that researchers are considerably more internationally-minded than teaching-oriented faculty. The findings of this initial analysis of the Carnegie survey data support this expectation, but to a surprisingly limited degree in some cases. Certainly, the news is good for research-oriented faculty—as the correlations in this analysis show that stronger teaching orientation is related to lower internationalism, they also show that stronger research orientation is related to stronger internationalism. However, together these trends suggest the potential for a substantial rift in the academic profession, between the "cosmopolitan" faculty and their "local" colleagues, over issues of curricular reform, institutional policy, and the overall priorities of the profession. How the professoriate address-es the issues raised here will certainly have lasting affects on the future of higher education.

Summing Up: Implications for Further Research on the Teaching-Oriented Professoriate

INTRODUCTION

This chapter reviews the findings presented in previous six chapters of this volume, and concludes that (1) teaching-oriented faculty differ from research-oriented faculty, and (2) there are international trends among these differences. In order to provide a context in which to present these findings, the chapter begins with a brief review of the study's theoretical framework, then suggests implications of the study's findings for the larger issues that confront faculty worldwide, and once again endorses the importance of international and comparative research on the academic profession. Looking at cross-national consistencies in the data helps to reduce complex levels to meaningful comparisons—such as culture, language and geography—and gain a collective understanding of issues shared by faculty across the major regions of the world. The international dimension of this study is both timely and useful for expanding our understanding of how faculty worldwide view academic work and life.

THE CONTEXT

This study is based upon a belief that teaching-oriented faculty are different from research-oriented faculty, and that these differences are likely to be shared among academics worldwide. This belief is supported by a considerable amount of existing literature on the academic profession. An important perspective in this area is provided by Gouldner's (1957) description of how some faculty emphasize their disciplinary affiliations (cosmopolitans) while others lean more toward their institutional loyalties (locals). Whether a professor responds to the question of "who are you?" with "an Associate Professor at Boston College" or "a Mathematician" says much about the nature of that professor's professional loyalties and views toward being a member of the academic profession. Haas (1996) draws many useful distinctions between a "research cohort" and a "teaching cohort" in the U.S. responses to the Carnegie survey. Making such a distinction has broad implications for our understanding of how faculty approach academic work. In an essay on management theory in higher education, Hughes (1985) observed that "the standards by which professionals judge their work are likely to be closely related to the intellectual discipline of their specialist field and less directly to the instrumental expediences of their employing organization. Loyalty to the organization is thus liable to take a second place to the concept of solidarity with professional colleagues outside the boundaries of the organization itself" (p. 3197). This study adds an important international dimension to the work of these researchers. As described later in this chapter, the distinction made between research-oriented "cosmopolitans" and teaching-oriented "locals" has implications for how we approach policies of change in higher education.

The attention paid to exploring and understanding the attitudes and work preferences of faculty has grown considerably over the past three decades, and the body of research on the academic profession as a sociological entity continues to expand. This study adds to this body of research, with an international look at many commonalities shared by teaching-oriented faculty, including demographic background, professional preparation, and views toward academic work and life, and toward national and international dimensions of higher education. The study set out to examine the validity of three general research hypotheses:

  1. Teaching-oriented faculty internationally share similar demographic profiles, academic rank, or other background variables that distinguish them from their research-oriented colleagues.

  2. Teaching-oriented faculty reflect different views than their research-oriented colleagues toward certain dimensions of academe, specifically their perspectives toward: (1) teaching and the assessment of teaching; (2) their institutional working conditions; (3) their academic disciplines and the profession; (4) the role of higher education in society; and (5) the international dimension of higher education.

  3. There are meaningful international trends in how teaching-oriented faculty responded to the Carnegie survey differently than research-oriented faculty.

According to the analyses presented in this volume, the Carnegie international survey data support each of these hypotheses at the $p < .05$ level of significance. It must be remembered here that where teaching orientation plays a significant role in how faculty responded to the Carnegie survey, so must its opposite—orientation towards research. Stronger research orientation is correlated in the opposite manner than stronger teaching orientation is. For example, where the findings indicate that teaching-oriented faculty are less internationally-minded, research-oriented faculty are seen as more internationally-minded.

THE FINDINGS

This international exploration of the Carnegie Foundation survey data has yielded several interesting data relationships concerning faculty orientation toward teaching. Using standard regression analysis techniques common to social sciences research, this study found that despite diverse regional, cultural, systemic, and other influences on faculty responding to the survey, descriptive information can be used to predict orientation towards teaching or research, and this orientation has a relationship with how faculty view several dimensions of academic work and life. The international trends observed in this analysis of the data include the following:

> 1. Teaching-oriented faculty share similar demographic backgrounds and views toward their training for the academic profession.
>
> 2. Teaching orientation is related to how faculty responded to survey questions about teaching and the assessment of teaching.
>
> 3. Teaching-oriented faculty feel differently than research-oriented faculty about their institutional working conditions.
>
> 4. Teaching orientation is associated with how faculty feel about their academic discipline and the academic profession.
>
> 5. Teaching orientation is related to how faculty feel about the role of higher education in society.
>
> 6. Teaching-oriented faculty are significantly less concerned than research-oriented faculty about the international dimensions of higher education.
>
> 7. There are significant international similarities in how teaching-oriented faculty responded to the Carnegie survey differently than research-oriented faculty.

This chapter explores each of these findings and their implications for our understanding of the academic profession. The findings are presented in a similar order as the chapters of the volume, for the sake of organizational consistency. Also, while several mixed and unique findings were produced by this analysis of the Carnegie data, this study adopts the research philosophy that cross-national *similarities* inform more of our understanding of the academic profession than do cross-national differences. Additionally,

"cross-national similarities lend themselves readily to sociological interpretation, while cross-national differences are much more difficult to interpret"
(Kohn, 1987: 31). Looking at cross-national consistencies in the data helps
to reduce complex levels to meaningful comparisons—such as culture, language and geography—and gain a collective understanding of issues shared
by faculty across the major regions of the world. Thus, national differences
can be largely set aside in this study, in looking for a shared phenomenon—
in this case, how orientation toward teaching is related to faculty perspectives toward various dimensions of academic work and life.

**Finding #1: Teaching-oriented faculty have similar demographic back-
grounds and views toward their professional preparation.**

Using multiple regression analysis for each country's data sample, this
study found several variables which collectively account for considerable
amounts of the variance in responses to the survey question on orientation
towards teaching or research, ranging from 35% in Chile to 11% in the
Netherlands (see Appendix B). This study found that throughout the survey
faculty who indicated a relatively stronger preference for teaching were
more likely to be female than male, and more likely to be older than their
colleagues. Tenure, rank, or other academic appointment variables were not
significant predictors of orientation towards teaching or research. That is,
teaching orientation appears equally strong among faculty of all ranks, both
tenured and untenured. Further, while part-time faculty rarely are expected
to engage in research activities, they are no more or less teaching-oriented
than their full-time colleagues.

The most important international predictor of teaching orientation found
in this study of the Carnegie data is a faculty member's professional training. This analysis found that in virtually every country surveyed:

> • Higher academic credentials are negatively correlated to
> teaching orientation—that is, holding a doctoral degree was
> found to be a significant predictor of lower preference for
> teaching.
> • Faculty who felt more positive about their training for teach-
> ing were significantly more likely to indicate a strong prefer-
> ence for teaching.
> • Faculty who felt more positive about their training for
> research were significantly less likely to indicate a strong pref-
> erence for teaching.

In most cases, the regression analysis showed correlations that were either
always positive or always negative across all countries' survey responses.
There are a few cases in which teaching orientation had a positive correlation in some countries, and a negative one in others, but overall the findings show that teaching orientation is correlated in much the same way

throughout all the countries surveyed. Thus, these findings provide an international insight into who teaching-oriented faculty are.

Implications

This analysis of the Carnegie survey data supports an existing body of literature that shows women and older professors are more inclined towards teaching activities than research. These findings also do not support assertions made by Sykes (1988) and others that tenure allows professors to sit back on their haunches and neglect their classrooms or avoid any future research productivity. These findings also raise questions about the research focus of typical doctoral degree programs, particularly in an era which has seen rising demands for improving teaching in postsecondary education. Indeed, there are efforts to redefine the role of the professor and to place more emphasis on teaching and less on research (Altbach, 1995).

It could largely be expected that faculty who feel well prepared to engage in a certain activity would enjoy that activity more than their colleagues who feel less prepared. The same would arguably hold true for any number of professions. Certainly, graduate training programs can play a prominent role in a faculty member's orientation towards teaching. The findings presented in this analysis support the argument made by Boyer (1990) and others that graduate training needs to incorporate a more 'teaching-friendly' focus. That is, without losing sight of the academic goal of creating knowledge through traditional research, future university and college faculty must be trained with an increased understanding of—and appreciation for—the importance of teaching. We have the intellectually challenging task of developing more comprehensive training programs for future faculty which address both disciplinary needs for research and institutional needs for effective teaching.

In showing that a faculty member's teaching orientation can be influenced by their training for the profession, we find a new importance in how these programs are designed and administered. As Kenneth Eble (1972) observed, "Upgrading the preparation of college teachers in graduate schools is fundamentally important not only to improving teaching but to refashioning higher education" (p. 180). Certainly, the research presented in this volume echoes these and other scholars' concerns, and provides an international dimension to the importance of examining and developing new approaches to training future academics.

Finding #2: Teaching orientation is significantly related with how faculty feel about teaching and the assessment of teaching.

In over half the countries in which this question was asked, teaching-oriented faculty were significantly more likely than their colleagues to indicate that faculty should spend more time with students outside the classroom. However, in general, faculty with stronger preference for teaching than for research are *not* significantly different from research-oriented faculty in their approaches to teaching—that is, teaching orientation does not appear to play a major role regarding the amount of the time they spend in their undergraduate classrooms on lectures, classroom discussions, or laboratory work. In contrast, teaching-oriented faculty worldwide are significantly more likely than their colleagues to support the use of teaching effectiveness as the primary criterion for the hiring and promotion of faculty. While a majority of faculty (regardless of orientation towards teaching or research) in every country surveyed felt that student opinions should be used in evaluating teaching effectiveness, support for this is stronger among teaching-oriented faculty in Europe, Japan, Australia and the United States, but not in Latin America. The international dimension of these findings brings an important element to our understanding of how faculty feel their teaching should be assessed. The Carnegie survey collected data from a diverse population of faculty, and yet there appears to be a great deal of similarity among their responses to questions on the assessment of teaching.

Implications

Research has shown that faculty who engage in research more than in teaching tend to be rewarded more prominently than faculty who primarily teach. Thus, this finding brings a new dimension to the ongoing debate over faculty roles, rewards, and tenure. In a recent analysis of teaching in the United States, Lewis (1996) noted that "for many academics, teaching is an intrinsically motivated activity . . . it is a task that motivates, not because of the promise of some external reward, but because it is something they simply enjoy doing" (p.147). This perspective may indeed be shared by faculty worldwide. According to the data collected by the Carnegie survey, there is considerable support among faculty worldwide for a stronger recognition of the importance of teaching effectiveness. There is certainly a need worldwide for new approaches to the assessment of teaching and faculty productivity. This study can be useful for informing strategies for evaluating teaching performance across disciplinary and geographic boundaries. The approach of this study—looking at predictors and outcomes of faculty preferences for teaching—is thus both timely and useful for both institutional and broader policy discussions.

Boyer's (1990) *Scholarship Reconsidered* summed up the situation nicely. "Today, at most four-year institutions, the requirements of tenure and promotion continue to focus heavily on research and on articles published in journals, especially those that are refereed. Good teaching is expected, but it is often inadequately assessed" (p.28). Boyer calls for redefining the term *scholarship* to incorporate the importance of effective teaching and college classroom interaction. However, the term *effective teaching* has yet to find a common definition in many academic circles. Indeed, anyone who carries out research on teaching effectiveness quickly runs into the problem of evaluating the outcomes of teaching (McKeachie, 1990). How do classroom processes affect learning outcomes? Students react differently to the same teacher, and yet the majority of current teaching assessment methods throughout the world rely on student evaluations. There is worldwide concern over the inadequacies of current methods for evaluating teaching, a concern which has fostered a growing body of research and suggestions. One idea for improving the assessment of teaching is provided in Murray's (1995) discussion of teaching portfolios. Also, Wright (1998) and others have continually advocated the use of instructional development workshops and institutes to bring faculty together around this issue, and for this "community" to decide how best to evaluate their teaching.

The notion of a unified "academic community" is particularly important when revisiting Gouldner's (1957) distinction between "local" and "cosmopolitan" academics. As earlier chapters of this volume have described, the Carnegie data appear to indicate that teaching-oriented faculty lean more toward "local" affiliations—particularly, their institution—while research-oriented faculty are more concerned with "cosmopolitan" affiliations—mostly, their academic discipline. Some researchers in academic management theory have adopted Gouldner's distinction in exploring differences between professional and administrative concerns. As Hughes (1979) observed, the standards by which professionals judge their work are likely to be closely related to the intellectual discipline of their specialist field and less directly to the instrumental expediences of their employing organization. Loyalty to the organization is thus liable to take a second place to the concept of solidarity with professional colleagues outside the boundaries of the organization itself.

In *A Teaching Doctorate?: The Doctor of Arts Degree, Then and Now*, Judith Glazer (1993) chronicles the failure of the DA—a teaching-centered degree—to make teaching more equal to research. She observes, "Neither Boyer's advocacy of the scholarship of teaching nor Bok's formulations for training graduate students as junior faculty addresses an extremely complex issue: the paradigmatic conflict between research and teaching. A resolution will occur not through better faculty-development programs in research universities or changes in promotion and tenure policies to give greater recognition to teaching but through a more fundamental restructuring of higher education" (p. 36). However, the findings of this study suggest that even "fundamental restructuring" will lead nowhere unless we first address the issue of how to recognize and appropriately reward each faculty member for engaging in activities in which they are most interested in doing. As Bensimon (1996) observes, "we need to think about faculty in terms of differences rather in terms of sameness" (p. 46). Instead of attempting to develop sweeping, universal changes in the academic profession, as many scholars have proposed, this study calls for a closer attention to the relationship between each faculty member's professional identity—and particularly, orientation towards research or towards teaching—and how their work is encouraged, assessed, and rewarded.

Higher education worldwide must engage teaching-oriented faculty in efforts to improve the evaluation of teaching, as they show the strongest concern for this issue among all faculty. Additionally, as teaching-oriented faculty appear to be significantly concerned about how teaching is rewarded in terms of faculty hiring and promotion, higher education administrators would do well to make new efforts at involving teaching-oriented faculty in hiring and promotion review committees and other related decision-making bodies. The amount of time faculty have available for spending with students outside the classroom also needs a closer look, and is certainly related to the overall need to more adequately recognize and reward the importance of teaching in the academy. Perhaps we should have different forms of assessment for different kinds of faculty, related to their orientation towards teaching or research. The underlying paradigms for how academics perceive their role and responsibilities as classroom teacher need serious exploration. As Boyer (1990) observed, scholarship is multidimensional, and the application, integration, and teaching of knowledge are part of its expanded definition. The findings of this study have several implications for further research that can inform these discussions and future efforts at re-engineering the reward systems for teaching in higher education.

Finding #3: Teaching-oriented faculty hold significantly different views about their institutional working conditions than research-oriented faculty.

Teaching-oriented faculty indicate significantly higher satisfaction than their colleagues with the courses they teach. One might expect teaching-oriented faculty to have stronger views than most faculty toward the courses they teach. Their interests lie primarily in teaching, and they teach more than their research-oriented colleagues. Thus, it is considerably important that this analysis found teaching-oriented faculty to be significantly more satisfied than their colleagues with the courses they teach. However, this raises a significant question of why research-oriented faculty are relatively dissatisfied with the courses they teach.

Teaching orientation is significantly related with how faculty rated the quality of their institution's resources, including the classrooms, laboratories, technology for teaching, computer facilities, and library holdings. The most international trends observed were that teaching-oriented faculty are significantly *more satisfied* than their research-oriented colleagues with their institution's technology for teaching, and are significantly *less satisfied* with their institution's computer facilities. Further, teaching-oriented faculty in a majority of countries surveyed were significantly *more likely* than their colleagues to agree with the statement, "The pressure to publish reduces the quality of teaching at this institution." This seems to reflect a stronger dissatisfaction among teaching-oriented faculty with the research-focused work environment found in colleges and universities worldwide.

Although not as internationally significant as the others presented here, two more trends observed in the data are noteworthy. Teaching-oriented faculty in Brazil, England, Germany, Israel, Sweden and the United States were significantly *less likely* to indicate satisfaction with their prospects for promotion. However, teaching-oriented faculty in Australia, England, Germany, Japan, Korea, the Netherlands and Sweden were *less likely* to indicate intentions of leaving their institution within the next five years. Taken together, these trends appear to indicate that teaching-oriented faculty are either more loyal to their institution than their research-oriented colleagues, or—more likely—that there are fewer opportunities to leave their institution. This has implications for how life in the academy is different for teaching-oriented faculty than for their research-oriented colleagues.

Implications

In looking at the responses from faculty in the United States, Haas (1996) observed that in general, faculty in the United States reflect a distinct contradiction in terms of job satisfaction:

> How can these professionals, specifically 78 percent of the respondents, be satisfied with their job situation as a whole while at the same time expressing dissatisfaction with so many elements of the setting in which they practice their profession? (p. 349)

This contradiction was observed throughout the responses to the Carnegie survey. The international dimension of this trend provides an important opportunity to explore how orientation towards teaching or research is related with faculty satisfaction with institutional working conditions, particularly those which may influence a decision to leave their institution. While teaching orientation does not have an internationally-similar relationship with faculty perspectives toward institutional working conditions altogether, the data relationships found here do lead to some suggestions for future research. As "the working conditions of faculty, inevitably, influence both productivity and morale" (Boyer, Altbach & Whitelaw, 1994: 13), understanding how different kinds of faculty feel about these conditions informs our understanding of the academic profession and higher education organizations.

Certainly, one might expect that teaching-oriented faculty have stronger views than their research-oriented colleagues toward the quality of resources they have to work with in their teaching. After all, teaching-oriented faculty spend more time in the classroom than their research-oriented colleagues. This analysis found that indeed, teaching orientation is significantly correlated with faculty satisfaction with their classrooms, their laboratories, their technology for teaching, their computer facilities, and their library holdings. While the nature of the relationships in the survey data on these items vary between country, it is nonetheless an important distinction to make for our understanding of how teaching orientation is related worldwide with how faculty view academic work.

It is also important to note that the teaching-oriented professoriate worldwide are significantly more satisfied than their research-oriented colleagues with the courses they teach. In other words, faculty who prefer to teach spend more time teaching and are significantly more satisfied with the courses they teach than is the case for their research-oriented colleagues. Thus, one important area for further research is why do research-oriented faculty worldwide indicate stronger *dissatisfaction* with the courses they teach? Is it because they would simply rather be researching than in the classroom, or is this an indication that they are not teaching the kinds of specialized courses that could be more closely associated with their research agenda? Are there significant differences worldwide between courses that teaching-oriented faculty teach, and courses that research-oriented faculty teach? Clearly, further research beyond the Carnegie survey data is necessary for addressing these compelling questions.

An important dimension to this issue concerns the relationship between research and effective teaching. There are two ideological camps in academe that bear different views toward the relationship between teaching and research in the academic profession. On one hand, there are academics who feel that teaching and research are necessarily complementary—good teaching informs good research, and vice versa—and, therefore, faculty should be hired and promoted on the basis of excellence in both areas. On the other hand, there are academics who argue that a faculty member's skills, interest, and available time permit excellence in only one or the other. Their argument is that, given naturally limited resources, one can excel only in teaching or in research, but not in both. Certainly, they argue, a professor's time is not infinite—more time spent on one activity must certainly leave less time to engage in another.

This analysis of the Carnegie data found that teaching orientation is internationally correlated with faculty views toward pressure to publish. Although the nature of the relationships in the survey data vary between countries, a majority of teaching-oriented faculty surveyed were significantly more likely than their research-oriented colleagues to agree with the statement, "the pressure to publish reduces the quality of teaching at this institution." At first glance, this relationship in the data seems intuitive—faculty whose interests lie more strongly in teaching can largely be expected to feel that research negatively impacts their teaching, while their research-oriented colleagues can be expected to feel that this is not the case. The Carnegie data provide a new, international dimension to this issue, and suggests that teaching-oriented faculty may not only have a weak interest in research, but also a somewhat negative view towards the impact of research on that which they hold dearly—classroom instruction. This has considerable implications for current discussions of faculty reward structures.

A recent study by the National Center on Postsecondary Teaching, Learning and Assessment (NCPTLA, 1995) found that faculty with the least amount of student contact hours earn the highest salaries, and that the more refereed publications a faculty member publishes, the higher their salary. If teaching-oriented faculty are more likely to emphasize the importance of teaching effectiveness in faculty hiring and promotion decisions (as observed in Chapter 5), one may wonder whether they are not less disillusioned with current academic reward systems, which typically emphasize research productivity. Further analysis and interpretation of the Carnegie survey data—as well as future studies on the influence of faculty reward systems on professional satisfaction—would be useful in addressing this and other related questions. Overall, these trends indicate a mixed relationship between teaching orientation and how faculty view their institutional working conditions, but there is considerable international dissatisfaction among teaching-oriented faculty with their prospects for promotion. It is likely that this dissatisfaction carries forward to other views they may have about life in the academic profession. The institutional context is but one of several—including the contexts of nation and discipline—that are important to faculty (Clark, 1987). Thus, we now widen the scope of this discussion to include issues beyond the institution, specifically concerning the academic discipline and the academic profession

Finding #4: Teaching-oriented faculty worldwide share similar views toward academic disciplines but in only a few countries are they different from their research-oriented colleagues in their views toward the academic profession.

In almost every country surveyed, teaching-oriented faculty were *less likely* to indicate that this is an especially creative and productive time to be in the academic profession. Further, in most countries surveyed, teaching-oriented faculty indicated more positive associations toward their institution and department than toward their academic discipline (see Chapter 1). As described throughout this study, the distinction made between research-oriented "cosmopolitans" and teaching-oriented "locals" has implications for how we approach policies of change in higher education.

Interestingly, teaching-oriented faculty around the world are not less satisfied with their job than research-oriented faculty—in most countries surveyed, there is no relationship between job satisfaction and teaching orientation, and in a small minority of countries, teaching-oriented faculty are more satisfied with their jobs. Further, despite their views toward the pressure to publish (observed in the previous section of this chapter), teaching-oriented faculty are not more likely to indicate that their job is a source of considerable strain. However, there are several intriguing differences among faculty in the different countries surveyed.

Teaching oriented faculty in Germany, Hong Kong, Mexico, and the United States were significantly less likely than their research-oriented colleagues to indicate that "This is poor time for a young person to begin a career in the academic profession." Teaching oriented faculty in Germany, Russia, the Netherlands, and the United States were significantly less likely than their research-oriented colleagues to agree with the statement, "If I had it do it again, I would not become an academic." Teaching-oriented faculty in Germany, Japan and the United States are *more likely* than their colleagues to indicate that academics are among the most influential opinion leaders. Throughout the survey, teaching orientation appears to have a significant relationship with faculty perspectives toward the academic profession most often among respondents from Germany, Japan and the United States. These differences suggest that while teaching-oriented faculty share much in common worldwide, a strong preference for teaching has a significantly different effect in some countries than in others.

Implications

These trends indicate a mixed relationship between teaching orientation and how faculty view their academic discipline and the academic profession in general. For the most part, significant international relationships between teaching orientation and faculty views toward the academic profession were not found. In other words, faculty appear to feel basically the same about the current status of their profession regardless of the strength of their preference for teaching or research. However, correlations were found in several countries between teaching orientation and attitudes toward a career in the academic profession, and toward how the public views academics. Further, an international relationship was found in the Carnegie data between teaching orientation and faculty perspectives toward this being a "creative and productive time" in their field. This supports the earlier findings in the Carnegie data which indicated that teaching-oriented faculty indicate stronger loyalty to their institution and research-oriented faculty are more focused on their disciplines, trends which lend some form of international validity to Gouldner's (1957) cosmopolitan/local paradigm.

However, while the differences overall are modest in international terms, there are some compelling questions which this study raises. In almost every country surveyed, teaching-oriented faculty were *less likely* to indicate that this is an especially creative and productive time in their field. We need to explore more fully why this is so, and develop new ways to change the situation. Certainly, faculty who prefer to teach are rarely mentioned by institutions or professional disciplines as "stars" or "experts"—rather, these labels are awarded most often to the productive researcher (Gumport, 1991). Thus, one implication of this analysis of the Carnegie international survey data is that we need to explore new avenues for teaching-oriented faculty to feel more connected with the creative and productive dimensions of their respective disciplines.

Higher education in many corners of the world rewards research productivity more than effective teaching. Thus, one might expect that teaching-oriented faculty would feel significantly different than their research-oriented colleagues about life in a profession which, some may feel, marginalizes the work which they hold most valuable. However, the Carnegie data do not support this expectation. Perhaps Lionel Lewis (1996) hit the nail on the head when observing that "for many academics, teaching is an intrinsically motivated activity . . . it is a task that motivates, not because of the promise of some external reward, but because it is something they simply enjoy doing" (p.147). Perhaps these same intrinsic rewards are what steer teaching-oriented faculty towards an academic career in the first place, and continue to drive them throughout their careers. This would explain in part why teaching-oriented faculty in several countries surveyed are more supportive of young people starting a career in the profession, and more likely to do so themselves if given the opportunity. Overall, despite all the research and hand-wringing over the disparities in rewards between research and teaching activities, faculty who prefer to teach do not appear to be significantly more negative in their views toward the academic profession. That is, faculty appear to feel basically the same about the current status of their profession regardless of the strength of their preference for teaching or research.

Finding #5: Teaching-oriented faculty worldwide share common views toward the role of higher education in society that are significantly different from their research-oriented colleagues.

Internationally, teaching-oriented faculty were considerably *less likely* than their colleagues to indicate that higher education should place a high priority on promoting intellectual inquiry and the creation of knowledge. Although this may not seem surprising, given the previous findings that showed teaching-oriented faculty have relatively less support for their academic disciplines, it is nonetheless an important additional dimension to our ongoing discussion regarding the differences between "cosmopolitan" and "local" faculty. Also, teaching-oriented faculty internationally were significantly *more likely* than their colleagues to indicate that higher education should place a high priority on lifelong learning for adults.

Several other less internationally-significant trends in the Carnegie data are worth noting. In half of the countries surveyed, teaching-oriented faculty are considerably *more likely* than their colleagues to indicate that higher education should place a high priority on preparing students for making productive contributions in the workplace. Teaching orientation is related internationally with how faculty responded to questions of higher education's role in addressing basic problems of society. However, in Brazil, Japan and the United States, teaching-oriented faculty were *more likely* than their colleagues to indicate that higher education should place a high priority on solving problems in society, while in Chile, Germany, Israel, and Sweden teaching-oriented faculty were *less likely* to agree with this statement.

Teaching-oriented faculty in Russia were significantly more likely than their colleagues to indicate that higher education in their country should give high priority to protecting free intellectual inquiry, while teaching-oriented faculty in most other countries surveyed were less likely than their colleagues to indicate this. Perhaps this indicates that in Russia, researchers are provided with more intellectual freedom than teachers. Certainly this would have some implications for the changes that need to be made in the approaches to higher education in that country's fledgling democratic society. Also, the United States bears the distinction of being the only country surveyed in which teaching orientation is related to faculty perspectives toward access to higher education. Here, teaching-oriented faculty expressed considerably more favorable views than their research-oriented colleagues towards providing more open access to higher education. This is perhaps related with our history as the most open, universally accessible system of higher education in the world.

Implications

These faculty responses support the distinction suggested by Gouldner (1957) and others between "local" and "cosmopolitan" faculty, based upon where a faculty member primary interests lie. Research-oriented faculty are relatively more supportive of higher education's role in promoting intellectual inquiry and scholarship—activities rooted in the academic disciplines, which is where their loyalties are the strongest. Teaching-oriented faculty appear more interested in ensuring that education helps students succeed in work and life, which reflects the concerns of institutions and departments where students and teachers interact the most. But this begs the question, why do research-oriented faculty appear relatively less concerned with whether their students are adequately equipped to "make productive contributions to the workplace" or for leadership? Does being "cosmopolitan" mean relatively less concern for students overall, while "locally-oriented" faculty are more concerned with the impact of higher education on students?

On the reverse side of this dimension, teaching-oriented faculty worldwide are less inclined to feel that protecting free intellectual inquiry or promoting research and scholarship are important priorities of higher education's role in society. How can the profession engage teaching-oriented faculty in a way that might strengthen their support for higher education's role in promoting intellectual inquiry and scholarship?

Teaching-oriented faculty worldwide feel more strongly than their research-oriented counterparts that preparing students for making productive contributions in the workplace should be a high priority for higher education. Teaching-oriented faculty are more in favor than their colleagues of higher education providing life-learning for adults. Thus, at two points where higher education and society interact most frequently, there is less support among research-oriented faculty. Is this an indication that researchers are relatively disengaged from institutional or social issues when compared to the teaching-oriented professoriate? As Stanley Hauerwaus (1988) points out, "teaching is a way to enhance our society through knowledge and wisdom. The moral authority of the teacher derives from this commitment . . ." (p.13). The Carnegie data appear to indicate that teaching-oriented faculty are more acclimated towards the "moral authority of the teacher" than their research-oriented colleagues. How the profession collectively grapples with these issues will surely have implications for the future of higher education.

Finding #6: Teaching-oriented faculty worldwide are less internationally-minded than their research-oriented colleagues.

Teaching-oriented faculty around the world were less likely than their colleagues to indicate that connections with foreign scholars are important, that scholars should read books published abroad, and that their institution should do more to promote international mobility. Teaching-oriented faculty worldwide were also significantly less likely to have engaged in any international-related activity, such as traveling to or working in another country, or collaborating with foreign scholars. However, despite their relative lack of international activity, teaching-oriented faculty in many countries surveyed were significantly less likely than their colleagues to indicate that their institution should do more to promote faculty and student mobility from one country to another. Most importantly, the teaching professoriate—those faculty who are most oriented towards teaching and spend considerably more time than their colleagues in the classroom—in many countries are considerably less supportive of the notion that their institution's curriculum should be more international in focus.

Implications

These findings have implications for the development of international curriculum, for international teaching exchanges, and our understanding of universal connections between faculty around the world. "Foreign students and scholars constitute an important academic resource in that they provide valuable expertise and a cross-cultural perspective" (Altbach, 1997: 222). However, according to the faculty perspectives reflected in the Carnegie survey data, we must find new ways to engage teaching-oriented faculty so that they feel more strongly that they are a part of a vibrant and exciting international academic profession. "We live in a world where the worldwide advancement of learning has become the single most influential factor affecting the human condition" (Kerr, 1990: 12). Our understanding of the academic responsibility of teaching needs to encompass an international dimension, in order for our students—and our colleagues—to adequately address the demands of this increasing global interdependence. The findings of this study provide insight into how faculty who prefer to teach see the world and their place in it. Unfortunately, the picture we are presented with is not good in terms of international perspectives among the teaching-oriented professoriate. Throughout this analysis of the Carnegie survey, teaching-oriented faculty were considerably less supportive of the international dimensions of higher education. This has implications for both research and policy on institutional, national, regional and international levels.

To begin with, institutions of higher education must find ways to engage the teaching professoriate in a way that encourages a stronger international perspective. For the reasons described in Chapter 9, as well as previous chapters of this volume, teachers must recognize and convey to their students the importance of a global perspective. For the sake of a nation's current generation of students, governmental policies should also pay heed to fostering an international dimension in the classroom. The findings presented in this chapter inform these efforts. At any institution of higher education, teaching-oriented faculty will play a key role in the development and adoption of an international curriculum. As teaching-oriented faculty are engaged more in campus-based activities than their research-oriented colleagues (Altbach & Lewis, 1996), they are considerably more likely to have a meaningful role in the adoption of a curriculum at any institution. However, according to the results of this analysis, there exists a significant challenge of convincing teaching-oriented faculty that an international curriculum is important. Thus, the findings of this analysis of the Carnegie data suggest that we must develop new ways to change the way the teaching professoriate views the international dimensions of higher education, if we are to be successful in moving the curriculum toward a more international direction. We must find ways to encourage teaching-oriented faculty to recognize the important "internationalization of learning" (Kerr, 1990) in ways that will enable future generations to be successful in an increasingly global marketplace.

Regionally, issues of language, economic and political cooperation, and social understanding require an international perspective among faculty, students, and society at large. One of the most common and effective means for developing an international perspective is to travel to and work in other countries. Indeed, at least among faculty in the United States, "the concept of learning by being there is extremely popular" (Haas, 1996: 378). However, if significant opportunities are not provided for teaching-oriented faculty to travel or work abroad, this can have negative implications for our efforts to internationalize our classrooms and our institutions—the arenas in which the loyalties of teaching-oriented faculty's are strongest. While opportunities are rare for teaching-oriented faculty to work abroad, they do not appear to feel that this is a significant problem. In fact, in most countries surveyed, they are considerably less likely than their research-oriented colleagues to see a need for opportunities for going abroad. Convincing the teaching-oriented professoriate otherwise is thus an important challenge to address in the coming years.

Overall, the findings presented in this study suggest that teaching-oriented faculty have much in common internationally, commonalities which provide an insight into what it means to prefer teaching over research worldwide. The importance of the international dimension of these findings cannot be overstated. Significant trends were found among faculty responses in virtually all of the countries surveyed by the Carnegie Foundation. Thus, despite significant structural or cultural differences, teaching-oriented faculty appear to feel the same around the world about the relative unimportance of the international dimension of higher education. These findings have particular significance for our growing understanding of academe as a truly international profession. While there is certainly an increasing amount of attention among research-oriented faculty towards the international dimension in higher education, this focus is not shared by teaching-oriented faculty. Indeed, how can this be any different? Teaching is basically an activity located within the institution, and is evaluated according to institutional guidelines of quality, whereas academic research is an activity generated primarily for the consumption of those outside the institution, and is thus compared with external measures of quality. The international dimension of this study provides an important addition the Gouldner's (1957) differentiation between "cosmopolitan" and "local" academics.

As international connections become increasingly common among academic disciplines, it may be expected that researchers are considerably more internationally-minded than teaching-oriented faculty. The findings of this initial analysis of the Carnegie survey data support this expectation, but to a surprisingly limited degree in some cases. Certainly, the news is good for research-oriented faculty—as the correlations in this analysis show that stronger teaching orientation is related to lower internationalism, they also show that stronger research orientation is related to stronger internationalism. However, together these trends suggest the potential for a substantial rift in the academic profession, between the "cosmopolitan" faculty and their "local" colleagues, over issues of curricular reform, institutional policy, and the overall priorities of the profession. How the professoriate addresses the issues raised here will certainly have lasting affects on the future of higher education.

Finding #7: There are important international similarities in how teaching-oriented faculty differ from research-oriented faculty in their perspectives toward many dimensions of academic work and life

This study found that throughout the academic world, orientation towards teaching or research is a useful attribution for describing meaningful differences between faculty. Further, despite a wide variety of cultural, organizational and structural issues among the various kinds of institutions and countries included in the Carnegie survey, this study found that teaching-oriented faculty share a great deal in common regarding their views toward the assessment of teaching, toward the courses they teach, toward their academic disciplines, toward the role of higher education in society, and toward the international dimensions of higher education. The likelihood of this phenomenon owing to chance is beyond possibility. Thus, the findings of this analysis lend an important international dimension to the study of the academic profession.

Implications

"Finding cross-national similarities greatly extends the scope of sociological knowledge" (Kohn, 1987: 31). The international dimension of the findings presented in this chapter are both timely and useful—studies of a comparative or international nature are undoubtedly useful for informing our understanding of the perspectives and ideas toward teaching and learning that are shared by academics across cultures and nations. This analysis represents the first study of the Carnegie survey responses to look at the dimension of teaching orientation internationally. Through this study, we can gain a more thorough understanding of both the academic profession and what it means for faculty to be teaching-oriented. As teaching orientation has a correlation internationally with how faculty answered survey items within each of these themes, one can say that teaching orientation is a useful way of looking at the academic profession internationally.

This international study of faculty perspectives toward teaching and learning presents a unique and timely opportunity to expand our understanding of the academic profession, and to "define priorities that could strengthen the academy worldwide" (Boyer, Altbach & Whitelaw, 1994: 1). The Carnegie data, representing the collective views of nearly 20,000 faculty from around the world, provide a unique and powerful source of information for our understanding of academics, in showing that "there is indeed an international academic profession with common perspectives and concerns, common problems and challenges" (Boyer, 1996: xv). The analysis of the Carnegie data provided in this study represents the first exploration into why some faculty prefer teaching more than others, and what this preference means in relation to how they responded to other questions on the survey.

To understand the academic profession, we must come to terms with the multiple interpretations that exist about it (Tierney & Bensimon, 1996). This analysis addresses several important dimension of faculty identity, first by determining similarities among teaching-oriented faculty which distinguish them from their research-oriented colleagues, and by identifying significant relationships between teaching orientation and faculty perspectives on a wide variety of issues and activities that impact their lives. As observed earlier in this discussion, studies have shown that faculty who prefer to teach do in fact teach more than their research-oriented colleagues. Thus, the findings presented here have implications for addressing the widespread concern over reforming classroom instruction, insofar as they add to our understanding of the faculty most engaged in this activity.

The international dimension of this study brings an important element to our understanding of how faculty feel their teaching should be assessed. The Carnegie survey collected data from a diverse population of faculty, and yet there appears to be a great deal of similarity among their responses to questions on the assessment of teaching. These findings support existing research on the common values embedded in teaching throughout much of academe worldwide. As Watkins (1998) observed, "Western conceptions of what constitutes good teaching seem to have a high degree of cross-cultural validity" (p. 21). These similarities in perspectives are significantly strengthened when this population is divided into teaching-oriented and research-oriented academics. Thus, it can be concluded that orientation toward teaching plays a considerable international role in how faculty feel about the assessment of teaching.

This analysis also determined that one does not often find regional similarities in the data collected by the Carnegie Foundation. For example, few similarities were found among the data on faculty from the Latin American countries, although teaching-oriented faculty in Brazil and Mexico do tend to share more of the same views than their Chilean colleagues. Teaching-oriented faculty responded to the Carnegie survey in similar ways in Sweden and the Netherlands, but differently in Germany and England. Also, cultural and academic traditions do not appear useful as a predictor of how teaching orientation affects faculty. For example, teaching-oriented faculty in England and the United States have much in common, but are noticeably different from their Australian counterparts in their views toward several topics addressed in this study.

It is anticipated that over time, a more rigorous analysis and interpretation of the data will find answers to the common question of why the trends found among faculty responses in most countries are not found in a select few. As well, further research will seek to compare these initial findings with other studies of the academic profession (where they exist) on both the national and international level. While research of this kind is necessary to confirm the validity of the Carnegie survey results, it will also be useful for comparing trends that may be associated with some time element at the time of the Carnegie data collection process. For example, during the survey administration in Israel, almost the entire postsecondary faculty were on strike. Surely, this had some influence on faculty responses to the Carnegie survey, an influence that may be noticeable when compared with similar data on the Israeli faculty collected at some other time. Thus, while the international similarities found in this study of the Carnegie faculty survey responses are important, a new study would be usful in determining any significant changes—or, perhaps more importantly—commonalities in the way teaching-oriented faculty view these issues today.

Overall, the most significant finding in this analysis is that there are international similarities in how teaching-oriented faculty differ from research-oriented faculty. These international trends have implications for our understanding of academic organizational culture, management and administrative policies relating to faculty, and organizational change within the academic profession, including the evolution of how a profession collectively defines the work they engage in, and how "excellent" examples of this work are framed. This research can lead to new discussions of how we may structure academic job descriptions that reward faculty for doing that which they most prefer to do.

SUMMARY AND RECOMMENDATIONS

"As information and expertise become increasingly central to contemporary societies, those involved in the knowledge industries and especially in higher education will inevitably play a key societal role" (Altbach, 1997: 144). The academic profession has always served as a provider of both expertise and information to their societies, and members of the profession are commonly viewed as having a certain amount of prestige. However, changes in the higher education environment worldwide, particularly along dimensions associated with national economic competitiveness and institutional accountability, present new challenges to members of the profession. According to this analysis of the Carnegie survey responses, the teaching-oriented professoriate is likely to respond to these changes differently than their research-oriented colleagues.

The Carnegie data appear to support the distinction made by Gouldner (1957) and subsequent researchers that there are two primary kinds of faculty: "cosmopolitans" and "locals." Research-oriented faculty are largely cosmopolitan, in that they express less affiliation with their institution than to their academic discipline, while their locally-oriented colleagues prefer teaching over research and express stronger loyalty to the institution than to the discipline. Past studies of this phenomenon have focused almost exclusively on the faculty within a single country, and sometimes—as was the case with Gouldner—a single institution. This study represents the first substantial international inquiry into the matter, and shows that cosmopolitans and locals worldwide differ considerably from each other in their views towards many dimensions of academic work and life. This has implications for efforts at organizational change within higher education worldwide.

In exploring reasons for the failure of organizational change, Arthur Levine (1980) refers to compatibility—defined as the degree of congruence between the norms, values and goals of an innovation and its host—as a major component. In the same sense, scholars and policy-makers calling for the improvement of college and university teaching should consider whether the policy changes they are calling for and attempting to implement will be compatible with the academics whose activities they hope to change. Thus, an understanding of faculty attitudes and orientations toward teaching becomes crucial for determining the compatibility of innovative teaching policies with the organizational participants—teaching-oriented faculty—with whom the success of these policies rest.

The findings of this analysis can certainly prove useful for informing organizational change. Indeed, observing all that teaching-oriented faculty have in common may help address what Boyer (1990) calls for in his *Scholarship Reconsidered*. An understanding of what influences faculty attitudes toward teaching and learning can facilitate the development of a framework within which to approach this complex issues in a manner acceptable to faculty in all corners of the world. One of the questions this raises, though, is how this information can inform new approaches to faculty career development and reward structures within all the different contexts involved. This study has found that, despite wide differences in academic traditions, national or regional culture, and many other environmental dimensions, teaching orientation plays a similar role internationally in how faculty responded to many of the Carnegie survey items. However, in order for these commonalities to be useful for developing models of change, one must incorporate these environmental differences into our interpretations of what teaching orientation means in each country. To this extent, the findings presented throughout this discussion provide a beginning, a groundwork upon which considerably more work is needed.

Recommendations

The chapters of this volume each tell a unique story about what it means to be oriented towards teaching in the countries surveyed by the Carnegie Foundation. Together, they help form the beginning of a comprehensive picture of who teaching-oriented faculty are and how they see the world of academe differently than their research-oriented colleagues. However, what we do with this new insight into the academic profession can have lasting impact on the future of higher education. The results of this exploration of the Carnegie survey data are useful for suggesting several recommendations about teaching oriented faculty:

1. **The profession must find ways to improve the strength of teaching orientation among younger, male faculty at all academic ranks.** Indeed, the young faculty of today are the future of the academic profession. As these faculty will continue to face growing demands for teaching accountability, we would do well to equip them with the training necessary to meet these challenges effectively, and it is hoped, in a way that is both intellectually and professionally rewarding. To this end, we must

improve our training programs for the profession in ways that enhance, rather than diminish, one's preference for teaching.

2. **Organizations must develop better ways to evaluate teaching effectiveness.** Faculty worldwide are in strong support of new and better ways to evaluate their teaching, and this support is even stronger among faculty who spend more time teaching than their research-oriented colleagues. Thus, given the literature on how preferences and attitudes can have significant implications for organizational change efforts, we would do well to engage teaching-oriented faculty on the highest levels for addressing this need for better ways to evaluate teaching effectiveness.

3. **Departments must pay considerable attention to the desire among teaching-oriented faculty to make teaching "the primary criterion for the hiring and promotion of faculty."** According to this analysis of the data, faculty who prefer teaching feel that teaching effectiveness, once properly assessed, should be more important than their record of publications for hiring and promoting faculty. On a related point, we would also do well to consider reducing the pressure to publish felt by teaching-oriented faculty. Thus, it would be useful to develop new policies and procedures within every department which recognizes and places value on effective teaching. Neglecting these important issues will certainly lead to greater dissatisfaction among the teaching professoriate, which is something from which no one benefits.

4. **We must explore new ways to engage teaching-oriented faculty so that they feel more strongly that this a creative and productive time in their academic disciplines.** Perhaps we need to re-evaluate our use of the word "productive" and the connotations it suggests, as mentioned in the previous recommendation. As well, creativity in the classroom is often hampered by administrative policies, bureaucratic procedures, over-subscribed courses, and lack of departmental leadership. Certainly, any discipline does not fare as well as it should when a considerable number of their members—those whose interests lie more in teaching than in research—feel less engaged. Perhaps one useful avenue to explore is within the growing trend of action research projects involving classroom instructors and their students. Certainly, if teachers feel that this is a creative and productive time in their discipline, this enthusiasm can have a considerable impact on how their students approach their studies in that field.

5. **Teaching-oriented faculty must be encouraged to recognize that they are part of a vibrant and exciting international academic profession.** The findings of this analysis suggest that there is not a single, universal academic profession, but rather, an international research-oriented academic profession, and many local teaching-oriented academic professions. Is there some sense of insularity or isolation among teaching-oriented faculty? We must determine why teaching-oriented faculty are less

inclined to foster connections with scholars in other countries or to read books and articles published abroad, and we must find ways to change these attitudes in a direction more positive towards the international dimension of higher education. Failure to do so will have lasting negative impacts on the way their students learn about the world and their place in it.

6. **We must convince the teaching-oriented professoriate that the curriculum needs to become more international in scope.** "The professoriate must be intimately involved in the changes and reforms taking place in many countries." (Boyer, 1996: xvi) This is most important when looking at the relationship between teaching-oriented faculty and efforts to make the curriculum more international. There is little doubt in the literature that this international dimension is necessary, but teaching-oriented faculty do not appear to be either connected or engaged with the research on this matter. Thus, new ways are needed to encourage changes in the attitudes and—as much as possible—the behaviors of teaching-oriented faculty toward a more internationally-favorable direction.

These are merely a few of the many possible recommendations that a thorough analysis of the Carnegie data—as well as future international studies of the professoriate—may yield. The findings presented in this study have implications for our understanding of organizational culture and change within the academic profession, how professors collectively define the work they engage in, and how "excellent" examples of this work are framed. The study also informs institutional administrative policies regarding faculty workload, and contributes to future international and comparative studies of the academic profession. Overall, the research presented in this volume represents some initial steps toward a much larger conversation, and hopefully will lead toward new research studies and policies that address the shared concerns and issues faced by teaching-oriented faculty worldwide. How the academic profession responds to the issues raised in this discussion will surely have implications for the future of higher education.

List of Tables and Diagrams

Statistical Analysis Results: Predictors of Teaching Orientation

The following pages (Tables: Chapter 4, pages 1-14) provide the results of a series of regression analyses for each country included the Carnegie survey. The variables used for these regressions were as follows:

Dependent Variables

q40new: 1 = low teaching orientation/high research orientation;
              4 = high teaching orientation/low research orientation

Independent Variable

age
Q1   gender: 1 = female 2 = male
Q3a*   Credentials: 1 = "no doctorate" 2 = "doctorate"
Q4a*   Training for Teaching: 1 = "Poor" 4 = "Excellent"
Q4b*   Training for Research: 1 = "Poor" 4 = "Excellent"
Q6   Years employed in higher education: real values for years
             employed
Q7   Years employed outside higher education: real values for years
             employed
Q9*   Academic Rank: 1 = "Visiting" 5 = "Assistant" 6 = "Associate" 7 =
             "Professor"
Q11a*   Working Time: 1 = "Part-time" 2 = "Full-time"
Q11b*   Tenure Status: 1 = "not tenures" 2 = "tenured"
Q12   Years employed at this institution: real values for years employed
Q14a*   Other Academic Positions: 1 = "No" 3 = "Yes, Full-time"
Q14b*   Other Nonacademic Positions: 1 = "No" 3 = "Yes, Full-time"

*indicates that this variable was re-coded.

For the multiple regression presented in Chapter 4, it was useful to recode the *dependent* variable so that the most preferred response (strong teaching orientation) would be assigned the highest number. However, for the remaining data analysis chapters (Chapters 5 through 9), the original data coding was used, as most of the correlation analyses conducted in those chapters relied on variables which used the same rank order of variables (1=high, 4=low) as does q40 (preference towards teaching). These issues of variable re-ordering must be taken into account before accurately reproducing the data analyses provided in this dissertation.

With the exception of Age and Gender, the "Predictor" variables are listed in order of their relative power in explaining the variance in response to the survey item on orientation towards teaching or research.

PLEASE NOTE: SPSS syntax and output for all chapters of this dissertation, including correlation tables and data frequencies, are available from the author. They are omitted here for the sake of keeping the overall publication within a manageable size. The analysis results for Chapter 4 are provided here to show the total variance in teaching orientation accounted for by different mixes of predictive variables.

Country: Australia

Predictor	Beta	R^2	R^2 Change	F Change	P
Significant Variables					
1. Q1 Gender	-.13	.02	.02	13.31	.0003
2. Age	.14	.04	.02	15.45	.0001
3. Q4b Quality of Training for Research	-.37	.17	.14	127.60	.0000
4. Q9 Academic Rank	-.28	.22	.05	48.99	.0000
5. Q4a Quality of Training for Teaching	.16	.25	.02	24.40	.0000
6. Q3a Holds a Doctoral degree	-.15	.26	.01	14.25	.0002
7. Q6 Years Employed in Higher Education	.15	.27	.01	8.83	.0031

Together, these variables account for 27% of the variance in orientation of interests towards teaching or research (F = 40.22, p<.001).

Variables that were _not significant_
Q7 - Number of years employed in non-academic work
Q11a - Working Time
Q11b - Tenure Status
Q12 - Number of years at current institution
Q14a - Holds other academic positions outside current institution
Q14b - Holds other non-academic positions outside current institution

Total number surveyed: 1420

NOTE: The variables are shown in the order of importance found through the hierarchical regression procedure. Variables that were not significant (at the P (.05 level of significance) were naturally excluded by the computer in this procedure, reflected under the SPSS output heading "Variables not in the equation." However, because gender and age were entered separately, they were included in the formula even if found to be statistically insignificant. This is reflected in the tables as well.

These tables indicate the percentage of variance that each variable accounts for (r^2), and the highest percentage indicates the strongest impact on preference choice. The numbers provided under the column hearing "beta" will indicate the direction of the respondent's preference toward teaching or research. To be significant, the P value must be below .05.

Country: Brazil

Predictor	Beta	R^2	R^2 Change	F Change	P
Significant Variables					
1. Q1 Gender *(Not significant)*	(-.06)	(.00)	(.00)	(1.52)	(.2184)
2. Age	.20	.04	.04	16.99	.0000
3. Q4b Quality of Training for Research	-.32	.14	.10	50.16	.0000
4. Q11a Working Time (FT/PT)	-.17	.17	.03	14.23	.0002
5. Q11b Tenure Status	.12	.18	.01	6.62	.0182
6. Q4a Quality of Training for Teaching	.11	.19	.01	4.19	.0400

Together, (excluding Gender) these variables account for 19% of the variance in orientation of interests towards teaching or research (F = 16.46, p<.001).

Variables that were not significant
Q1 - Gender
Q6 - Number of years employed in higher education
Q7 - Number of years employed in non-academic work
Q9 - Rank
Q12 - Number of years at current institution
Q14a - Holds other academic positions outside current institution
Q14b - Holds other non-academic positions outside current institution

Total number surveyed: 989

**NOTE: The survey data on Academic Rank were not included in the results submitted to the Carnegie Foundation.

Country: Chile

Predictor	Beta	R^2	R^2 Change	F Change	P
Significant Variables					
1. Q1 Gender	-.18	.03	.03	12.55	.0004
2. Age	.27	.11	.07	30.93	.0000
3. Q4b Quality of Training for Research	-.39	.25	.15	73.57	.0000
4. Q3a Holds a Doctoral degree	-.24	.30	.05	26.29	.0000
5. Q4a Quality of Training for Teaching	.22	.34	.04	21.33	.0000
6. Q9 Academic Rank	-.15	.35	.01	7.54	.0063

Together, these variables account for 35% of the variance in orientation of interests towards teaching or research (F = 33.77, p<.001).

Variables that were not significant
Q6 - Number of years employed in higher education
Q7 - Number of years employed in non-academic work
Q11a - Working Time
Q11b - Tenure Status
Q12 - Number of years at current institution
Q14a - Holds other academic positions outside current institution
Q14b - Holds other non-academic positions outside current institution

Total number surveyed: 1071

Country: England

Predictor	Beta	R^2	R^2 Change	F Change	P
Significant Variables					
1. Q1 Gender	-.11	.01	.01	17.74	.0000
2. Age	.26	.08	.07	96.36	.0000
3. Q3a Holds a Doctoral Degree	-.36	.20	.13	214.70	.0000
4. Q7 Years Employed in Non-Academic Work	.10	.21	.01	13.50	.0002
5. Q12 Number of Years at Current Institution	.12	.22	.01	9.07	.0026
6. Q9 Academic Rank	.07	.22	.01	7.13	.0077

Together, these variables account for 22% of the variance in orientation of interests towards teaching or research (F = 64.17, p<.001).

Variables that were not significant
Q6 - Number of years employed in higher education
Q11a - Working Time
Q11b - Tenure Status
Q14a - Holds other academic positions outside current institution
Q14b - Holds other non-academic positions outside current institution

Total number surveyed: 1946

**NOTE: The survey data on quality of training for teaching or research were not included in the results submitted to the Carnegie Foundation.

Country: Germany

Predictor	Beta	R^2	R^2 Change	F Change	P
Significant Variables					
1. Q1 Gender - *(Not Significant)*	(.01)	(.00)	(.00)	(0.05)	(.8236)
2. Age	.24	.06	.06	27.66	.0000
3. Q4b Quality of Training for Research	-.27	.13	.07	37.87	.0000
4. Q4a Quality of Training for Teaching	.23	.18	.05	26.84	.0000
5. Q11a Working Time (FT/PT)	.16	.20	.02	11.42	.0008
6. Q3a Holds a Doctoral degree	-.18	.22	.02	12.41	.0005
7. Q9 Academic Rank	.14	.23	.01	5.64	.0180

Together (excluding Gender), these variables account for 23% of the variance in orientation of interests towards teaching or research (F = 19.16, p<.001).

Variables that were <u>not significant</u>
Q1 - Gender
Q6 - Number of years employed in higher education
Q7 - Number of years employed in non-academic work
Q12 - Number of years at current institution
Q14a - Holds other academic positions outside current institution
Q14b - Holds other non-academic positions outside current institution

Total number surveyed: 2801

**NOTE: The survey data on tenure status were not included in the results submitted to the Carnegie Foundation.

Country: Hong Kong

Predictor	Beta	R²	R² Change	F Change	P
Significant Variables					
1. Q1 Gender	-.26	.07	.07	23.00	.0000
2. Age - *(Not Significant)*	(.08)	(.07)	(.01)	(2.04)	(.1539)
3. Q4b Quality of Training for Research	-.38	.21	.14	57.01	.0000
4. Q3a Holds a Doctoral degree	-.23	.25	.04	16.49	.0001
5. Q11a Working Time (FT/PT)	-.10	.26	.01	4.31	.0387
6. Q12 Number of Years at Current Institution	.12	.27	.01	4.57	.0334

Together (excluding Age), these variables account for 27% of the variance in orientation of interests towards teaching or research (F = 19.74, p<.001).

Variables that were __not significant__
Age
Q4a - Quality of Training for Teaching
Q6 - Number of years employed in higher education
Q7 - Number of years employed in non-academic work
Q11b - Tenure Status
Q14a - Holds other academic positions outside current institution
Q14b - Holds other non-academic positions outside current institution

Total number surveyed: 471

**NOTES: On survey question Q11a in the Hong Kong survey, participants were coded as (2) substantiated or (1) other, instead of according to tenure status.

Country: Israel

Predictor	Beta	R^2	R^2 Change	F Change	P
Significant Variables					
1. Q1 Gender	-.27	.07	.07	11.34	.0010
2. Age	.18	.11	.03	4.87	.0290
3. Q9 Academic Rank	-.36	.20	.10	16.67	.0001
4. Q4a Quality of Training for Teaching	.24	.26	.06	10.70	.0014
5. Q4b Quality of Training for Research	-.24	.30	.04	8.60	.0039

Together, these variables account for 30% of the variance in orientation of interests towards teaching or research (F = 11.89, p<.001).

Variables that were <u>not significant</u>
Q3A - Holds a Doctoral degree
Q6 - Number of years employed in higher education
Q7 - Number of years employed in non-academic work
Q11a - Working Time
Q11b - Tenure Status
Q12 - Number of years at current institution
Q14a - Holds other academic positions outside current institution
Q14b - Holds other non-academic positions outside current institution

Total number surveyed: 502

Country: Japan

Predictor	Beta	R²	R² Change	F Change	P
Significant Variables					
1. Q1 Gender	-.07	.01	.01	4.09	.0436
2. Age	.24	.06	.06	50.31	.0000
3. Q3a Holds a Doctoral degree	-.33	.17	.11	110.60	.0000
4. Q11a Working Time (FT/PT)	-.08	.17	.01	6.77	.0094
5. Q4b Quality of Training for Research	-.08	.18	.01	5.84	.0159
6. Q6 Years Employed in Higher Education	-.09	.19	.00	5.73	.0169
7. Q12 Number of Years at Current Institution	.08	.19	.00	4.57	.0328

Together, these variables account for 19% of the variance in orientation of interests towards teaching or research (F = 28.45, p<.001).

Variables that were not significant
Q4a - Quality of Training for Teaching
Q7 - Number of years employed in non-academic work
Q9 - Academic Rank
Q11b - Tenure Status
Q14a - Holds other academic positions outside current institution
Q14b - Holds other non-academic positions outside current institution

Total number surveyed: 1889

Country: Korea

Predictor	Beta	R^2	R^2 Change	F Change	P
Significant Variables					
1. Q1 Gender - *(Not Significant)*	(-.03)	(.00)	(.00)	(0.41)	(.5216)
2. Age	.25	.06	.06	42.65	.0000
3. Q4b Quality of Training for Research	-.22	.11	.05	35.49	.0000
4. Q4a Quality of Training for Teaching	.21	.14	.03	26.43	.0000
5. Q3a Holds a Doctoral degree	-.09	.15	.01	5.42	.0202
6. Q6 Years Employed in Higher Education	.12	.15	.01	4.25	.0396
7. Q9 Academic Rank	-.15	.16	.01	7.91	.0051

Together, these variables account for 16% of the variance in orientation of interests towards teaching or research (F = 18.63, p<.001)

Variables that were <u>not significant</u>
Q1 - Gender
Q7 - Number of years employed in non-academic work
Q11a - Working Time
Q11b - Tenure Status
Q12 - Number of years at current institution
Q14a - Holds other academic positions outside current institution
Q14b - Holds other non-academic positions outside current institution

Total number surveyed: 903

Country: Mexico

Predictor	Beta	R^2	R^2 Change	F Change	P
Significant Variables					
1. Q1 Gender - *(Not Significant)*	(.07)	(.00)	(.00)	(1.48)	(.2244)
2. Age - *(Not Significant)*	(-85)	(.00)	(.00)	(.00)	(.9874)
3. Q4b Quality of Training for Research	-.32	.11	.10	40.17	.0000
4. Q3a Holds a Doctoral degree	-.20	.14	.03	13.91	.0002
5. Q12 Number of Years at Current Institution	.21	.17	.03	10.94	.0010
6. Q7 Holds other Non-Academic Position	.08	.20	.03	13.52	.0003
7. Q4a Quality of Training for Teaching	.15	.22	.02	7.94	.0051

Together (excluding Age and Gender), these variables account for 22% of the variance in orientation of interests towards teaching or research (F = 13.62, p<.001).

Variables that were not significant
Q1 - Gender
Q6 - Number of years employed in higher education
Q7 - Number of years employed in non-academic work
Q11a - Working Time
Q11b - Tenure Status
Q14a - Holds other academic positions outside current institution

Total number surveyed: 1027

**NOTE: In Mexico, the actual number of faculty and the kinds of their academic appointments remain unknown, since one person often holds several posts (Antón, Manuel Gil "The Mexican Academic Profession" in Altbach, Philip G. (ed.) *The International Academic Profession: Portraits of Fourteen Countries*, p. 314).

Country: The Netherlands

Predictor	Beta	R^2	R^2 Change	F Change	P
Significant Variables					
1. Q1 Gender - *(Not Significant)*	(.04)	(.00)	(.00)	(1.58)	(.2084)
2. Age	.20	.04	.04	33.16	.0000
3. Q4b Quality of Training for Research	-.21	.08	.04	41.67	.0000
4. Q11b Tenure Status**	.13	.09	.01	9.59	.0020
5. Q3a Holds a Doctoral degree	-.10	.10	.01	6.84	.0090
6. Q14a Holds other Academic Positions	.08	.11	.01	5.34	.0211

Together (excluding Gender), these variables account for 11% of the variance in orientation of interests towards teaching or research (F = 16.96, p<.001).

Variables that were not significant
Q1 - Gender
Q6 - Number of years employed in higher education
Q12 - Number of years at current institution
Q14b - Holds other non-academic positions outside current institution

Total number surveyed: 1364

**NOTES: Survey data on quality of training for teaching, on working time (full-time/part-time), on academic rank, and on years employed in non-academic work were not included in the results submitted in the Carnegie Foundation. Also, "tenure status" is not an accurate description of the nature of a Dutch academic appointment; rather, survey responses were coded into (3) permanent, (2) permanent qualified, or (1) non-permanent.

Country: Russia

Predictor	Beta	R^2	R^2 Change	F Change	P
Significant Variables					
1. Q1 Gender	-.25	.06	.06	19.31	.0000
2. Age	.13	.08	.02	5.01	.0259
3. Q4b Quality of Training for Research	-.33	.18	.10	35.90	.0000
4. Q3a Holds a Doctoral degree	-.20	.21	.03	12.24	.0005
5. Q4a Quality of Training for Teaching	.15	.23	.02	7.10	.0081

Together, these variables account for 23% of the variance in orientation of interests towards teaching or research (F = 17.33, p<.001).

Variables that were not significant
Q6 - Number of years employed in higher education
Q7 - Number of years employed in non-academic work
Q9 - Academic Rank
Q11a - Working Time
Q11b - Tenure Status
Q12 - Number of years at current institution

Total number surveyed: 438

**NOTE: Questions on holding other academic or non-academic positions were omitted from the survey in Russia.

Country: Sweden

Predictor	Beta	R^2	R^2 Change	F Change	P
Significant Variables					
1. Q1 Gender	-.10	.01	.01	5.91	.0153
2. Age	.18	.04	.03	19.01	.0000
3. Q3a Holds a Doctoral degree	-.37	.17	.12	82.82	.0000
4. Q4b Quality of Training for Research	-.16	.19	.02	16.18	.0001
5. Q4a Quality of Training for Teaching	.13	.20	.01	9.77	.0019
6. Q11b Tenure Status	.11	.21	.01	6.90	.0089
7. Q7 Years Employed in Non-Academic Work	.08	.22	.01	3.90	.0489
8. Q12 Number of Years at Current Institution	.12	.23	.01	5.52	.0191

**Together, these variables account for 23% of the variance in orientation of interests towards
teaching or research (F = 20.32, p<.001).**

Variables that were not significant
Q6 - Number of years employed in higher education
Q9 - Academic Rank
Q11a - Working Time
Q14a - Holds other academic positions outside current institution
Q14b - Holds other non-academic positions outside current institution

Total number surveyed: 1122

Country: United States

Predictor	Beta	R^2	R^2 Change	F Change	P
Significant Variables					
1. Q1 Gender	-.13	.02	.02	38.37	.0000
2. Age	.18	.05	.03	79.47	.0000
3. Q4b Quality of Training for Research	-.32	.15	.10	262.90	.0000
4. Q3a Holds a Doctoral degree	-.23	.19	.05	138.80	.0000
5. Q4a Quality of Training for Teaching	.13	.21	.02	47.73	.0000
6. Q9 Academic Rank	-.11	.22	.01	24.09	.0000
7. Q11b Tenure Status	.11	.23	.01	18.20	.0000
8. Q7 Years Employed in Non-Academic Work	.07	.23	.00	10.98	.0009
9. Q12 Number of Years at Current Institution	.12	.23	.00	16.77	.0000
10. Q11a Working Time (FT/PT)	-.05	.24	.00	4.63	.0316

Together, these variables account for 24% of the variance in orientation of interests towards teaching or research (F = 71.13, p<.001).

Variables that were not significant
Q6 - Number of years employed in higher education
Q14a - Holds other academic positions outside current institution
Q14b - Holds other non-academic positions outside current institution

Total number surveyed: 3529

References

Chapter 1

Altbach, P.G. and Lewis, L. (1996). The Academic Profession in International Perspective. In Altbach, P.G. (ed.), *The International Academic Profession: Portraits of 14 Countries*. Princeton, NJ: Carnegie Foundation for the Advancement of Teaching.

Altbach, P.G. (1979). *Comparative Higher Education: Research Trends and Bibliography*. London: Mansell Publishing.

Austin, A.E. (1990). Faculty Cultures, Faculty Values. *Assessing Academic Climates and Cultures*. New Directions for Institutional Research 68 (Winter), p. 61-74.

Bensimon, E. (1996). Faculty Identity: Essential, Imposed or Constructed? In *Integrating Research on Faculty: Seeking New Ways to Communicate About the Academic Life of Faculty* (NCES Conference Report). Washington, DC: OERI, U.S. Department of Education.

Boyer, E.L., Altbach P.G. and Whitelaw, M.J. (1994). *The Academic Profession: International Perspectives*. Princeton, NJ: Carnegie Foundation for the Advancement of Teaching.

Boyer, E.L. (1996). Foreword. In Altbach, P.G. (ed.), *The International Academic Profession: Portraits of 14 Countries*. Princeton, NJ: Carnegie Foundation for the Advancement of Teaching.

Clark, B.R. (1992). Faculty Differentiation and Dispersion. In Levine, A. (ed.), *Higher Learning in America*. Baltimore, MD: Johns Hopkins University Press, p. 163-177.

Clark, B.R. (ed.). (1987). *The Academic Profession: National, Disciplinary, and Institutional Settings*. Berkeley: University of California Press.

Denzin, N.K. (1989). *The Research Act: A Theoretical Introduction to Sociological Methods*. Englewood Cliffs, NJ: Prentice-Hall, Inc.

Enders, J. and Teichler, U. (1996). The Academic Profession in Germany. In Altbach, P.G. (ed.), *The International Academic Profession: Portraits of 14 Countries.* Princeton, NJ: Carnegie Foundation for the Advancement of Teaching.

Finkelstein, M.J. (1984). *The American Academic Profession: A Synthesis of Social Science Inquiry since World War II.* Columbus, OH: Ohio State University Press.

Gottlieb, E.E. and Keith, B.E. (1996). The Academic Research-Teaching Nexus in Advanced-Industrialized Countries. *Higher Education* 25.

Gouldner, A.W. (1957). Cosmopolitans and Locals: Toward an analysis of latent social roles. *Administrative Sciences Quarterly* 2, p. 281-306.

Greenfield, T.B. (1975). Theory about organization: A new perspective and its implications for schools. In Hughes, M.G. (ed.), *Administering Education: International Challenges.* London: Athlone Press, p. 71-99.

Grimes A.J. and Berger, P.K. (1970). Cosmopolitan-local: Evaluation of the construct. *Administrative Science Quarterly* 15, p. 407-16.

Gumport, P. (1991). The Research Imperative. In Tierney, W.G. (ed.), *Culture and Ideology in Higher Education: Advancing a Critical Agenda.* New York: Praeger Publishers.

Hughes, M.G. (1979). Management Theory: Reconciling Professional and Administrative Concerns in Education. *Studies in Educational Administration* 13 (December).

Kember, D. and Gow, L. (1994). Orientations to teaching and their effect on the quality of student learning. *Journal of Higher Education* 65(1), p. 58-74.

Kerr, C. (1990). The Internationalisation of Learning and the Nationalism of the Purposes of Higher Education: Two 'laws of motion' in conflict? *European Journal of Education* 25(1).

Kohn, M.L. (1987). Cross-National Research as an Analytical Strategy. *American Sociological Review* 52(6), p. 713-31.

Levine, A. (1980). *Why Innovation Fails: The Institutionalism and Termination of Innovation in Higher Education.* Albany, NY: SUNY Press.

Lewis, L. (1996). *Marginal Worth: Teaching and the Academic Labor Market.* New Brunswick, NJ: Transaction Publishers.

McKeachie, W.J. (1990). Research on College Teaching: The Historical Background. *Journal of Educational Psychology* 82(2), p.189-200.

Murray, H.G., Rushton, J.P. and Paunonen, S.V. (1990). Teacher Personality Traits and Student Instructional Ratings in Six Types of University Courses. *Journal of Educational Psychology* 82(2), p. 250-261.

Rokkan, S. (1976). Cross-Cultural, Cross-Societal, and Cross-National Research. In *Main Trends of Research in the Human and the Social Sciences.* Paris: UNESCO.

Sherman, B.R. and Blackburn, R.T. (1975). Personal Characteristics and Teaching Effectiveness of College Faculty. *Journal of Educational Psychology* 67(1), p. 124-131.

Shulman, L. (1993). Teaching as Community Property: Putting an End to Pedagogical Solitude. *Change* (November/December).

Tierney, W. and Bensimon, E.M. (1996). *Promotion and Tenure: Community and Socialization in Academe*. Albany, NY: State University of New York Press.

Toomey, D. and Child, D. (1971). The development of local-cosmopolitan attitudes among undergraduates and sixth formers. *Sociology Review* 19, p. 325-41.

Chapter 2

Altbach, P.G and Lewis, L. (1996). The Academic Profession in International Perspective. In Altbach, P.G. (ed.), *The International Academic Profession: Portraits of 14 Countries*. Princeton, NJ: Carnegie Foundation for the Advancement of Teaching.

Altbach, P.G. (1995). Problems and Possibilities: The US Academic Profession. *Studies in Higher Education* 20(1), p. 27-44.

Altbach, P.G. (1992). Patterns in Higher Education Development: Towards the Year 2000. In Altbach, P.G. and Morsy, Z. (eds.), *Higher Education in International Perspective*. New York: UNESCO/Advent Books.

Altbach, P.G. (1987). *The Knowledge Context: Comparative Perspectives on the Distribution of Knowledge*. Albany, NY: State University of New York Press.

Altbach, P.G. (1985). Perspectives on Comparative Higher Education: A survey of research and literature. In Altbach, P.G. and Kelly, D. (eds.), *Higher Education in International Perspective: Survey and Bibliography*. London: Mansell, pp. 3-51.

Altbach, P.G. (1984). The Management of Decline. *Higher Education in Europe* 9 (October-December), p. 58-64.

Altbach, P.G. (1979). *Comparative Higher Education: Research Trends and Bibliography*. London: Mansell Publishing.

Angelo, T.A. (1993). A "Teacher's Dozen": Fourteen general, research-based principles for improving higher learning in our classrooms. AAHE *Bulletin*, 45(8).

Anwyl, J. and McNaught, C. (1993). Awards for Teaching Excellence at Australian Universities. *Higher Education Review* 25(1).

Austin, A.E. (1990). Faculty Cultures, Faculty Values. *Assessing Academic Climates and Cultures*. New Directions for Institutional Research 68 (Winter), p. 61-74.

Astin A. (1991). *Assessment for Excellence: The Philosophy and Practice of Assessment and Evaluation in Higher Education*. American Council on Education/Macmillan Series on Higher Education. Washington, DC: American Council on Education.

Bane, C.L. (1925). The Lecture vs. the Class Discussion Method of College Teaching. *School and Society* 21, p. 300-302.

Bayer, A.E. (1973). *Teaching Faculty in Academe*. American Council on Education, Research Reports 8(2).

Becher, T. (1989). *Academic Tribes and Territories: Intellectual Enquiry and the Cultures of Disciplines.* Cambridge, UK: Open University Press.

Belenky, M.F., Clinchy, B.M., Glodberger, N.R., and Tarule, J.M. (1986). *Women's Ways of Knowing: The Development of Self, Voice, and Mind.* New York: Basic Books.

Ben-David, J. (1977). *Centers of Learning: Britain, France, Germany and the United States.* New York: McGraw-Hill.

Bensimon, E. (1996). Faculty Identity: Essential, Imposed or Constructed? In *Integrating Research on Faculty: Seeking New Ways to Communicate About the Academic Life of Faculty* (NCES Conference Report). Washington, DC: OERI, U.S. Department of Education.

Bess, J.L. (1982). *University Organization: A Matrix Analysis of the Academic Professions.* New York: New York University.

Boyer, E.L. (1996). Foreword. In Altbach, P.G. (ed.), *The International Academic Profession: Portraits of 14 Countries.* Princeton, NJ: Carnegie Foundation for the Advancement of Teaching.

Boyer, E.L., Altbach, P.G., and Whitelaw, M.J. (1994). *The Academic Profession: An International Perspective.* Princeton, NJ: The Carnegie Foundation for the Advancement of Teaching.

Boyer, E.L. (1990). *Scholarship Reconsidered: Priorities of the Professoriate.* Princeton, NJ: Carnegie Foundation for the Advancement of Teaching.

Brown, L. (1992). Higher Education and the Reality of Interdependence. *International Journal of Educational Development* 12(2).

Chaffee, E.E. and Tierney, W.G. (1988). *Collegiate Culture and Leadership Strategies.* New York: Macmillan Publishing.

Chickering, A.W. and Gamson, Z.F. (1987). *Seven Principles for Good Practice in Undergraduate Education.* Milwaukee: Johnson Foundation.

Clark, B.R. (1987). *The Academic Life: Small Worlds, Different Worlds.* Princeton, NJ: Carnegie Foundation for the Advancement of Teaching.

Clark, B.R. (ed.). (1987). *The Academic Profession: National, Disciplinary, and Institutional Settings.* Berkeley: University of California Press.

Clark, B.R. (1983). *The Higher Education System: Academic Organization in Cross-National Perspective.* Berkeley, CA: University of California Press.

Damrosch, D. (1995). *We Scholars: Changing the Culture of the University.* Cambridge, MA: Harvard University Press.

Edmondson, J.B., and Mulder, F.J. (1924). Size of class as a factor in university instruction. *Journal of Educational Research* 9, p. 1-12.

El-Khawas, E. (1991). Senior Faculty in Academe: Active, Committed to the Teaching Role. *Research Briefs*, 2(5). Washington, D.C.: American Council on Education, Division of Policy Analysis and Research.

El-Khawas, E. (1994). *Campus Trends, 1994.* Washington, DC: American Council on Education.

Fairweather, J.S. (1993). *Teaching, Research and Faculty Rewards: A Summary of the Research Findings of the Faculty Profile Project.* University Park, PA: National Center for Postsecondary Teaching, Learning, and Assessment.

Feldman, K.A. (1986). The Perceived Instructional effectiveness of College Teachers as Related to Their Personality and Attitudinal Characteristics: A review and synthesis. *Research in Higher Education* 24(2).

Finkelstein, M.J. (1984). *The American Academic Profession: A Synthesis of Social Science Inquiry since World War II.* Columbus, OH: Ohio State University Press.

Forest, J.J.F. (ed.). (1998). *University Teaching: International Perspectives.* New York: Garland Publishing.

Fulton, O. and Trow, M. (1974). Research Activity in American Higher Education. *Sociology of Education* 47 (Winter), p. 29-73.

Furniss, W.T. (1981). *Reshaping Faculty Careers.* Washington, DC: American Council on Education.

Gaff, Jerry G. (1975). *Toward Faculty Renewal: Advances in Faculty, Instructional and Organizational Development.* San Francisco, CA: Jossey-Bass.

Glass, G.V. and Smith, M.L. (1979). Meta-Analysis of Research on Class Size and Achievement. *Educational Evaluation and Policy Analysis* 1, p. 2-16.

Goodwin, L.D. and Stevens, E.A. (1993). The influence of gender on university faculty members' perceptions of "good" teaching. *Journal of Higher Education* 64(2).

Gouldner, A.W. (1957). Cosmopolitans and Locals: Toward an analysis of latent social roles. *Administrative Sciences Quarterly* 2, p. 281-306.

Greenfield, T.B. (1975). Theory about organization: A new perspective and its implications for schools. In Hughes, M.G. (ed.), *Administering Education: International Challenges.* Londong: Athlone Press, p. 71-99.

Grimes A.J. and Berger, P.K. (1970). Cosmopolitan-local: Evaluation of the construct. *Administrative Science Quarterly* 15, p. 407-16.

Gumport, P.J. (1993). Fired Faculty: Reflections on Marginalization and Academic Identity. In McLaughlin and Tierney (eds.), *Naming Silenced Lives.* London: Routledge.

Gumport, P.J. (1993). The Contested Terrain of Academic Program Reduction. *Journal of Higher Education* 64 (May-June), p. 283-311.

Gumport, P.J. (1991). E *Pluribus Unum?* Academic Structure, Culture, and the Case of Feminist Scholarship. *Review of Higher Education* 15 (Fall) p. 9-29.

Halpern, Diane F., and Associates. (1994). *Changing College Classrooms New Teaching and Learning Strategies for an Increasingly Complex World.* San Francisco, CA: Jossey-Bass.

Hauerwaus, S.M. (1988). The Morality of Teaching. In A.L. Deneef, C.D. Goodwin and E.S. McCrate (eds.), *The Academic's Handbook.* Durham, NC: Duke Press, p. 19-28.

Hughes, M.G. (1979). Management Theory: Reconciling Professional and Administrative Concerns in Education. *Studies in Educational Administration* 13 (December).

Kerr, C. (1990). The Internationalisation of Learning and the Nationalism of the Purposes of Higher Education: Two 'laws of motion' in conflict? *European Journal of Education* 25(1).

Ladd, E.C. (1979). The Work Experience of American College Professors: Some Data and an Argument. *Current Issues in Higher Education*. Washington, DC: American Association for Higher Education.

Ladd, E.C. (1976). The General Periodicals Professors Read. *Chronicle of Higher Education* (January 19), p. 14.

Ladd, E.C. (1975). How do Faculty Members Take Their Responsibilities as Citizens? *Chronicle of Higher Education* (December 22), p. 13.

Ladd, E.C., Jr. and Lipset, S.M. (1975). *The Divided Academy: Professors and Politics*. New York: McGraw Hill.

Levine, A. (1980). *Why Innovation Fails: The Institutionalism and Termination of Innovation in Higher Education*. Albany, NY: SUNY Press.

Lewis, L. (1977). Studies of the Academic Profession. In Knowles, A. (ed.), *The International Encyclopedia of Higher Education*, Vol. 8. San Francisco, CA: Jossey-Bass, p. 3876-3879.

Macomber F.G. and Seigel, L. (1960). Experimental Study in Instructional Procedures (Final Report) Oxford, OH: Miami University.

Macomber F.G. and Seigel, L. (1957a). A Study of Large-Group Teaching Procedures. *Educational Research* 38, p. 220-229.

Macomber F.G. and Seigel, L. (1957b). *Experimental Study in Instructional Procedures* (Progress Report No. 2). Oxford, OH: Miami University.

McKeachie W.J. (ed.). (1994). *Teaching Tips: Strategies, Research and Theory for College and University Teachers*, 9th ed. Lexington, MA: D.C. Heath Co.

McKeachie, W.J. (1990). Research on College Teaching: The Historical Background. *Journal of Educational Psychology* 82(2), p. 189-200.

McKeachie, W.J, Pintrich, P.R., Lin, Y. and Smith, D.A. (1986). *Teaching and Learning in the College Classroom: A Review of the Research Literature*. Ann Arbor: University of Michigan, National Center for Research to Improve Postsecondary Teaching and Learning.

Meyer, J.W. and Rowan, B. (1978). Institutionalized Organizations: Formal Structure as Myth and Ceremony. *American Journal of Sociology* 83(2), p. 340-363.

Miller, H. (1992). The State of the Academic Profession: An Australia-United Kingdom Comparison. *Australian Universities' Review* 35(2), p. 21-25.

Murray, H.G., Rushton, J.P. and Paunonen, S.V. (1990). Teacher Personality Traits and Student Instructional Ratings in Six Types of University Courses. *Journal of Educational Psychology* 82(2), p. 250-261.

NCPTLA (1995). *Realizing the Potential: Improving Postsecondary Teaching, Learning and Assessment*. University Park, PA: National Center for Postsecondary Teaching, Learning and Assessment.

Neave, G. (1994). The Politics of Quality: Developments in Higher Education in Western Europe 1992-1994. *European Journal of Education* 29(2), p. 115-34.

Neave, G. (1992). On Instantly Consumable Knowledge and Snake Oil. *European Journal of Education* 27(2), p. 5-27.

Neave, G. (1983). The Changing Face of the Academic Profession in Western Europe. *European Journal of Education* 18(3), p. 217-228.

Newton, R. (1992). The Two Cultures of Academe: An Overlooked Planning Hurdle. *Planning for Higher Education* 21 (Fall), p. 8-14.

Nora, A. and Olivas, M.A. (1988). Faculty Attitudes Toward Industrial Research on Campus. *Research in Higher Education* 29(2), p. 125-147.

Ornstein, A.C. (1995). The New Paradigm in Research on Teaching. *Educational Forum*, 59 (Winter), p. 124-129.

Panitz, T. and Panitz P. (1998). Encouraging the Use of Collaborative Learning in Higher Education. In Forest, J.J.F. (ed.), *University Teaching: International Perspectives*. New York: Garland Publishing, p. 161-202.

Parsons, T. and Platt, G.M. (1973). *The American University*. Cambridge, MA: Harvard University Press.

Pelczar, R. (1977). The Latin American Professoriate: Progress and Prospects. In Altbach, P.G. (ed.), *Comparative Perspectives on the Academic Profession*. New York: Praeger, p. 125-44.

Perkin, H. (1987). The Historical Perspective. In Clark, B.R. (ed.), *Perspectives on Higher Education: Eight Disciplinary and Comparative Views*. Berkeley, CA: University of California Press.

Perry, W.G. (1970). *Forms of Intellectual and Ethical Development in the College Years: A Scheme*. New York: Holt, Rinehart and Winston.

Peterson, M. (1985). Emerging Developments in Postsecondary Organization Theory and Research: Fragmentation or Integration. *Educational Researcher* 14(3).

Ruscio, K.P. (1987). Many Sectors, Many Professions. In Burton R. Clark (ed.), *The Academic Profession, National, Disciplinary and Institutional Settings*. Berkeley, CA: University of California Press, p. 331

Schuster, J.H. and Bowen, H.R. (1985). The Faculty at Risk. *Change* (September/October), p. 21.

Sherman, B.R. and Blackburn, R.T. (1975). Personal Characteristics and Teaching Effectiveness of College Faculty. *Journal of Educational Psychology* 67(1), p. 124-131.

Shils, E. (1983). *The Academic Ethic*. Chicago, IL: University of Chicago Press.

Simpson, E.L. (1990). *Faculty Renewal in Higher Education*. Malabar, FL: Krieger Publishing.

Slaughter, S. (1985). From Serving Students to Serving the Economy: Changing Expectations of Faculty Role Performance. *Higher Education* 14, p. 41-56.

Smith, K. (1998). Portfolios as an Alternative Assessment Practice in Higher Education. In Forest, J.J.F. (ed.), *University Teaching: International Perspectives*. New York: Garland Publishing, p. 137-160

Stuart, A. and Whetten, D.A. (1985). Organizational Identity. *Research in Organizational Behavior* 7, p. 263-295.

Taylor, W.H. (1993). Educating British Children for European Citizenship. *European Journal of Education* 28(4), p. 439.

Tierney, W. and Bensimon, E.M. (1996). *Promotion and Tenure: Community and Socialization in Academe*. Albany, NY: State University of New York Press.

Tierney, W.G. (1993). *Building Communities of Difference: Higher Education in the Twenty-First Century*. Westport, CT: Bergin and Garvey.

Tierney, W.G. (1988). Organizational Culture in Higher Education: Defining the Essentials. *Journal of Higher Education* 59(1), p. 2-21.

Toomey, D. and Child, D. (1971). The Development of Local-Cosmopolitan Attitudes among Undergraduates and Sixth Formers. *Sociology Review* 19: 325-41.

Van Maanen, J. (1976). Breaking In: Socialization to Work. In Dubin, R. (ed.), *Handbook of Work, Organization and Society*. Chicago, IL: Rand McNally.

Wilson, E.K. (1982). Power, Pretense, and Piggybacking: Some Ethical Issues in Teaching. *Journal of Higher Education* 53 (May/June), p. 268-281.

Wilson, L. (1993). TEMPUS as an Instrument of Reform. *European Journal of Education* 28(4), p. 429-36

Wilson, L. (1942). *The Academic Man*. London: Oxford University Press.

Chapter 3

Altbach, P.G and Lewis, L. (1996). The Academic Profession in International Perspective. In Altbach, P.G. (ed.), *The International Academic Profession: Portraits of 14 Countries*. Princeton, NJ: Carnegie Foundation for the Advancement of Teaching.

Boyer, E.L. (1996). Foreword. In Altbach, P.G. (ed.), *The International Academic Profession: Portraits of 14 Countries*. Princeton, NJ: Carnegie Foundation for the Advancement of Teaching.

Denzin, N.K. (1989). *The Research Act: A Theoretical Introduction to Sociological Methods*. Englewood Cliffs, NJ: Prentice-Hall, Inc.

Enders, J. and Teichler, U. (1996). The Academic Profession in Germany. In Altbach, P.G. (ed.), *The International Academic Profession: Portraits of 14 Countries*. Princeton, NJ: Carnegie Foundation for the Advancement of Teaching.

Gottlieb, E.E. and Keith, B.E. (1996). The Academic Research-Teaching Nexus in Advanced-Industrialized Countries. *Higher Education* 25.

Hyland, T. (1998). Work-Based Experience and Higher Professional Learning in British Universities. In Forest, J.J.F. (ed.), *University Teaching: International Perspectives*. New York: Garland Publishing, p. 161-202.

Levin-Stankevich, B.L. and Savelyev, A. (1996). The Academic Profession in Russia. In Altbach, P.G. (ed.), *The International Academic Profession: Portraits of 14 Countries*. Princeton, NJ: Carnegie Foundation for the Advancement of Teaching.

Whitelaw, M.J. (1996). The International Study of the Academic Profession, 1991-1993: Methodological Notes. In Altbach, P.G. (ed.), *The International Academic Profession: Portraits of 14 Countries*. Princeton, NJ: Carnegie Foundation for the Advancement of Teaching.

Chapter 4

Aisenberg, N. and Harrington, M. (1988). *Women of Academe: Outsiders in the Sacred Grove*. Amherst, MA: The University of Massachusetts Press.

Altbach, P.G. (ed.). (1996). *The International Academic Profession: Portraits of 14 Countries*. Princeton, NJ: Carnegie Foundation for the Advancement of Teaching.

Altbach, P.G and Lewis, L. (1996). The Academic Profession in International Perspective. In Altbach, P.G. (ed.), *The International Academic Profession: Portraits of 14 Countries*. Princeton, NJ: Carnegie Foundation for the Advancement of Teaching.

Altbach, P.G. (1995). Problems and Possibilities: The US Academic Profession. *Studies in Higher Education* 20(1), p. 27-44.

Altbach, P.G. (1995). The Pros and Cons of Hiring Taxicab Professors. *The Chronicle of Higher Education* (January 6), p. B3.

Altbach, P.G. (1993). The Academic Profession. In Altbach, P.G. (ed.), *International Higher Education: An Encyclopedia*. New York: Garland Press, p. 23-44.

Antón, G. (1996). The Mexican Professoriate. In Altbach, P.G. (ed.), *The International Academic Profession: Portraits of 14 Countries*. Princeton, NJ: Carnegie Foundation for the Advancement of Teaching.

Austin, A. (1990). New Directions for Institutional Research. In Tierney, W. (ed.), *Assessing Academic Climates and Cultures*. San Francisco: Jossey-Bass, Inc.

Bensimon, E. (1996). Faculty Identity: Essential, Imposed or Constructed? In *Integrating Research on Faculty: Seeking New Ways to Communicate About the Academic Life of Faculty* (NCES Conference Report). Washington, DC: OERI, U.S. Department of Education.

Bloom, A. (1987). *The Closing of the American Mind: How Higher Education has Failed Democracy and Impoverished the Souls of Today's Students*. New York: Simon and Schuster.

Boyer, E.L., Altbach, P.G. and Whitelaw, M.J. (1994). *The Academic Profession: An International Perspective*. Princeton, NJ: Carnegie Foundation for the Advancement of Teaching.

Boyer, E.L. (1990). *Scholarship Reconsidered: Priorities of the Professoriate*. Princeton, NJ: Carnegie Foundation for the Advancement of Teaching.

Caplan, P.J. (1994). *Lifting a Ton of Feathers: A Woman's Guide to Surviving in the Academic World*. Toronto: University of Toronto Press.

Carter, D. and Wilson, R. (1992). *Minorities in Higher Education*. Washington, DC: American Council on Education.

Chait, R.P. (1997). Thawing the Cold War Over Tenure: Why academe needs more employment opportunities. *Chronicle of Higher Education* (February 2), p. B4-5.

Chait, R.P. (1995). The Future of Academic Tenure. *Priorities* 3 (Spring) p. 1-11

Chait, R.P. and Ford, A.T. (1982). *Beyond Traditional Tenure*. San Francisco: Jossey-Bass.

Clark, S.M., and Corcoran, M. (1986). Perspectives on the professional socialization of women faculty: A case of accumulative disadvantage? *Journal of Higher Education* 57(1), p. 20-43.

Deutsch, K.W. (1978). Achievements and Challenges in 2000 Years of Comparative Research. In Dierkes, M., Weiler, H.N., and Antal, A.B. (eds.), *Comparative Policy Resarch: Learning from Experience*. New York: St. Martins Press.

Dey, E.L., Ramirez, C.E., Korn, W.S., and Astin, A.W. (1993). *The American College Teacher: National Norms for the* 1992-93 HERI *Faculty Survey*. Los Angeles: Higher Education Research Institute.

El-Khawas, E. (1991). Senior Faculty in Academe: Active, Committed to the Teaching Role. *Research Briefs* 2(5). Washington, D.C.: American Council on Education, Division of Policy Analysis and Research.

Enders, J. (1998). Academic Staff Mobility in the European Community: The ERASMUS Experience. *Comparative Education Review* 42(1), p. 46-60.

Enders, J. and Teichler, U. (1996). The Academic Profession in Germany. In Altbach, P.G. (ed.), *The International Academic Profession: Portraits of 14 Countries*. Princeton, NJ: Carnegie Foundation for the Advancement of Teaching.

Eble, K.E. (1972). *Professors as Teachers*. San Francisco: Jossey-Bass.

Fairweather, J.S. (1993). *Teaching, Research and Faculty Rewards: A Summary of the Research Findings of the Faculty Profile Project*. University Park, PA: National Center for Postsecondary Teaching, Learning and Assessment.

Forest, J.J.F. (ed.), (1998). *University Teaching: International Perspectives*. New York: Garland Publishing.

Furniss, W.T. (1981). *Reshaping Faculty Careers*. Washington, DC: American Council on Education.

Gao, L.B. (1996). A validity study of the Teachers' Conception of School Physics Teaching Questionnaire. Unpublished manuscript, University of Hong Kong.

Goodwin, L.D. and Stevens, E.A. (1993). The Influence of Gender on University Faculty Members' Perceptions of "Good" Teaching. *Journal of Higher Education* 64(2).

Gottlieb, E.E. and Keith, B.E. (1996). The Academic Research-Teaching Nexus in Advanced-Industrialized Countries. *Higher Education* 25.

Gouldner, A.W. (1957). Cosmopolitans and Locals: Toward an analysis of latent social roles. *Administrative Sciences Quarterly* 2, p. 281-306.

Hess, R.D. and Azuma, H. (1991). Cultural support for schooling. *Educational Researcher* 20(9), p. 2-12.

Higher Education Research Institute. (1995). *The American College Teacher*. HERI, UCLA Graduate School of Education and Information Studies.

Johnsrud, L.K. and Des Jarlais, C.D. (1994). Barriers to tenure for women and minorities. *Review of Higher Education* 17(4), p. 335-353.

Kember, D. and Gow, L. (1994). Orientations to teaching and their effect on the quality of student learning. *Journal of Higher Education* 65(1), p. 58-74.

Kohn, M.L. (1987). Cross-National Research as an Analytical Strategy. *American Sociological Review* 52(6), p. 713-31.

Lewis, L.S. (1996). *Marginal Worth: Teaching and the Academic Labor Market*. New Brunswick, NJ: Transaction Publishers.

Lo, L. and Siu, T. (1990). Teacher's perception of a good teacher. Paper presented at the Annual Conference of the Hong Kong Educational Research Association, City University of Hong Kong.

Main, A.N. (1985). Higher Education: Faculty Training for Teaching. In Husen, T. and Postlethwaite, T. (eds.), *The International Encyclopedia of Education* (Vol. 4). New York: Pergamon Press, p. 2212-6.

Marton, F., Dall'Alba, G. and Tse, L.K. (1996). Memorizing and understanding: The keys to the paradox? In Watkins, D. and Biggs, J. (eds.), *The Chinese learner: Cultural, Psychological, and Contextual Influences*. Hong Kong and Melbourne: Comparative Education Research Center/Australian Council for Educational Research.

Murray, H.G., Rushton, J.P. and Paunonen, S.V. (1990). Teacher Personality Traits and Student Instructional Ratings in Six Types of University Courses. *Journal of Educational Psychology* 82(2), p. 250-261.

National Center for Education Statistics. (1994). NCES *Survey Report: 1993 National Study of Postsecondary Faculty*. Washington, DC: U.S. Department of Education, Office of Research and Improvement.

NCPTLA. (1995). *Realizing the Potential: Improving Postsecondary Teaching, Learning and Assessment*. University Park, PA: National Center for Postsecondary Teaching, Learning and Assessment.

Olsen, D., Maple, S.A., and Stage, F. (1995). Women and Minority Faculty Job Satisfaction. *Journal of Higher Education* 66(3).

Postiglione, G.A. (1996). The Future of the Hong Kong Academic Profession. In Altbach, P.G. (ed.), *The International Academic Profession: Portraits of 14 Countries*. Princeton, NJ: Carnegie Foundation for the Advancement of Teaching.

Prichard K.W. and Sawyer, R.M. (1994). *Handbook of College Teaching: Theory and Applications*. Westport, CT: Greenwood Press.

Purdie, N., Hattie, J. and Douglas, G. (1996). Student conceptions of learning and their use of self-regulated learning strategies: A cross-cultural comparison. *Journal of Educational Psychology* 88(1), p. 87-100.

Schlegel, A. (1996). Gender Issues and Cross-Cultural Research. In Inkeles, A. and Sasaki, M. (eds.), *Comparing Nations and Cultures: Readings in a Cross-Disciplinary Perspective*. Englewood Cliffs, NJ: Prentice Hall.

Schwartzmann, S. and Balbachevsky, E. (1996). The Academic Profession in Brazil. In Altbach, P.G. (ed.), *The International Academic Profession: Portraits of 14 Countries*. Princeton, NJ: Carnegie Foundation for the Advancement of Teaching.

Sherman, B.R. and Blackburn, R.T. (1975). Personal Characteristics and Teaching Effectiveness of College Faculty. *Journal of Educational Psychology* 67(1), p. 124-131.

Simpson, E.L. (1990). *Faculty Renewal in Higher Education*. Malabar, FL: Krieger Publishing.

Sykes, C.J. (1988). *ProfScam: Professors and the Demise of Higher Education*. New York: St. Martin's Press.

Tierney, W.G. (1997). Organizational Socialization in Higher Education. *Journal of Higher Education* 68(1), p. 1-16.

Tierney, W.G. and Bensimon, E.M. (1996). *Promotion and Tenure: Community and Socialization in Academe*. Albany, NY: SUNY Press.

Tierney, W.G. (1993). *Building Communities of Difference: Higher Education in the Twenty-First Century*. Westport, CT: Bergin and Garvey.

Tierney, W.G. (1991). *Culture and Ideology in Higher Education: Advancing a Critical Agenda*. New York: Praeger.

Toomey, D. and Child, D. (1971). The development of local-cosmopolitan attitudes among undergraduates and sixth formers. *Sociology Review* 19, p. 325-41.

Turner, C.S. and Thompson, J.R. (1993). Socializing women doctoral students: Minority and majority experiences. *The Review of Higher Education* 16(3), p. 355-370.

U.S. Department of Education. (1994). *Integrating Research on Faculty: Seeking New Ways to Communicate About the Academic Life of Faculty*. Conference Report: Results from the 1994 Forum. Washington, DC: U.S. Department of Education, Office of Research and Improvement.

Watkins, D. (1998). A Cross-Cultural Look at Conceptions of Good Teaching. In Forest, J.J.F. (ed.), *University Teaching: International Perspectives*. New York: Garland Publishing.

Watkins, D. and Biggs, J.B. (eds.). (1996). *The Chinese learner: Cultural, Psychological, and Contextual Influences*. Hong Kong and Melbourne: Comparative Education Research Centre/Australian Council for Educational Research.

Welch, A. (1998). The End of Certainty? The Academic Profession and the Challenge of Change. *Comparative Education Review* 42(1), p. 1-14.

Welch, L. (ed). (1992). *Perspectives on Minority Women in Higher Education*. New York: Praeger Publishers.

Whitelaw, M.J. (1996). The International Study of the Academic Profession, 1991-1993: Methodological Notes. In Altbach, P.G. (ed.), *The International Academic Profession: Portraits of 14 Countries*. Princeton, NJ: Carnegie Foundation for the Advancement of Teaching.

Chapter 5

Altbach, P.G and Lewis, L. (1996). The Academic Profession in International Perspective. In Altbach, P.G. (ed.), *The International Academic Profession: Portraits of 14 Countries*. Princeton, NJ: Carnegie Foundation for the Advancement of Teaching.

Altbach, P.G. (1995). Problems and Possibilities: The US Academic Profession. *Studies in Higher Education* 20(1), p. 27-44.

Antón, G. (1996). The Mexican Professoriate. In Altbach, P.G. (ed.), *The International Academic Profession: Portraits of 14 Countries*. Princeton, NJ: Carnegie Foundation for the Advancement of Teaching.

Arimoto, A. (1996). The Japanese Professoriate. In Altbach, P.G. (ed.), *The International Academic Profession: Portraits of 14 Countries*. Princeton, NJ: Carnegie Foundation for the Advancement of Teaching.

Bane, C.L. (1925). The Lecture vs. the Class Discussion Method of College Teaching. *School and Society* 21, p. 300-302.

Beecher, R.A. (1985). Higher Education Systems: Structure. In Husen, T. and Postlethwaite, T. (eds.), *The International Encyclopedia of Education* (Vol. 4). New York: Pergamon Press.

Boyer, E.L., Altbach P.G. and Whitelaw, M.J. (1994) *The Academic Profession: International Perspectives*. Princeton, NJ: Carnegie Foundation for the Advancement of Teaching.

Boyer, E.L. (1990). *Scholarship Reconsidered: Priorities of the Professoriate*. Princeton, NJ: Carnegie Foundation for the Advancement of Teaching.

Brufee, K. (1993). *Collaborative Learning: Higher Education, Interdependence and the Authority of Knowledge*. Baltimore, MD: Johns Hopkins Press.

Caplow , T. and McGee, R.J. (1958). *The Academic Marketplace*. New York: Basic Books, p. 221.

Chen, S. Gottlieb, E. and Yakir, R. (1996). The Academic Profession in Israel. In Altbach, P.G. (ed.), *The International Academic Profession: Portraits of 14 Countries*. Princeton, NJ: Carnegie Foundation for the Advancement of Teaching.

Cross, K.P. and Angelo, T.A. (1988). *Classroom Assessment Techniques: A Handbook for Faculty*. Ann Arbor, MI: National Center for Research to Improve Postsecondary Teaching and Learning.

Crouch, M.K. and Fontaine, S.I. (1994). Student Portfolios as an Assessment Tool. In Halpern, D.F. and Associates, *Changing College Classrooms: New Teaching and Learning Strategies for an Increasingly Complex World*. San Francisco: Jossey-Bass, p. 306-328.

Ekeler, W.J. (1994). The lecture method. In Prichard, K.W. and Sawyer, R.M. (eds.), *Handbook of College Teaching: Theory and Applications*. Westport, CT: Greenwood Press.

Enders, J. and Teichler, U. (1996). The Academic Profession in Germany. In Altbach, P.G. (ed.), *The International Academic Profession: Portraits of 14 Countries*. Princeton, NJ: Carnegie Foundation for the Advancement of Teaching.

Fairweather, J.S. (1993). *Teaching, Research and Faculty Rewards: A summary of the research findings of the Faculty Profile Project*. University Park, PA: National Center for Postsecondary Teaching, Learning, and Assessment.

Gottlieb, E.E. and Keith, B.E. (1996). The Academic Research-Teaching Nexus in Advanced-Industrialized Countries. *Higher Education* 25.

Gouldner, A.W. (1957). Cosmopolitans and Locals: Toward an analysis of latent social roles. *Administrative Sciences Quarterly* 2, p. 281-306.

Haas, E. (1996). The United States Academic Profession. In Altbach, P.G. (ed.), *The International Academic Profession: Portraits of 14 Countries*. Princeton, NJ: Carnegie Foundation for the Advancement of Teaching.

Halpern, D.F., and Associates. (1994). *Changing College Classrooms: New Teaching and Learning Strategies for an Increasingly Complex World*. San Francisco, CA: Jossey-Bass.

Howe, H. (1993). Classroom without Walls. *Earthwatch Magazine*.

Hughes, M.G. (1979). Management Theory: Reconciling Professional and Administrative Concerns in Education. *Studies in Educational Administration* 13 (December).

Kember, D. and Gow, L. (1994). Orientations to teaching and their effect on the quality of student learning. *Journal of Higher Education* 65(1), p. 58-74.

Lee S. (1996). The Korean Academic Profession. In Altbach, P.G. (ed.), *The International Academic Profession: Portraits of 14 Countries*. Princeton, NJ: Carnegie Foundation for the Advancement of Teaching.

Lewis, L. (1996). *Marginal Worth: Teaching and the Academic Labor Market*. New Brunswick, NJ: Transaction Publishers.

Macomber F.G. and Seigel, L. (1957). A Study of Large-Group Teaching Procedures. *Educational Research* 38, p. 220-229.

McKeachie W.J. (ed.). (1994). *Teaching Tips: Strategies, Research and Theory for College and University Teachers*, 9th ed. Lexington, MA: D.C. Heath Co.

McKeachie, W.J., Pintrich, P.R., Lin, Y-G, Smith, D.A.F., and Sharma, R. (1990). *Teaching and Learning in the College Classroom: A Review of the Research Literature*, 2nd ed. Ann Arbor: University of Michigan, National Center for Research to Improve Postsecondary Teaching and Learning.

McKeachie, W.J. (1990). Research on College Teaching: The Historical Background. *Journal of Educational Psychology* 82 (2), p. 189-200.

McKeachie, W.J, Pintrich, P.R., Lin, Y. and Smith, D.A. (1986). *Teaching and Learning in the College Classroom: A Review of the Research Literature*. Ann Arbor: University of Michigan, National Center for Research to Improve Postsecondary Teaching and Learning.

Murray, H.G., Rushton, J.P. and Paunonen, S.V. (1990). Teacher Personality Traits and Student Instructional Ratings in Six Types of University Courses. *Journal of Educational Psychology* 82(2), p. 250-261.

Murray, J.P. (1995). *Successful Faculty Development and Evaluation: The Complete Teaching Portfolio*. ASHE-ERIC Higher Education Report No. 8. Washington, DC: The George Washington University.

Murray, H.G. (1987). Classroom teaching behaviors related to college teaching effectiveness. In Aleamoni, L.M. (ed.), *Techniques for Evaluating and Improving Instruction*. New Directions for Teaching and Learning 31. San Francisco, CA: Jossey-Bass, p. 9-24.

Olson, G.A. and Ashton-Jones, E. (1992). "Doing" Gender: (En)Gendering Academic Mentoring. *Journal of Education* 174(3), p. 114-127.

Panitz, T. and Panitz P. (1998). Encouraging the Use of Collaborative Learning in Higher Education. In Forest, J.J.F. (ed.), *University Teaching: International Perspectives*. New York: Garland Publishing, p. 161-202.

Penner, J.G. (1984). *Why Many College Teachers Cannot Lecture.* Springfield, IL: Charles C. Thomas.

Postiglione, G.A. (1996). The Future of the Hong Kong Academic Profession. In Altbach, P.G. (ed.), *The International Academic Profession: Portraits of 14 Countries.* Princeton, NJ: Carnegie Foundation for the Advancement of Teaching.

Sherman, B.R. and Blackburn, R.T. (1975). Personal Characteristics and Teaching Effectiveness of College Faculty. *Journal of Educational Psychology* 67(1), p. 124-131.

Smith, K. (1998). Portfolios as an Alternative Assessment Practice in Higher Education. In Forest, J.J.F. (ed.), *University Teaching: International Perspectives.* New York: Garland Publishing, p. 137-160.

Solomon, D., Rosenberg, L., and Bezdek, W.E. (1964). Teacher Behavior and Student Learning. *Journal of Educational Psychology* 55, p.23-30.

Tierney, W. and Bensimon, E.M. (1996). *Promotion and Tenure: Community and Socialization in Academe.* Albany, NY: State University of New York Press.

Watkins, D. (1998). A Cross-Cultural Look at Conceptions of Good Teaching. In Forest, J.J.F. (ed.), *University Teaching: International Perspectives.* New York: Garland Publishing.

Wright, A.W. (1998). Improving Teaching by Design: Preferred Policies, Programs and Practices. In Forest, J.J.F. (ed.), *University Teaching: International Perspectives.* New York: Garland Publishing.

Chapter 6

Abrahamson, M. (1967). *The Professional in the Organization.* Chicago, IL: Rand McNally.

Altbach, P.G. (1997). Professors and Politics: An International Perspective. In Altbach, P.G. (ed.), *Comparative Higher Education.* Chestnut Hill, MA: Boston College Center for International Higher Education.

Altbach, P.G and Lewis, L. (1996). The Academic Profession in International Perspective. In Altbach, P.G. (ed.), *The International Academic Profession: Portraits of 14 Countries.* Princeton, NJ: Carnegie Foundation for the Advancement of Teaching.

Antón, G. (1996). The Mexican Professoriate. In Altbach, P.G. (ed.), *The International Academic Profession: Portraits of 14 Countries.* Princeton, NJ: Carnegie Foundation for the Advancement of Teaching.

Bloom, A. (1987). *The Closing of the American Mind: How Higher Education has Failed Democracy and Impoverished the Souls of Today's Students.* New York: Simon and Schuster.

Boyer, E.L., Altbach P.G. and Whitelaw, M.J. (1994) *The Academic Profession: International Perspectives.* Princeton, NJ: Carnegie Foundation for the Advancement of Teaching.

Chait, R.P. and Ford, A.T. (1982). *Beyond Traditional Tenure.* San Francisco: Jossey-Bass.

Clark, B.R. (1992). Faculty Differentiation and Dispersion. In Levine, A. (ed.), *Higher Learning in America*. Baltimore, MD: Johns Hopkins University Press, p. 163-177.

Clark, B.R. (1987). *The Academic Life: Small Worlds, Different Worlds*. Princeton, NJ: Carnegie Foundation for the Advancement of Teaching.

Damrosch, D. (1995). *We Scholars: Changing the Culture of the University*. Cambridge, MA: Harvard University Press.

de Witt, H. (1996). European Internationalization Programs. *International Higher Education* 2.

Drucker, P.F. (1952). Management and the Professional Employee. *Harvard Business Review* 30(3), p. 84-90.

Enders, J. and Teichler, U. (1996). The Academic Profession in Germany. In Altbach, P.G. (ed.), *The International Academic Profession: Portraits of 14 Countries*. Princeton, NJ: Carnegie Foundation for the Advancement of Teaching.

Furniss, W.T. (1981). *Reshaping Faculty Careers*. Washington, DC: American Council on Education.

Gouldner, A.W. (1957). Cosmopolitans and Locals: Toward an analysis of latent social roles. *Administrative Sciences Quarterly* 2, p. 281-306.

Gottlieb, E.E. and Keith, B.E. (1996). The Academic Research-Teaching Nexus in Advanced-Industrialized Countries. *Higher Education* 25.

Greenfield, T.B. (1975). Theory about organization: A new perspective and its implications for schools. In Hughes, M.G. (ed.), *Administering Education: International Challenges*. London: Athlone Press, p. 71-99.

Gumport, P. (1991). The Research Imperative. In Tierney, W.G. (ed.), *Culture and Ideology in Higher Education: Advancing a Critical Agenda*. New York: Praeger Publishers.

Haas, E. (1996). The United States Academic Profession. In Altbach, P.G. (ed.), *The International Academic Profession: Portraits of 14 Countries*. Princeton, NJ: Carnegie Foundation for the Advancement of Teaching.

Hughes, M.G. (1979). Management Theory: Reconciling Professional and Administrative Concerns in Education. *Studies in Educational Administration* 13 (December).

Kohn, M.L. (1987). Cross-National Research as an Analytical Strategy. *American Sociological Review* 52(6), p. 713-31.

Kornhauser, W. (1962). *Scientists in Industry: Conflict and Accommodation*. Berkeley, CA: University of California Press.

Lewis, L. (1996). *Marginal Worth: Teaching and the Academic Labor Market*. New Brunswick, NJ: Transaction Publishers.

Levin-Stankevich, B.L. and Savelyev, A. (1996). The Academic Profession in Russia. In Altbach, P.G. (ed.), *The International Academic Profession: Portraits of 14 Countries*. Princeton, NJ: Carnegie Foundation for the Advancement of Teaching.

NCPTLA. (1995). *Realizing the Potential: Improving Postsecondary Teaching, Learning and Assessment*. University Park, PA: National Center for Postsecondary Teaching, Learning and Assessment.

Panitz, T. and Panitz P. (1998). Encouraging the Use of Collaborative Learning in Higher Education. In Forest, J.J.F. (ed.), *University Teaching: International Perspectives*. New York: Garland Publishing, p. 161-202.

Scott, W.R. (1966). Professionals in Bureaucracies: Areas of Conflict. In Vollmer, H.M. and Mills, D.L. (eds.), *Professionalization*. Englewood Cliffs, NJ: Prentice-Hall.

Sherman, B.R. and Blackburn, R.T. (1975). Personal Characteristics and Teaching Effectiveness of College Faculty. *Journal of Educational Psychology* 67(1), p. 124-131.

Shils, E. (1983). *The Academic Ethic*. Chicago: University of Chicago Press.

Simpson, E.L. (1990). *Faculty Renewal in Higher Education*. Malabar, FL: Krieger Publishing.

Tierney, W. and Bensimon, E.M. (1996). *Promotion and Tenure: Community and Socialization in Academe*. Albany, NY: State University of New York Press.

Zemsky. R. (1996). The Impact of Higher Education's New Climate on Faculty Perceptions. In *Integrating Research on Faculty: Seeking New Ways to Communicate About the Academic Life of Faculty* (NCES Conference Report). Washington, DC: OERI, U.S. Department of Education.

Chapter 7

Altbach, P.G and Lewis, L. (1996). The Academic Profession in International Perspective. In Altbach, P.G. (ed.), *The International Academic Profession: Portraits of 14 Countries*. Princeton, NJ: Carnegie Foundation for the Advancement of Teaching.

Arimoto, A. (1996). The Japanese Professoriate. In Altbach, P.G. (ed.), *The International Academic Profession: Portraits of 14 Countries*. Princeton, NJ: Carnegie Foundation for the Advancement of Teaching.

Becher, T. (1989). *Academic Tribes and Territories: Intellectual Enquiry and the Cultures of Disciplines*. Cambridge, UK: Open University Press.

Clark, B.R. (1992). Faculty Differentiation and Dispersion. In Levine, A. (ed.), *Higher Learning in America*. Baltimore, MD: Johns Hopkins University Press, p. 163-177.

Clark, B.R. (1987). *The Academic Life: Small Worlds, Different Worlds*. Princeton, NJ: Carnegie Foundation for the Advancement of Teaching.

Enders, J. and Teichler, U. (1996). The Academic Profession in Germany. In Altbach, P.G. (ed.), *The International Academic Profession: Portraits of 14 Countries*. Princeton, NJ: Carnegie Foundation for the Advancement of Teaching.

Furniss, W.T. (1981). *Reshaping Faculty Careers*. Washington, DC: American Council on Education.

Gouldner, A.W. (1957). Cosmopolitans and Locals: Toward an analysis of latent social roles. *Administrative Sciences Quarterly* 2, p. 281-306.

Gumport, P. (1991). The Research Imperative. In Tierney, W.G. (ed.), *Culture and Ideology in Higher Education: Advancing a Critical Agenda*. New York: Praeger Publishers.

Haas, E. (1996). The United States Academic Profession. In Altbach, P.G. (ed.), *The International Academic Profession: Portraits of 14 Countries*. Princeton, NJ: Carnegie Foundation for the Advancement of Teaching.

Lewis, L. (1996). *Marginal Worth: Teaching and the Academic Labor Market*. New Brunswick, NJ: Transaction Publishers.

NCPTLA. (1995). *Realizing the Potential: Improving Postsecondary Teaching, Learning and Assessment*. University Park, PA: National Center for Postsecondary Teaching, Learning and Assessment.

Schuster, J.H. and Bowen, H.R. (1985). The Faculty at Risk. *Change* (September/October), p. 21.

Sherman, B.R. and Blackburn, R.T. (1975). Personal Characteristics and Teaching Effectiveness of College Faculty. *Journal of Educational Psychology* 67(1), p. 124-131.

Shils, E. (1983). *The Academic Ethic*. Chicago, IL: University of Chicago Press.

Tierney, W. and Bensimon, E.M. (1996). *Promotion and Tenure: Community and Socialization in Academe*. Albany, NY: State University of New York Press.

Chapter 8

Altbach, P.G. (1997). The New Internationalism: Foreign Students and Scholars. In Altbach, P.G., *Comparative Higher Education: Knowledge, the University, and Development*. Chestnut Hill, MA: Boston College Center for International Higher Education.

Altbach, P.G and Lewis, L. (1996). The Academic Profession in International Perspective. In Altbach, P.G. (ed.), *The International Academic Profession: Portraits of 14 Countries*. Princeton, NJ: Carnegie Foundation for the Advancement of Teaching.

Bergendal, G. (1979). Higher Education: Impact on Society. In Husen, T. and Postlethwaite, T. (eds.) *The International Enclyclopedia of Education* (Vol. 4). New York: Pergamon Pres, p. 2220-3.

Boyer, E.L., Altbach P.G. and Whitelaw, M.J. (1994). *The Academic Profession: International Perspectives*. Princeton, NJ: Carnegie Foundation for the Advancement of Teaching.

Clark, B.R. (1995). *Places of Inquiry: Research and Advanced Education in Modern Universities*. University of California Press, Berkeley.

Clark, B.R. (1993). Faculty Differentiation and Dispersion. In Levine, A. (ed.), *Higher Learning in America*. Baltimore, MD: Johns Hopkins University Press, p. 163-177.

Enders, J. and Teichler, U. (1996). The Academic Profession in Germany. In Altbach, P.G. (ed.), *The International Academic Profession: Portraits of 14 Countries*. Princeton, NJ: Carnegie Foundation for the Advancement of Teaching.

Gouldner, A.W. (1957). Cosmopolitans and Locals: Toward an analysis of latent social roles. *Administrative Sciences Quarterly* 2, p. 281-306.

Schiefelbein, E. (1996). The Chilean Academic Profession. In Altbach, P.G. (ed.), *The International Academic Profession: Portraits of 14 Countries*. Princeton, NJ: Carnegie Foundation for the Advancement of Teaching.

Schwartzmann, S. and Balbachevsky, E. (1996). The Academic Profession in Brazil. In Altbach, P.G. (ed.), *The International Academic Profession: Portraits of 14 Countries*. Princeton, NJ: Carnegie Foundation for the Advancement of Teaching.

Trow, M. (1970). Reflections on the transition from mass to universal higher education. *Daedalus* 99, p. 1-42.

Chapter 9

Altbach, P.G. (1997). The New Internationalism: Foreign Students and Scholars. In Altbach, P.G., *Comparative Higher Education: Knowledge, the University, and Development*. Chestnut Hill, MA: Boston College Center for International Higher Education.

Altbach, P.G. (1997). The University as Center and Periphery. In Altbach, P.G., *Comparative Higher Education: Knowledge, the University, and Development*. Chestnut Hill, MA: Boston College Center for International Higher Education.

Altbach, P.G. and Lewis, L. (1996). The Academic Profession in International Perspective. In Altbach, P.G. (ed.), *The International Academic Profession: Portraits of 14 Countries*. Princeton, NJ: Carnegie Foundation for the Advancement of Teaching.

Enders, J. (1998). Academic Staff Mobility in the European Community: The ERASMUS Experience. *Comparative Education Review* 42(1), p. 46-60.

Gouldner, A.W. (1957). Cosmopolitans and Locals: Toward an analysis of latent social roles. *Administrative Sciences Quarterly* 2, p. 281-306.

Haas, E. (1996). The United States Academic Profession. In Altbach, P.G. (ed.), *The International Academic Profession: Portraits of 14 Countries*. Princeton, NJ: Carnegie Foundation for the Advancement of Teaching.

Kerr, C. (1990). The Internationalisation of Learning and the Nationalism of the Purposes of Higher Education: Two 'laws of motion' in conflict? *European Journal of Education* 25(1).

Taylor, W.H. (1993). Educating British Children for European Citizenship. *European Journal of Education* 28(4), p. 439.

Chapter 10

Altbach, P.G. (1997). The New Internationalism: Foreign Students and Scholars. In Altbach, P.G., *Comparative Higher Education: Knowledge, the University, and Development*. Chestnut Hill, MA: Boston College Center for International Higher Education.

Altbach, P.G. and Lewis, L. (1996). The Academic Profession in International Perspective. In Altbach, P.G. (ed.), *The International Academic Profession:

Portraits of 14 Countries. Princeton, NJ: Carnegie Foundation for the Advancement of Teaching.

Altbach, P.G. (1995). Problems and Possibilities: The US Academic Profession. *Studies in Higher Education* 20(1), p. 27-44.

Bensimon, E. (1996). Faculty Identity: Essential, Imposed or Constructed? In *Integrating Research on Faculty: Seeking New Ways to Communicate About the Academic Life of Faculty* (NCES Conference Report). Washington, DC: OERI, U.S. Department of Education.

Boyer, E.L., Altbach P.G. and Whitelaw, M.J. (1994). *The Academic Profession: International Perspectives.* Princeton, NJ: Carnegie Foundation for the Advancement of Teaching.

Boyer, E.L. (1990). *Scholarship Reconsidered: Priorities of the Professoriate.* Princeton, NJ: Carnegie Foundation for the Advancement of Teaching.

Clark, B.R. (1987). *The Academic Life: Small Worlds, Different Worlds.* Princeton, NJ: Carnegie Foundation for the Advancement of Teaching.

Eble, K.E. (1972). *Professors as Teachers.* San Francisco: Jossey-Bass.

Glazer, J. (1993). *A Teaching Doctorate?: The Doctor of Arts Degree, Then and Now.* Washington, DC: American Association for Higher Education.

Gouldner, A.W. (1957). Cosmopolitans and Locals: Toward an analysis of latent social roles. *Administrative Sciences Quarterly* 2, p. 281-306.

Gumport, P. (1991). The Research Imperative. In Tierney, W.G. (ed.), *Culture and Ideology in Higher Education: Advancing a Critical Agenda.* New York: Praeger Publishers.

Haas, E. (1996). The United States Academic Profession. In Altbach, P.G. (ed.), *The International Academic Profession: Portraits of 14 Countries.* Princeton, NJ: Carnegie Foundation for the Advancement of Teaching.

Hauerwaus, S.M. (1988). The Morality of Teaching. In Deneef, A.L., Goodwin, C.D. and McCrate, E.S. (eds.), *The Academic's Handbook.* Durham, NC: Duke Press, p. 19-28.

Hughes, M.G. (1985). Management Theory: Reconciling Professional and Administrative Concerns in Education. In Husen, T. and Postlethwaite, T. (eds.), *The International Encyclopedia of Education* (Vol. 4). New York: Pergamon Press, p. 3197-8.

Kerr, C. (1990). The Internationalisation of Learning and the Nationalism of the Purposes of Higher Education: Two 'laws of motion' in conflict? *European Journal of Education* 25(1).

Kohn, M.L. (1987). Cross-National Research as an Analytical Strategy. *American Sociological Review* 52(6), p. 713-31.

Levine, A. (1980). *Why Innovation Fails: The Institutionalism and Termination of Innovation in Higher Education.* Albany, NY: SUNY Press.

Lewis, L. (1996). *Marginal Worth: Teaching and the Academic Labor Market.* New Brunswick, NJ: Transaction Publishers.

McKeachie, W.J. (1990). Research on College Teaching: The Historical Background. *Journal of Educational Psychology* 82(2), p. 189-200.

Murray, J.P. (1995). *Successful Faculty Development and Evaluation: The Complete Teaching Portfolio*. ASHE-ERIC Higher Education Report No. 8. Washington, DC: The George Washington University.

NCPTLA. (1995). *Realizing the Potential: Improving Postsecondary Teaching, Learning and Assessment*. University Park, PA: National Center for Postsecondary Teaching, Learning and Assessment.

Sykes, C.J. (1988). *ProfScam: Professors and the Demise of Higher Education*. New York: St. Martin's Press.

Tierney, W. and Bensimon, E.M. (1996). *Promotion and Tenure: Community and Socialization in Academe*. Albany, NY: State University of New York Press.

Watkins, D. (1998). A Cross-Cultural Look at Conceptions of Good Teaching. In Forest, J.J.F. (ed.), *University Teaching: International Perspectives*. New York: Garland Publishing.

Wright, A.W. (1998). Improving Teaching by Design: Preferred Policies, Programs and Practices. In Forest, J.J.F. (ed.), *University Teaching: International Perspectives*. New York: Garland Publishing.

Index

3